WHERE IS JULIET STUART POYNTZ?

A VOLUME IN THE SERIES
Culture in Politics in the Cold War and Beyond

EDITED BY
Edwin A. Martini and Scott Laderman

WHERE IS JULIET STUART POYNTZ?

Gender, Spycraft, and Anti-Stalinism in the Early Cold War

DENISE M. LYNN

UNIVERSITY OF MASSACHUSETTS PRESS
Amherst and Boston

Printed in the United States of America

ISBN 978-1-62534-548-6 (paper); 547-9 (hardcover)

Designed by Deste Roosa
Set in Adobe Garamond Pro, Eurostile, and Futura
Printed and bound by Books International, Inc.

Cover design by TG Design
Cover photo: Juliet Stuart Poyntz, Press Photo, 1949, ACME Telephoto.

Library of Congress Cataloging-in-Publication Data
A catalog record for this book is available from the Library of Congress.

British Library Cataloguing-in-Publication Data
A catalog record for this book is available from the British Library.

TO ANDREW

CONTENTS

ACKNOWLEDGMENTS

I began my research on Poyntz many years ago while still writing my dissertation. It remained a tangential project as I focused my research on women in the Communist Party and began to work toward my academic career. But as I moved toward trying to understand the veracity of anti-communist politics in the United States, Poyntz was always present in my thoughts.

I must first thank the teachers who encouraged my work on American communism and allowed me to focus on the growing field of post–Cold War communist studies. My graduate school advisors, Melvyn Dubofsky, Elisa Camiscioli, Arleen de Vera, and Sarah Elbert, were enormously important in keeping me focused, shaping my research, and providing critical feedback. Many of my fellow graduate students also influenced my thinking and interpretations of communism and anti-communism. My friend Greg Geddes's work on outsiders among the New York intellectuals was particularly important in challenging the limited literature on anti-Stalinists. My fellow gender historians, also known as the Goats, have been supportive and influential in shaping my thinking on gender: Gaylynn Welch, Melyssa Wrisley, Dee Gillespie, Mary Weikum, and Andrea Dekoter. Other members of my cohort who have remained engaged in my life and in history include Shannon King, Jenn Cubic, Marian Horan, Meg Egitto, Gulhan Erkaya Balsoy, Jeff Hall, Melissa Madera, Shelley Rose, Gul Karagoz Kizilca, and Attila Ayetkin.

American communist history often invokes palpable fears among those who came of age during the Cold War. I am thankful for the historians who paved the way for a more critical analysis regarding the party and its impact on American politics. Scholars such as Van Gosse, Kate Weigand, Erik McDuffie, Robin Kelley, Kathryn Olmsted, Landon Storrs, and Ellen Schrecker have expanded our thinking and inserted new voices into the historiography. I particularly thank Vernon Pederson and Beth Slutsky, both excellent historians of American communism, whose work has directly influenced mine. Additionally, I thank them both for taking the time to read and offer feedback on my work on Poyntz.

Many of my colleagues at the University of Southern Indiana deserve thanks, if only for keeping me grounded and on task. I am grateful to my department chair, Jason Hardgrave, for supporting my research endeavors and my fellow historians Stella Ress, Cacee Hoyer, and Anya King for always encouraging intellectual curiosity and critical thinking among our students and our colleagues. My philosophy colleague Mary Lyn Stoll deserves thanks for her friendship and her constant challenges to my thinking. I am grateful to my intimate friends and colleagues Sakina Hughes and Adrian Gentle for being my greatest cheerleaders. Both read various documents and manuscripts related to this project, listened to presentations on Poyntz, and kept pushing me when I was ready to walk away.

I would like to extend my deep appreciation to the archivists and librarians who are an essential part of historical research. As I tried to piece together the life of a missing woman, many people across the country helped me find the clues that brought Poyntz into the story. The archivists at the Douglas County Historical Society in Omaha, Nebraska, and the Delaware County Historical Society in Muncie, Indiana, helped enormously. Lynn Sullivan at the W. Dale Clark Main Library in Omaha, Nebraska, not only helped me locate the Points family gravesites but also responded to my inquiries when I failed to record page numbers for local records. The archivists at Kansas State University, Oberlin College, Barnard College, and Columbia University located and shared important information about Poyntz's parents and her academic career. Librarians and archivists are the backbone of historical research, and I extend my deepest thanks to those just mentioned and any that my memory failed to include.

My family members, both biological and not, deserve many thanks. I often do not burden them with details of my research, but they have been constantly present in encouraging my path as a historian. My dear friends Angela Reap and Jess Bacon-Reap, Danielle Copeland, Colleen McGowan, Nicole Russell, and Sue Wee-Hickman have been a constant presence in my life for nearly thirty years. Without them I would have certainly floundered. My brother Dan, my sister-in-law Angie, my sister Corinne, and my niece and nephews Megan, Ryan, and Callan have been there through it all. Thanks to my cuz-bro Andrew to whom this book is dedicated; we miss you always, and you are ever present to us. Special thanks to my parents, Judi Lynn and Jack Lynn, without whom it would quite literally never have happened. My daughter Cybele deserves special praise for being my inspiration. Without her, none of my written work might have seen the light of day.

Many people have influenced me along this path, both positively and negatively, and I have no doubt neglected to name many of them. But special recognition should go to Juliet Stuart Poyntz, a long-missing, voiceless prop in America's long war against a faceless enemy. I have often wondered what she would have wanted as her legacy; probably not what it turned out to be. Her entire life was devoted to social justice, and thus I hope that this book will contribute in some small way to making that her legacy: her mission to find fairness and hope for all, despite race, gender, and economic condition.

A NOTE ON THE TEXT

The subject of this study was born Juliet Stewart Points. During her college years, she changed the spelling of her name to Juliet Stuart Points before finally settling on Juliet Stuart Poyntz. Acquaintances often referred to her as Julia. After marrying Frederick Franz Ludwig Glaser in 1913, she went by Juliet Glazer or Juliet Glaser. By 1924, the couple had become estranged, but Poyntz continued to use variations of his name. In the documentation that mentions her, her name has no uniformity, which could certainly have been useful for a spy. However, throughout this book, for the sake of consistency and narrative flow, I will refer to her as Juliet Stuart Poyntz.

WHERE IS JULIET STUART POYNTZ?

INTRODUCTION

Sometime in the spring of 1937, telephone operators at the American Woman's Association Clubhouse at 353 West 57th Street in Manhattan began noticing that a man with a deep, German-sounding voice was calling daily for a resident named Juliet Stuart Poyntz. Poyntz was by all accounts a good resident. She was well educated, articulate, and had a background in teaching at Columbia University, where she was also working on a historical research project. She paid her rent on time and kept her room tidy. It was not particularly unusual for residents to get phone calls, but the man with the deep voice called so frequently that the clubhouse employees remembered him. Poyntz took the calls every time, so she must have known him. These daily calls did not raise any alarms, until Poyntz disappeared.

The clubhouse had opened in 1929 with the stated purpose of creating a place for single professional women to live in comfort and safety. The brainchild of Anne Morgan, daughter of J. Pierpont Morgan, it was centrally located in the city and could house five hundred women. Residents could rent a single room for $12 a week, each sharing a bath with one other resident. The clubhouse offered entertainment facilities for both residents and association members, including a gymnasium, a swimming pool, dining rooms, a cafeteria, and a ballroom. Poyntz, widowed when she moved in in 1935, seemed to be a perfect fit.[1]

As it turned out, however, she was not a typical resident. Throughout the 1920s and into the early Depression years, Poyntz was a leading American communist. In 1934, she left the American branch of the Communist Party (CPUSA) and joined the Soviet underground. Her task was to recruit German and Italian students who were attending Columbia University, convincing them to return to their homelands and work in the anti-fascist underground. In other words, unbeknownst to the clubhouse property manager, Mr. Thackerberry, one of his residents was a Soviet spy.[2]

Still, there was nothing to alert him to her unusual life—except for those daily phone calls. the telephone operators noticed that Poyntz took the calls throughout the spring and into the early summer. Then, on a hot June evening, after speaking briefly to the man, she left the clubhouse and reportedly walked in the direction of Central Park, three short blocks away. She did not return that day, or the next. After the rent went unpaid for several weeks, Thackerberry realized that something was wrong. He went to her deserted room and found an open jar of Jell-O on the desk, stale breadcrumbs on the table, and her belongings still in their places. The operators told him about the calls from the deep-voiced man and said that he had never called the clubhouse again after the June evening she had disappeared.[3]

Thackerberry called Poyntz's emergency contact, Marie B. MacDonald, a former co-worker and a long-time friend. MacDonald contacted Poyntz's attorney, Elias Lieberman, also a former co-worker, and the two went to her room to look around. There was no indication that Poyntz had planned to be away from her room for long: she had left behind her passport and her citizenship papers and had not withdrawn any money from her skimpy bank account. The two contacted another friend of Poyntz's, and together they packed up her belongings and put them into storage. They decided not to alert authorities because they knew that Poyntz was working for the underground and they did not want the police or FBI tracking her.

Seven months passed, and still no formal missing person's report was made. MacDonald, concerned that Poyntz had failed to contact her, claimed that she had pressed Lieberman to contact the police, but he never did. Eventually, it was Thackerberry who unintentionally alerted them. After he mentioned to a police officer friend that one of his tenants had gone missing, that officer or another employee of the New York City police leaked the news to the press. Poyntz's disappearance was formally announced in the *New York World Telegram* on December 17, 1937. Only a week before, an American couple, Mr. and Mrs. Donald Robinson, had been arrested in Moscow on suspicion of spying. Poyntz's months-long disappearance was suddenly connected to the Robinsons', and many people began to envision a vast Stalinist conspiracy unfolding in the United States.

The U.S. State Department frantically tried to locate the Robinsons, but neither the feds nor the police showed much interest in Poyntz. A former top communist leader was missing, but the New York state police hardly seemed concerned about it. Meanwhile, the Robinsons were also not whom they had claimed to be. Officials discovered that they were, in fact, A. A. and Ruth Rubens. A. A. was a Latvian who worked as a Soviet agent producing fake passports, such as the ones the pair had used to travel to the USSR. Ruth was an American citizen and a Communist Party member. Now some began to wonder if Poyntz knew the Rubens. Or was it merely a coincidence that American communists with links to the Soviet underground were going missing?

The year 1937—the height of Josef Stalin's show trials and the purge known as the Great Terror—was an especially dangerous one to be in the employ of the Soviets. Between the spring of 1937 and the fall of 1938, the American press posited that American citizens Ruth Rubens and Juliet Stuart Poyntz had been caught up in the purges. They cited witnesses who claimed that Poyntz, in her role as an agent for the Soviet secret police, had interrogated accused show trial defendants. Known as the Joint State Political Directorate (OGPU), the police organization was originally an arm of the Commission to Combat Counter-Revolution and Sabotage and dealt primarily with external threats to the USSR. In 1934, it merged with the People's Commissariat for Internal Affairs (NKVD), which concentrated on internal security issues. Poyntz's friends believed that her involvement with the interrogations must have led her to express doubts about Stalin's leadership and the socialist promises embodied by the Soviet Union—doubts that might have gotten her killed.[4]

Poyntz was never found, and there was no substantive evidence about what had happened to her. Nonetheless, in the days, months, and years after her disappearance, a full cast of characters emerged, and a story was constructed around her disappearance, one that emphasized Soviet terror and the dangers of communism. Meanwhile, the Robinson-Ruben story dominated the headlines, forever linking Poyntz's tale to theirs. Anti-Stalinists on the left—specifically Carlo Tresca and Herbert Solow—used the disappearances to warn Americans that the Soviet terror was spilling across American borders. But the rise of fascism in Germany and Italy was now capturing the nation's attention; a few missing or incarcerated communists did not cause either the intelligence community or the public much alarm. By the Cold War years, however, Americans had become obsessed with communism. Well-known anti-communists such as Whittaker Chambers, Elizabeth Bentley, and others turned again to Poyntz's disappearance and suspected murder, invoking them as proof that communism was a threat. In fact, Poyntz's disappearance played a prominent role in inspiring one-time leftists to turn to anti-communism.

Anti-Stalinism to Anti-Communism

Much Cold War scholarship focuses on the ascendency of the Republican Party and conservatives and the dismantling of the New Deal coalition. There continues to be limited research on the prewar American left's contribution to the production and dissemination of Cold War ideology. But both Cold War conservatism and liberal anti-communism have their roots in the 1930s American left wing. Poyntz's 1937 disappearance was a defining moment for the prewar anti-Stalinist left, influencing those who produced and reified anti-communist discourses to shift their political allegiances from Marxism to liberal and conservative anti-communism.[5]

As soon as Poyntz's disappearance was reported in the newspapers, Tresca, a well-known anarchist, publicly accused the CPUSA of killing her. Supported by his friend Solow, an independent leftist writer, the two began a vigorous investigation into the case. Tresca and Solow were part of a growing anti-Stalinist movement that emerged in the 1930s. In their view, Stalin, the Soviet premier, had corrupted Marxist communist ideology. They were not alone in this belief. While many in the American left, particularly members of the CPUSA, had initially looked to the Soviet Union with hope, that optimism began to erode under Stalin's leadership. By the 1930s, his paranoia and brutality were on full display, and American leftists began to defect from the Communist Party and its circles. The show trials and the purges between the spring of 1937 and the fall of 1938 cemented the belief that Stalin was a threat and that American Communists were his puppets.

According to the scholar Judy Kutulas, liberals (that is, those who want to effect serious reform) and radicals (people or groups who want to overthrow the existing system) are traditionally hostile toward one another. But between 1935 and 1939, they created an anti-fascist popular front, finding common ground and working together in organizations (often Communist-led) and on various anti-fascist campaigns. That honeymoon would be brief. By 1937, internal conflicts had begun to destroy their unity, and a renewed hostility had emerged. Kutulas argues that this rupture led to postwar anti-communism. The unraveling began with the CPUSA's attempts to explain the new party line, even as its own membership had doubts. Rather than trying to account for the show trials, it chose to issue "revelations" about Leon Trotsky, Stalin's number-one enemy, and emphasize the growing fascist threat. Kutulas calls the party's line on the trials "managed confusion." Some on the left began to argue that violence and brutality were inevitable in the Soviet revolutionary vision and an inherent part of Marxist-Leninism. Stalin was blocked by no "moral or ethical considerations" in his goal to eliminate class. In other words, the seeds for anti-Stalinism and liberal anti-communism lay not only in the premier's actions but also in liberals' interpretation of Marxist revolution. To them, revolutionary change was necessarily violent, and Stalin was proof.[6]

Solow and Tresca believed that the CPUSA was complicit in the Soviets' revolutionary violence and that the American branch of the party was purging its own ranks under orders from Moscow. Working under this assumption, Tresca was instrumental in constructing the argument that the Soviets had either killed or kidnapped Poyntz because she was disillusioned. He claimed that she had directly told him that she intended to leave the Soviet underground, and he wondered if her alleged disillusionment and her association with anti-Stalinists had led to her elimination. He told the press, law enforcement, and anyone else who would listen that in June 1937 she had either been killed on American soil or taken to a Soviet gulag. This story, which Tresca, with help from Solow, fashioned from unverifiable evidence and an abundance of hearsay, persists to this day and has been regurgitated by anti-communist witnesses, journalists, and conservatives.

In 1943, Tresca was assassinated by a still-unknown killer. Now Solow took the lead in pushing authorities to discover who had killed Poyntz and then Tresca. As his investigations deepened, his "anti-Stalinism gradually transformed into anti-communism." Solow and other anti-Stalinists believed that Stalin was corrupting Marxism; by the postwar years many came to believed that Marxism had corrupted Stalin. This political shift to the right among Solow and other former activists severely damaged liberal organizations and causes and eviscerated the American left. The historian Ellen Schrecker argues that the damage from postwar repression destroyed any possibility that radicals could create a "more authentic American radicalism." By the time a new civil rights movement began to emerge in the 1950s, liberal organizations such as the American Civil Liberties Union and the National Association for the Advancement of Colored People had ousted the radicals in their ranks, and the older generation had been effectively silenced. For Schrecker, perhaps the most important legacy of the Cold War was the way in which it showed political leaders how to effect "political repression" within a "democratic society."[7] Poyntz's alleged murder had become a rationale for silencing social justice activists, a reversal for many leftists who had devoted their younger years to achieving equity.

Ex-Communist Witnesses

Former communists and leftists were instrumental in the postwar anti-communist repression that silenced radical voices. During the Cold War, individuals who at one time had been fervently devoted to communism became just as passionate against it. For many of the leading ex-communist witnesses who were essential in the production and distribution of anti-communism, Poyntz's disappearance was central. In their eyes, it confirmed America's growing fears that communism was inherently violent, atheistic, and above all anti-American, though these claims were often illustrated with exaggerated accounts not based in actual evidence. Speculation about Poyntz's fate was enough to feed anti-communist hysteria; evidence was not necessary. Many of these people became conservative darlings and mouthpieces, with a public stage on which to voice their disillusionment and shape national attitudes.

The spy trials and legislative hearings that dominated American politics from the end of World War II well into the 1950s put disillusioned former spies on public display and gathered the American people behind new U.S. foreign and domestic policies. The scholars John Earl Haynes and Harvey Klehr write that the Soviet espionage trials at which ex-communist witnesses sold their wares "became a U.S. obsession" and came to dominate "public discourse." The hearings "shaped public perception" of the Cold War and convinced Americans that they faced a "serious issue of domestic security."[8]

In 1938, when the Soviet Union was liquidating the old Bolshevik leadership and killing some of its former agents abroad, Americans working in the Soviet underground were beginning to grow wary about maintaining their ties. One of them, Whittaker Chambers, afraid for his life and those of his wife and children, extricated himself and remained in hiding during the war years. Eventually he contacted his old friend Herbert Solow and confessed that Poyntz's disappearance had motivated his decision. As tensions between the United States and the Soviet Union intensified the Cold War, Chambers would emerge as a public anti-communist who garnered, according to Haynes and Klehr, "intense political attention" at a time of "shifting political context." He and other ex-communist witnesses convinced the nation that communism had already infiltrated American government, schools, and social justice organizations. In these arguments, Chambers gave Poyntz's alleged murder pride of place, arguing that it had sparked the Great Terror and subsequent purges.[9]

With the tide changing in American postwar politics, more former communists began to come forward to confirm mainstream politicians' claims that communists wanted to create a Soviet America. Many cited Poyntz's disappearance as a reason for fear. Benjamin Gitlow, who had been expelled from the party in 1929, claimed to have stayed in touch with members of the Soviet apparatus; in his 1948 book *The Whole of Their Lives,* he wrote about Poyntz's last hours in horrifying but questionable detail. Paul Crouch, once a friend of Poyntz's, left the party much later than Gitlow had. Crouch said he was told of Poyntz's murder directly by party insiders. Louis Budenz, the former editor of the CPUSA's daily newspaper, made a public religious conversion away from the party. He testified that he had been instructed not to print the pictures or names of the liquidated, including Poyntz, in the paper. Elizabeth Bentley, one of the best known and most controversial of the ex-communist witnesses, said that a fellow Soviet agent had told her that Poyntz was dead. The details of these various accounts diverged, but without evidence all claimed it was an open secret that the CPUSA had collaborated with the Soviet underground to silence Poyntz.

The witnesses described communists as subservient to Moscow's orders, traitors to their nation, and trapped by the communist conspiracy. They held up Poyntz as an example of the danger of trying to escape; and Schrecker writes that stories about her disappearance "regularly turned up" in their testimony and written work, which offered "vivid" though "obviously fictionalized" descriptions of her disappearance. Their graphic descriptions were intended to convince people that communism itself was violent. Thus, following this logic, conservative attacks on the Democratic Party, civil rights, women's rights, and other social justice movements were justified in the larger quest to preserve the American status quo.[10] There is still no evidence that Poyntz was murdered. The witnesses offered nothing but innuendo and rumor regurgitated from Tresca's original claims. Nonetheless, they effectively stoked anti-communist fears, and Poyntz served as a useful prop.

Gender and Anti-Communism

Poyntz had been a forceful, independent voice in the CPUSA, but her former comrades focused so much on what they suspected had happened to her that they lost sight of the person herself. As they speculated on her brutal victimization, they forgot that Poyntz, at least until her disappearance, had been a devoted communist willing to sacrifice her life to defeat fascism and usher in an anti-racist, anti-sexist, socialist America. This Poyntz did not make it into the anti-communist narratives; she was erased by the gendered constructions that were central to anti-communism.

As the scholar Nick Fischer writes, anti-communism has actively targeted labor and civil rights groups since the 1870s. With the dawn of feminism, it found a new target, though the historian Kirsten Delegard argues that the specifically gendered characteristics of anti-communism were not on full display until 1919. That year the U.S. Senate convened the Overman Committee, which was mandated to track the causes of the 1917 Bolshevik revolution. The committee went further and focused on the fate of Russian women, thus fueling the anti-radicalism that would characterize the rest of the century and creating hysteria about the fate of women under communist regimes.[11] The Overman Committee called witnesses who testified that the Bolsheviks were intent on destroying the nuclear family and declared that the regime's new divorce laws encouraged men to "discard" their wives. Perhaps the most sensational claim, and the one that would most influence later anti-communist sentiment, was that women and children were "nationalized" under the new regime; therefore, a woman did not belong to just one man. Witnesses described a new agency, the Bureau of Free Love, which they said had been created specifically to distribute women to men, regardless of love or emotional sentiment. Meanwhile, they asserted, children were sent off to be raised in state institutions. Both the bureau and the institutions were pure fiction, and the Soviets, along with Americans who had traveled to the USSR, ridiculed stories about nationalizing sexual relations. But the truth hardly mattered. The Overman Committee stoked a gendered fear that communism sanctioned "mass murder, desecration of churches, rape of upper-class women, corruption of children . . . and the corruption of marital bonds and parental authority." The revolution was sounding the death knell of the nuclear family.[12]

Anti-communist conservatives believed that the nuclear family was an institution that could help "reinforce self-control" and social control as well as prevent social discord. They feared that the destruction of that sacred institution would trigger the end of American values. The Overman Committee's findings confirmed for many that communism would erase families and gender differentiation, emasculating men and encouraging the working class to give in to "unfettered sexual desires." Committee witnesses claimed that upper-class women in the Soviet Union were made available to working men who had never before had access to such women. Because mainstream Americans continued to see the working class, especially immigrants and Black men, as sexually degenerate, these tales invoked race, gender, and class fears. Fueling public anxieties, stories in the press alleged that all Soviet women who were over the age of eighteen had to register with the fictitious Bureau of Free Love and then were "forced into sexual and marital relationships." Rape was, in these accounts, "routine official policy." The Overman Committee publicized the paradoxical claims that Soviet women were both sexual slaves and encouraged to take over the "harsh physical labor" of men. Anti-communists parroted this contradiction, alleging that communism both enslaved and emancipated women.[13]

One aspect of the committee's misogyny was its assumption that women were so politically naïve that they would be especially vulnerable to communist propaganda. Women were cast as both "victims and villains": as unwitting recruits, they would be drawn into communist politics; yet they also served as communist agents, which made them enemies of the state. Like the sexual contradictions just described, this paradox contributed to the creation of a foreign policy that was "grounded in [the] patriarchal nuclear family." It also informed later constructions of former female communists, including Poyntz.[14]

Conservatives were not wrong. American communists in the 1920s and 1930s did want to destroy gender and racial inequality. Many leftists traveled to the Soviet Union during those years and returned with promising stories about Soviet women's liberation, their access to birth control and abortion, and the availability of maternity leave.[15] The CPUSA lobbied for labor legislation that would secure women's right to work and demolish Jim Crow barriers to Black economic advancement. It welcomed women and people of color, not just as members but as leaders. Scandalizing conservatives, the party approved of, even encouraged, interracial dating, sex, and marriage. It openly advocated for women's right to voluntary motherhood and for access to safe and reliable birth control and abortion. Communist theorists argued that the American family was not a bulwark against communism but the locus for beginning revolutionary political change. In other words, the party *was* the nightmare that conservatives imagined. Red Scare anti-feminists saw its radicalism as a web of "economic, gender, sexual and racial chaos," and they energetically worked to stifle its power and influence. Together, mainstream anti-communism and grassroots anti-radicalism ensured that communism's foothold in American politics would be limited.[16]

But then capitalism failed. At least that was how the CPUSA framed the Great Depression. The 1930s became the party's golden era. Economic depression challenged the gender order and created opportunities for the American left to assault sexist and racist institutions. As male unemployment reached crisis levels, gendered female jobs stayed relatively secure, so women became breadwinners. Because women needed to keep these jobs, they put off marriage and motherhood in order to avoid getting fired. Already-married couples were having fewer children, and the legal restrictions on birth control were beginning to loosen ever so slightly. Panicked conservatives watched with dismay as women assumed masculine roles in the household. During these years, conservatism was perceived as "confused and unpopular," the left as "dynamic and intellectual." The CPUSA was actively organizing against fascism, advocating for equal rights, and attracting diverse artists and writers. Anti-communism did remain potent in American political culture, but it was not yet the dominant ideology it would become. For the moment, the rise of fascism in Europe, with its devoted opposition to communism and the left, made American conservatives appear "passé."[17]

Because the party was enjoying some influence at the time when Poyntz and Ruth Rubens disappeared, neither woman, though both were thoroughly embedded in communism, was held accountable for her political sympathies. In the press and among leftist male writers, they were infantilized, stripped of agency, and constructed as victims. The reality was that the fifty-year-old Poyntz had spent her entire adult life working in the left. She was no fool, and some colleagues described her as intimidating and overzealous. Yet after her disappearance, the real Poyntz—the hard-nosed communist who was rumored to have participated in show trial interrogations, frightened fellow communists, and badgered politicians—was forgotten. Instead, she was described as bookish, matronly, vulnerable, and nervous. Even as law enforcement refused to waste resources on locating a communist, the press and former comrades forgot her political leadership and absolved her of guilt.

This is remarkable, if we compare similar situations involving Cold War–era female communist spies. They were treated as gender traitors who had intentionally attacked the nuclear family and rejected their "natural" roles as mothers and housewives. According to the scholar Kathryn Olmsted, they were depicted as "shrewish wives, neurotic old maids, and voluptuous young vixens." American audiences were so distracted by their appearance that few ever really understood how these women had actually worked in the Soviet underground. Some, such as Ethel Rosenberg and Priscilla Hiss, who never admitted their involvement or never recanted, were depicted as ruthless or domineering or constructed as femmes fatales. Elizabeth Bentley, an ex-communist witness who tried to have a career in anti-communism, was constantly under assault because of her inability to conform to gendered expectations. She was the only former communist who used her first-person accounts of Poyntz as opportunities for personal attack. But Bentley's attempts to control her image failed because of the era's preoccupation with women's appearance and stereotypes about aggressive and unfeminine spies.[18] As the historian Elaine Tyler May argues, the postwar racialized construction of womanhood helped to contain communism abroad and the white American family at home. A new emphasis on restraining women's sexuality and conforming to heteronormativity limited women's roles. Social justice agitation for civil rights, women's equality, and peace were seen as threats to national security and suppressed. Activists were labeled as Bolsheviks, and social justice movements were dismissed as communist plots. Yet Poyntz's reputation remained mostly intact because she was believed to be a victim and not a perpetrator of communist evil.[19]

CHAPTER ONE
THE FAMILY

When Juliet Stuart Poyntz disappeared in 1937, the woman she was became lost in hysterical accounts of Soviet murder plots, female victimization, and the communist infiltration of America. In reality, Poyntz was a devoted communist who had deliberately chosen to operate as a spy for a foreign apparatus. She spent her entire adult life working for radical social change. Along the way, she became alienated from her family, and she made a disastrous marriage that ended because she refused to submit to traditional gender roles. Poyntz intimidated others in the Communist Party. She would not back down when others accused her of misdeeds, and intelligence agencies considered her to be one of the top-ten American communists. She was neither weak, vulnerable to influence, nor a victim. Until her last known moments, she was in total control of her life and was willing to endanger it to maintain that control.

It is likely that Poyntz inherited her tenacity and forceful personality from her parents and grandparents, some of whom were activists in their own right, all of whom were successful. Poyntz was descended from pioneers who had moved west at a time when the federal government was suppressing Native Americans and filling their land with white settlers. Her family benefited from that federal interference and, by gaining a foothold in the West, secured their place in middle-class white America and assured Poyntz's economic stability. But somewhere along the way, she rejected her bourgeois roots and embraced Marxism. Likely influenced by her abolitionist grandfather, her Populist father, and her strong-willed mother, she chose to devote her life to radical social change.

The Points Family

Poyntz's willfulness became apparent at a young age. She was born Juliet Stewart Points in Omaha, Nebraska, on November 20, 1886, to John J. Points and Alice Stewart Points. As I have mentioned, she used various spellings of her given name over the course of her life—perhaps an expression of independence or youthful rebellion that later became useful in the Soviet underground.[1] Whatever her motivations, she was clearly interested in controlling her own narrative.

Poyntz's father John had been born in Liberty, Indiana, in 1845 to Thomas Points and Talitha Guthrie. He was named after his grandfather, John Points, a military veteran from Campbell County, Kentucky, who had served with Huston's battalion of mounted volunteers in 1794 and with Boswell's militia in the War of 1812.[2] In 1823, the elder John Points took advantage of a government land-grant program to purchase eighty acres in Brookside, Indiana, located in Delaware County. The land had been taken from the Lenape tribe in 1818.[3]

Points, his wife Sarah, and their young children, including Thomas, packed up their goods and moved from Kentucky to begin their new life in Indiana. Two decades later, in 1842, Thomas, now thirty years old, purchased forty acres from his parents and set out to farm on his own. He was an educator and had worked as a teacher in the Delaware County public schools with "much success." (Both his son John and granddaughter Juliet would follow him into that occupation.) Contemporaries remembered him as an "earnest advocate" of all "educational interests," especially of the common school, which he believed was essential for society's advancement and for cultivating the individual for "the benefit of his fellow man." He was also a Baptist preacher, an "ardent republican," a devoted abolitionist, and a supporter of the temperance movement.[4]

On May 6, 1844, Thomas married Talitha Guthrie.[5] Little is known about Talitha's life before marriage except that she had been born in Montgomery County, Virginia, in October 1824. She spent her married years running the family household, which on a frontier farm was time-consuming and arduous. Yet her labor contributed to the success of the farm, which by 1850 was valued at $600.[6] Talitha and Thomas had eight children, five of whom survived to adulthood.[7] Juliet Stuart Poyntz's father, John, was the eldest, born in 1844, followed by Margaret and Sarah. Then, on October 1, 1849, there was a disruption: leaving Talitha and the children behind, Thomas departed for California with a company of twenty-eight men to try his luck as a gold miner.[8] His adventure was short-lived. By 1850, he was back in Indiana with his wife and children, who now included the baby Charles.[9] But Thomas did not stay put for long. In 1856, he moved his family to Iowa and soon thereafter to Pottawatomie, Kansas, where they settled.[10]

At this time, the territory of Kansas was embroiled in a tumultuous internal debate over whether it would join the union as a free state or a slave state. Passage of the 1854 Kansas-Nebraska Act had allowed voters to make the decision, and anti-slavery advocates, known as free-soilers, were determined to keep the state free. As a devoted Christian and a "staunch anti-slavery man," Thomas Points may have deliberately moved his family to Pottawatomie so that he could join them.[11] Already the battle over slavery in Kansas had become violent. In May 1856, just before the Points family arrived in Pottawatomie, the abolitionist John Brown, later famous for his failed raid on the federal arsenal in Harper's Ferry, Virginia, decided to act after pro-slavery forces attacked the abolitionist stronghold in Lawrence. Believing that at least five free-soilers had been killed and frustrated by a lack of militancy among his fellow abolitionists, Brown decided to avenge their deaths. Between the evening of May 24 and the morning of May 25, he and seven others abducted five pro-slavery settlers in their neighborhood near Pottawatomie Creek and murdered them. While Brown was never indicted for the murders, his homestead was burned in retaliation, and violence continued to erupt in Kansas. Points's commitment to abolition must have been powerful indeed if he was willing to move his family into the middle of this bloody conflict. Given that example, it is small wonder that his granddaughter became a formidable activist herself.[12]

In 1857, Pottawatomie County was incorporated, and Thomas Points became an early superintendent and commissioner. As a member of the territorial legislature, he was credited with helping to get rid of the "bogus pro-slavery laws." In 1859, Thomas built one of the "finest houses then to be found in Kansas," a two-story brick home that local lore later claimed was haunted.[13] Eventually, Kansas voters rejected slavery, and the territory entered the union as a free state in 1861.[14] Meanwhile, the Points family continued to grow, with its youngest daughter, Juliette, born in 1866. When Thomas died suddenly in March 1896, at the age of eighty-three, the community felt a deep loss. His obituary described him as a man of "sterling quality, just, upright, and farseeing." The writer recalled his efforts in the slavery debates during the 1850s and celebrated him as a man who had settled in a place where "laws are weak and disorder runs riot" but had battled against "error and injustice" to create peace for his community and his family.[15] Talitha died ten years later, "fifteen years beyond the allotted time of man," at the age of eighty-two.[16]

Rather than follow his family into farming, Poyntz's father John took up Thomas's commitment to education and public service. In 1863, he began attending Kansas State Agricultural College in Manhattan.[17] Four years later, he received his bachelor of arts degree as a member of the college's first graduating class. In 1871, he earned a master's degree in law from the college.[18] During this time he met his future wife, Alice Stewart, who attended the college until 1875. She then transferred to Oberlin College, graduating with a literary degree in 1878. (Oberlin was not yet issuing bachelors' degrees to women; the literary degree served as its equivalent.) Stewart returned to Kansas State Agricultural College and earned a master's degree in science in 1883.[19] The couple's commitment to education was rare at that time and in that place. As the two raised their family, it remained a priority in their household, empowering their daughters at a time when young women's aspirations were limited.

The Stewart Family

Poyntz's grandfather Thomas Points was a committed educator, religious leader, and abolitionist. Her maternal grandfather was quite the opposite. Alice Stewart was the youngest child of Charles Fanning Stewart and Juliette Slate Stewart. Both were from Connecticut. Charles was born in Voluntown, near New London, in 1814. At the age of sixteen, he left home for New Orleans and spent five years as a clerk for wholesale merchants. In 1841, he moved to Doaksville, in the Choctaw Nation in Oklahoma Territory, where he continued to work as a clerk. Here he met his first wife, Tryphena Wall, who was from a "prominent Choctaw mixed-blood family" and had been educated at local mission schools. With this marriage, Charles officially became a member of the Choctaw Nation.[20]

Charles and Tryphena opened a "general merchandise establishment" in Boswell, a town in Choctaw County, located between Fort Towson and Fort Washita. The business did well, and Charles was able to build a

Figure 1. Alice Stewart, Kansas State Agricultural College, 1883. Courtesy of Morse Department of Special Collections, Kansas State University Libraries.

new home and a new store and to purchase two slaves, seventy-five cattle, fifty-five hogs, and ten horses. The couple had four children together: Charles, Lavinia, Mariah, and Henry, all born between 1843 and 1848. By 1845, their holdings included a tavern, five slaves, "400 to 500 head of cattle, horses, and hogs." Stewart described himself as a "tolerable big bug for this country."[21]

In July 1849, Tryphena died in childbirth. She was buried in a grave in the Doaksville cemetery under a stone simply inscribed "Tryphena." Four months later, Charles married Juliette Slate from Norwich, Connecticut, in a ceremony at the Choctaw Nation town of Goodwater.[22] Perhaps Charles had traveled back to his home state to find a wife; perhaps it was a coincidence that the two Connecticut natives had met in Native American territory. In any case, Charles was unable to manage multiple businesses, slaves, and four children on his own. Together, he and Juliette would add two more children to the family. Arthur, the elder, was born in 1850. The younger, Alice Eulalia Stewart, was born in 1854.[23]

Charles's business continued to grow, and in 1851 he purchased his own steamer to transport goods upriver from New Orleans. Then, in 1855, one of his stores caught fire, and Charles rushed in to rescue his safe. He never "recovered from the exertion" and died in July, leaving Juliette with six children to raise. She brought three of her stepchildren and her own two back to Connecticut. With a sizable estate, she had enough money to take care of her large family.[24] In 1870, after Charles's children had reached adult age, Juliette traveled with Arthur and Alice to Manhattan, Kansas, where she set up a household with Rosana Slate, her older unmarried sister.[25]

Omaha

In 1874, John Points moved to Omaha, Nebraska, to take up a job as a schoolteacher. Omaha was a fast-growing town. Between the 1870s and 1900 the area transformed from a "frontier railroad center into a regional metropolis." Although growth slowed during the Panic of 1873 and the 1893 depression, much of the rest of that period was characterized by "tremendous progress" as the city developed a "clearly defined business community" and "transportation, commerce and industry flourished."[26]

Points, too, was making rapid progress. By 1877, he was the county superintendent of schools, a position he held for six years. He became a school-board member for Omaha's third ward and served on committees that oversaw the district's finances, teachers, and textbooks. In 1883, he was elected vice-president of the school board.[27]

If Omaha is any indication, growth often outpaced what western schools could handle. Between 1882 and 1883, the district gained 817 new students, a surge that required a "prompt response" from the school board. It needed to provide more teachers, more buildings, and more supplies.[28] Alice Stewart was one of those who answered Omaha's desperate call for new teachers. She had started her teaching career while still living in Kansas. In 1883, after earning her master's degree, she moved to Omaha and took up teaching at Central School, the district's largest. Throughout most of her career, Alice worked with the "grammar and primary grades," which included grades 1 through 8. Her starting salary was $700 per year, and she lived in a boardinghouse on California Street with other teachers.[29] The following winter, just two days before Christmas, John and Alice were married. Alice and her mother moved into his boardinghouse until they could set up their own household.[30]

By 1886, John Points had become president of the Omaha Board of Education. Under his leadership, the board provided free textbooks for all students, which lifted a "considerable burden" from the very poor, who had been compelled "to accept the bounty of the public."[31] After completing his term as president, Points stepped down but continued to serve as a board member. He moved his family to a house at 1218 South Twenty-Eighth Street, and Alice took a hiatus from teaching as the couple started their family.[32] Their first child, John T. Points, was born on October 12, 1885. Juliet Stewart Points was born thirteen months later, on November 20, 1886. Young John died of heart failure on August 29, 1887, and a second son, Charles, was born on April 6, 1889.[33] At the age of nine months, Charles contracted pneumonia and died on July 28, 1890.[34] Both boys were buried next to their grandmother Juliette, who had passed away in 1885, at Forest Lawn Cemetery. The Points's youngest child, Margaret, was born on September 16, 1891. Called Eulalie, she outlived everyone in the family, dying in 1967 at the age of seventy-five.[35]

Like his father, John Points was politically active. He was involved in the local Democratic Party and in 1888 was elected secretary of Douglas County's Democratic delegation to the state convention.[36] By the 1890s, he had become caught up in the Populist fervor that was sweeping the West and the South. Populism grew out of the farmers' alliance movement that, by the 1880s, was advocating for the creation of farmers' cooperatives to eliminate price gouging by middlemen, merchants, and railroads. In 1889, a farmers' alliance convention in St. Louis was calling for "currency reform, government ownership of the railroads and telegraph, equitable taxation, governmental economy, and sub treasury plan." In Kansas, a new Populist Party emerged from the alliance movement, and in the 1890 election its candidates for state office "swept the state." In neighboring Nebraska, however, town and rural voting patterns "diverged dramatically." By 1890, Nebraska Republicans were capturing urban votes, and Points was supporting a political minority.[37] At the 1897 Populist Party convention in Omaha, he was nominated as a candidate for county superintendent, though he declined to accept, for unclear reasons—possibly personal ones.[38]

For those who are trying to understand individual lives, the historical record is often inadequate—particularly in the case of women. Like her mother-in-law and her mother, Alice led a less public life than her husband did; thus, we know far less about her. We do know that, against the typical gender expectations of her time, she chose to return to teaching, even though she had two small children (only one of whom was school-aged) and a career-minded and politically active husband. After working in several other schools, she was assigned to Train School in 1896, where she taught the seventh and eighth grades—earning the same $700 salary that she had made when she first started teaching in Omaha thirteen years earlier. It was her final job in the district. In 1897, Alice left her husband, headed east with their two daughters, and settled in Jersey City, New Jersey. It is not known what happened to fracture the Points's marriage, though they never legally divorced. Nor is it known if the daughters had any contact with their father after the move. Poyntz was nine years old when her parents separated.[39]

For a time after his family left, John Points continued to move forward with his community work and career. In 1900, he again served as a Populist Party delegate. In 1902, he and his fellow Populists submitted a proposed platform for the state convention. In 1904, he was elected chairman of the Omaha Populist convention and ran as an independent to become a presidential elector. He failed to win that election.[40] But Points's career prospects waxed and waned during the first decade of the twentieth century. For years he had his own law firm and even served as a judge, but by 1914 he was a law clerk, and by 1915 he was working as a bookkeeper. By that time, he was seventy years old and probably ready for retirement. Nonetheless, his professional decline and erratic work history is difficult to understand. Perhaps they were linked to his wife and daughters' departure, for his public service declined as well. Still, he did remain active in a few causes. In 1912, he was one of a small group of individuals who discussed Henry George's single-tax proposal for funding federal spending. In 1914, he attended an organizational meeting to advocate for women's suffrage, a movement that his faraway elder daughter was also involved in.[41]

Jersey City and New York

Alice's reasons for bringing her daughters to New Jersey are unclear. Her older brother Arthur may have died in Kansas in 1894.[42] Her half-brother Henry and half-sister Lavinia had moved back to Oklahoma, where Henry had problems with the law; in August 1879 he was executed by hanging in an Arkansas prison. Lavinia had married and settled on Choctaw Nation territory.[43] Alice's eldest half-sister, Mariah, called Mary, was the only immediate family Alice had left on the East Coast, but she was living with her husband and two of her three children in Hampden, Massachusetts.[44]

Whatever her reasons, Alice settled her daughters in Jersey City, and she restarted her own teaching career in the city's public school system. Her elder daughter entered brand-new Public School 9, built in 1896. Early on, Juliet Poyntz showed a penchant for leadership. In May 1898, the eleven-year-old sang a solo titled "Forest Hymn" at the school's Arbor Day festival. After eighth grade, she attended Dickinson High School, where she was a smart and motivated student.[45] She was a member of the school's Delphian Society, an organization promoting women's education, and recited poems, engaged in debates, and attended lectures associated with the society. In March 1903, her senior year, Poyntz participated in a debate on whether the college course should be reduced from four years to three. She was opposed. In April, she served as "critic" for her fellow Delphians' presentations. That same year she served on a committee that hosted an entertainment and dance at the school. The *Jersey City Journal* reported that the event was a "financial and social success," which it attributed to the size and popularity of the class of 1903.[46]

Poyntz's academic achievements were impressive. She was valedictorian of her class and received the Dickinson Medal, awarded annually to the student with the highest average in all four years. Notably, she also won the Forensic Medal, the most "coveted prize" at commencement, which had never before gone to the winner of the Dickinson Medal. The prize was intended to honor the best orator at commencement and was usually given to a "conventional and conservative" speaker, which the valedictory speaker typically was not. Nonetheless, Poyntz managed to earn the coveted medal and add yet "another honor to [her] . . . long list."[47]

Poyntz was sixteen when she graduated from high school. In the fall of 1903, she entered Barnard College as a freshman. The college, located in New York City, was close to her home in Jersey City. Barnard was a relatively new college at the time, having opened in 1889 as the sister school to Columbia College. Poyntz was a busy student, involved in many activities that would later be useful in her political career. In her first semester at Barnard, she was elected class treasurer and worked on the scenery committee of the student theater. In the spring semester she was elected class president. She served as a class officer during all four years at Barnard and also joined and served as an officer for the Beta Epsilon chapter of the Kappa Gamma fraternity.[48]

During this era, many educated middle- and upper-class young women were attracted to progressivism, a catch-all movement that encompassed a variety of reforms but shared a common desire to "reshape society." Progressives focused on issues such as immigration and the effects of industrialization and urbanization.[49] Barnard College gave its students plenty of opportunities to explore progressivism. In 1906, Poyntz's junior year, its chapter of the College Settlements Association sponsored a tea with nationally known speakers, including Florence Kelley of the Consumers' Union, to speak about settlement houses and child labor. Another presenter at the tea was Mary Van Kleeck, then a Smith College fellow, who spoke about her investigations into women's working conditions in New York City. Though Van Kleeck was never officially a member of the CPUSA, she worked closely with it during the time that Poyntz was a public figure in the party. It is not known if Poyntz attended the tea, but she certainly had many opportunities at Barnard to engage with progressive reforms and well-known activists.[50]

Poyntz had been raised in a household that valued social reform and education, but she had to negotiate the divide that often existed between would-be reformers and the populations they wanted to reform. As a Barnard delegate at a student conference sponsored by the Young Women's Christian Association, she participated in a session on "Home Missions" that focused on working with "classes of people peculiar to the United States": Native Americans, immigrants, Mormons, and the "Mountain Whites of the South." In an article about the conference, the Barnard newspaper referred to them as "these people," thus driving home the notion of difference. Well-meaning conference leaders wanted to teach the privileged college students how to educate such "classes" in order to enhance their "patriotism" and give them "intelligent information about their country."[51] Yet a condescending manner often prevented progressives from understanding the people they were attempting to help. As a young activist, Poyntz, too, was infected with this paternalism. Though radical socialist politics later disabused her of that attitude, she continued to take a self-righteous approach to effecting social change.

Poyntz seems to have made an impression among her college peers. In April of her senior year, she was elected to serve a five-year term as alumnae officer for the class of 1907. At the class's celebration in June, she was voted "most popular, diplomatic and the best all-round." She also delivered the "valedictory address." In it she counseled her fellow graduates to "never forget that we are human beings—intensely human beings" and told them that Barnard had given them a "training in living," one that would help them achieve their goals "in the frame of the real world around us." Her speech revealed both her youthful idealism and her progressive desire to reform in her own image. Though she suggested that Barnard's location had given its students an upper hand in understanding the plight of the urban poor, she forgot that they were merely privileged observers. It would take her many years to shed that idealism; but when she did, she would embrace the need for revolutionary change, not piecemeal reform.[52]

CHAPTER TWO

THE COMMUNIST

Poyntz became an adult at a time of rapid economic, political, and social change, and progressive responses to that upheaval were a strong influence on her generation. Both during and after college, she was involved in the women's suffrage movement; she was also drawn to working-class politics in the form of unionism and unemployment relief. Although these early forays into reform were not particularly radical, eventually her political evolution would take a serious turn to the left and lead her directly to the American Communist Party.

Early Causes

Poyntz's first job after graduating from Barnard was teaching English at the Bergen School for Girls in Jersey City. She did not stay at the school for very long. Instead, she broke away from "the respectable middle classes," as she described them, and spent two years in the "slums" with "the lowest of the low delightful immigrants," where she worked as a special agent for the U.S. Immigration Commission. Many Progressive Era reformers believed that unrestricted immigration was leading to "the

Figure 2. Juliet Stuart Poyntz, Barnard College, 1907. Photograph appeared in *Mortarboard*. Barnard College Archives and Special Collections.

growth of slums and bossism." Some called for a literacy requirement for incoming migrants; others proposed forming a commission to study the immigration problem. As a result, the U.S. Immigration Commission (1907–11), also known as the Dillingham Commission, came into being. During Poyntz's years with the commission, she traveled to cities with large immigrant populations such as Chicago, Milwaukee, Philadelphia, and Utica to collect data. The commission's final forty-two-volume report concluded that a difference existed between old and new immigrants and thus "supported the prevailing beliefs" of those who advocated immigration restriction. Essentially, these "findings" legitimized the urge to "stereotyp[e] millions of Americans." They also revealed an inherent problem within progressivism: it promoted a patronizing view of people of color and working people and saw them as inherently flawed.[1] Poyntz, too, was convinced that reformers knew better than the immigrants themselves about how to create change. The stereotypes codified by the Dillingham Commission would remain with her for years as she began to hone her political commitments. Even at the end, she was always certain she knew best about how to fix the world.

As a young woman, Poyntz committed an increasing amount of time to political activism, and by 1911 she was describing herself as a suffragist, a feminist, and a socialist "of the worst brand."[2] She joined the Socialist Party in 1909, but suffrage captured most of her attention in her early post-college years. She worked as an organizer and a speaker for the College Equal Suffrage League, founded in Boston in 1900 by women college students and graduates who wanted to "take a positive stand" for women's voting rights. League branches emerged at a number of campuses across the United States. At a 1908 meeting in Buffalo, the organization "formed a national association" and became an affiliate of the National American Woman Suffrage Association. The association's aims were "educational rather than political," though many of its satellites did get involved in state political campaigns. Still, its primary goal was to "gain the attention" of young women. It was not a radical organization, and it discouraged any "canvassing, street speaking," or "spectacular and dramatic deeds" done in its name.[3]

As the association's representative, Poyntz traveled to college campuses to recruit young women into the suffrage movement. She believed it was their responsibility to take part, and her recruiting style foreshadowed her approach to leadership in the CPUSA. In February 1910, she spoke to students at Syracuse University about the history of the movement and then upbraided them for being the only university in the state that had not formed a suffrage organization. The students, either inspired or shamed by her, formed a branch the next day.[4]

In April 1910, Poyntz attended a national suffrage convention in Washington D.C. She was listed prominently as a speaker alongside well-known suffragists such as Alice Paul of the Congressional Union and Carrie Chapman Catt of the National American Woman Suffrage Association. The delegates were welcomed by President William Howard Taft, the first U.S. president to ever address a women's suffrage convention. But to the dismay of the delegates, he told them that he did not support their mission, primarily because he believed women were not interested in voting. Moreover, he said, granting women the vote would empower certain members of the "less desirable classes." As one reporter wrote, the "walls of the convention hall echoed a chorus of feminine hisses" that "sounded as if a valve on a steam engine had broken." In response, Taft condescendingly scolded the "ladies," telling them, "You must show yourselves capable of suffrage by exercising that degree of restraint which is necessary in the conduct of government by not hissing." In a letter to Taft the next day, the conventioneers officially apologized.[5]

What Poyntz thought of Taft's behavior is not known, but in general she had little patience for men's patronizing remarks about women's rights. In a 1914 article for the *Barnard Bear,* she described the difficulties she had faced as a student when she tried to establish a campus suffrage organization. She castigated "weak and timid" men who "cling blindly to things as they are" and make "suffragette" seem like a bad word. During her student days, anyone who admitted to being a suffragist was met with "kindly indulgence and ill-concealed superiority." They were reminded that men had "no use for 'suffragettes'" and that clever women were "bad enough." Poyntz worried that young female students were hesitant to openly support suffrage if it meant social ostracism. But she encouraged them to take the plunge, assuring them that, since her own graduation, suffrage had become not only tolerated but "fashionable."[6]

Poyntz made it clear that she was disappointed in the many Barnard students who had failed to embrace the mission. Her tone matched the one she had taken with the Syracuse students. Perhaps, she wrote, their reluctance could be traced to a "general indifference bred of inexperience"; perhaps it was a sign of "intellectual snobbishness." But probably it stemmed from their "lack of appreciation" for the "deep and wide significance" of the movement. Most students, she wrote, were not familiar "theoretically" with the "woman question." That phrase, commonly used to describe suffrage, also covered a variety of other reforms such as workplace protections, decent wages, voluntary motherhood, and access to education. Poyntz argued that Barnard students needed not only a general education about suffrage but also courses on women's history and the "general economic and social position" of women. No "Barnard girl" could be justified in "turning a deaf ear": all must join the "advance army" so that women could "march upward and onward."[7]

As Poyntz engaged in her work with the Dillingham Commission and the women's suffrage movement, she also continued her studies. In 1910, she earned a master's degree at Columbia. Her thesis essay, titled "Conditions among the Immigrants of Milwaukee, Wisconsin," included data compiled from her commission investigations into the racial and ethnic makeup and living conditions among that city's immigrant populations. Referring to each national group as a "race," she examined the most "congested blocks" of the German, Bohemian, Polish, Jewish, and Italian neighborhoods, focusing on about "200 families" in each national group. As a means of comparison, she also included data about a hundred "American families" with similar economic backgrounds.[8]

Poyntz's thesis reveals her general ignorance about poverty, immigration, and ethnic stereotypes and reflects the Dillingham Commission's stereotypes about various immigrant groups. She accused Poles and Italians of being unable to integrate and derided them for living in poorer housing, ignoring the fact that the housing was rented and thus the landlords were responsible for conditions. She claimed that the Germans and Bohemians tended to live in "better . . . conditions" with "less congestion," and said that they immediately moved out of neighborhoods once they became too crowded. The Poles, on the other hand, had "little tendency" to move out of such areas and thus apparently did not prefer better living conditions. Likewise, the Italians showed "no sign whatsoever" of pursuing better living conditions. Poyntz claimed that the city industries were not to blame for congestion; it was the racial groups themselves. In contrast, the Germans, she argued, were very like Americans in that they sought "individual betterment" more often than other races did.[9]

Poyntz's thesis failed to address any economic conditions that certainly influenced both overcrowding and dilapidation. It ignored the role of local industry in pollution and housing conditions and failed to recognize that prejudice was keeping certain communities out of better neighborhoods. She parroted an oft-cited stereotype that older immigrants were different from newer ones because of their level of integration. The Germans, Bohemians, and Jews, she wrote, saw themselves as American and had few remaining ties to the old country. She claimed that the Germans were "superior to the other races" and were quick to adopt American practices. The Poles, she wrote, saw themselves as sojourners rather than as permanent residents; and the Italians, "it was said," always had enough money to return to Italy. She saw them as "densely ignorant," "low on the social scale," and almost completely unable to Americanize. Poyntz's future radical socialism was nowhere evident in her thesis.[10]

Frederick Franz Ludwig Glaser

While Poyntz was working on her master's degree at Columbia, she was appointed assistant professor of history at Barnard. She taught there until 1910, when she was awarded a prestigious scholarship sponsored by the General Federation of Women's Clubs. The scholarship process followed "the exact forms" of the all-male Rhodes Scholarship, and officers of the Rhodes Trust examined the applicants. The General Federation made the final decision, with the ultimate goal of identifying a woman with the "highest promise of distinction." The winner received funds for a full year of study at an English institution of her choice.[11]

Poyntz chose to study at both the London School of Economics and Oxford University in order to study how the Industrial Revolution had affected "the labor of women." She wrote later her experience in England was "most illuminating" and said that she had met some "very interesting people." She must have enjoyed herself because she opted to stay for an additional year of study beyond the scholarship period. She was active in her studies, and she published an introduction to a book of essays on "seasonal unemployment" edited by Sidney Webb. She also traveled around Europe, visiting France, Denmark, Belgium, and Holland and spending the summer of 1911 in Germany with her mother.[12]

Responding to an alumnae committee's "'steenth appeal" for information about her post-college years, Poyntz claimed that she was not engaged and "never shall be though I may sometime persuade myself into marrying." She was either being coy or simply dishonest because by the time she returned from England she was engaged to Frederick Franz Ludwig Glaser. She may have avoided discussing her relationship because he was still married when they met. But many things are mysterious about her relationship with Glaser. Poyntz kept it so secret that some of her friends did not know she had ever been married. Glaser, too, was secretive about the marriage: his family never knew about his second wife until after his death.[13]

Glaser was born in Mannheim, Germany, in July 1879. His father, Carl Glaser, was part of the Farberindustrie Trust, also known as IG Farben, a conglomeration of chemical companies created in 1925. The elder Glaser hoped his son would join him in the business, but Frederick had no interest in joining his father. This decision, coupled with his commitment to socialism, led to an estrangement from his family that lasted until his death. Instead of business, Glaser chose a career in journalism. He met Poyntz while he was in London serving as a foreign correspondent and she was working at the London Library of Economics. When her studies were over and she returned to America, he followed her. On October 8, 1913, the two were married in New York City.[14]

Since 1855, foreign-born women who married American men had been granted American citizenship. The rationale was that men were expected to exercise "husbandly protectiveness" over their wives and thus their citizenship held more value than women's did. The law did not, however, specify what would happen to American women who married foreigners. Until 1907, that was left up to the courts. There was no consistency in these decisions: some women retained their citizenship, and others lost it. Finally, with passage of the Expatriation Act, the question was answered. Women who married foreign-born men would lose their

American citizenship. As the historian Nancy Cott explains, Congress assumed that women should naturally adopt their husbands' "national allegiance," even though the law "ma[d]e aliens of their countrywomen." By this time, many European nations, including Germany, had passed similar legislation. However, Germany did not welcome the naturalization of the wives of its foreign nationals. This left Poyntz stateless.[15]

Glaser and Poyntz's marriage was not a happy one. Glaser expected his wife to respect her husband's authority. Poyntz would have none of that, and their clash of wills created tension. During World War I, she became more and more involved with politics, and the couple had conflicting views about the war as well as divided national loyalties. They split up and reunited several times. Finally, in 1924, Poyntz permanently moved out and rented her own apartment. For reasons known only to the two of them, they (like Poyntz's parents) never officially divorced. But when the marriage dissolved, Poyntz went through the naturalization process to regain her American citizenship, which she obtained on March 14, 1924.[16]

Despite the failed marriage, Glaser played an important role in the mystery of Poyntz's disappearance. There is no indication that the pair had any contact between their final split in 1924 and his death in 1935. Nevertheless, because they had never divorced, Poyntz, with the help of her lawyer, Elias Lieberman, claimed Glaser's estate, which was worth between $10,000 and $20,000. Because Glaser's assets were in Nazi Germany, Poyntz, then working as a Soviet agent, found herself in direct contact with the Nazis. To complicate matters, Glaser had been working since 1933 as a foreign correspondent for the Associated Press at the German consulate in New York City. Questions emerged about his loyalty. Some asked if he was now loyal to the Nazi regime? Officials at the consulate knew he was a socialist, which cast doubts on the Nazi theory. Whatever the truth, the links among Poyntz, her former husband, and the Nazis led to questions about whether they had had a role in her disappearance.[17]

As a Soviet agent, Poyntz used her ex-husband's last name. This was not the first time she had assumed an alternate label. Since college, she had used various versions of her name to control her identity; and because she was inconsistent, some people knew her by multiple names. At Barnard, she began to play with different spellings of Stewart and Stuart. By 1914, she had changed Points to Poyntz. She once told a reporter that Poyntz was an "old English name, as you will find out by reading Shakespeare's comedies." Her real reasons for these changes remain murky. Perhaps she wanted to protect her family from any association with socialists. But even among her colleagues she was mercurial. In her political work she used Juliet Stuart Poyntz; in the underground and on her naturalization papers she went by Juliet Glaser. Some of her friends believe that, a full decade before she actually entered the underground, she was being groomed for the underground. Certainly, by 1924, she had a connection to Germany and was fluent in the language.[18]

Unionism and Socialism

After Poyntz returned from Europe, she went back to teaching at Barnard College, but she soon found a way to wed her political commitments to her career goals. In 1914, she began working for the Rand School of Social Science, offering history classes on labor and women. The Rand School was the brainchild of the American Socialist Party's board of directors. Their goal was to use the social sciences as a vehicle for studying socialism. The school's founders all belonged to the centrist wing of the Socialist Party: that is, they believed reform and the "electoral process" could be used to achieve "gradual, non-violent, international revolution." Though the Rand School was less radical, it provided a place of study for people who would eventually embrace more revolutionary goals.[19]

Poyntz also became involved with the American Association for Labor Legislation, founded in 1905. The organization was the first to advocate for a federal health plan; however, its goals were broader, based on the belief that the costs of "industrial progress" fell disproportionately onto the poorest and most disenfranchised workers. Poyntz worked with the association on unemployment issues and spoke on that topic at a number of conventions. In February 1915, as a featured speaker at the Woman's City Club of Boston, she told her audience that unemployment was not the result of an individual's inefficiency; rather, industry was to blame. She also emphasized that underemployment was a central problem as many people were unable to secure work that could provide for their families year round.[20]

Poyntz earned a reputation at the Rand School as an effective researcher and speaker. But after a male co-worker was chosen over her as editor for the school's labor yearbook, she became frustrated with her job. Morris Hillquit, one of the school's founders, believed in her potential and recruited her as a union researcher. Hillquit was the attorney for Local 25 of the Waist and Dressmakers' Union of New York, an affiliate of the International Ladies Garment Workers Union (ILGWU), with a membership of over 25,000. The Waist and Dressmakers' Union was seeking higher wages for its members; and as part of the arbitration process, Hillquit needed data on their current wages and cost of living. Although the workload was not heavy, Poyntz undertook the research, which introduced her to the labor movement. Then, in 1915, Hillquit recommended her for an opening as the local's first education director. The job suited her background and her growing commitment to progressive causes, and she accepted.[21]

One of the union's biggest challenges was that most of its members were immigrants and few were fluent in English. So Poyntz reached out to public school teachers and asked them to offer classes in English. She asked the historian Charles Beard to give a series of lectures on American history, and she hosted dances and recreation activities for union members. Like other union activists in the early twentieth century, she was committed to adult education as a fundamental aspect of effective union organization. This belief in teaching workers the "rudiments of trade unionism" would flourish until the 1920s, when conservatism became ascendant. An important part of the approach was encouraging union members to participate in building a "new and better world." In Poyntz's view, radical change could come only from unifying and organizing the workers, and she hoped her educational programs would inspire them to reach toward that change. Her "dynamic leadership" became an inspiration for other such programs aimed at women workers.[22]

Poyntz was committed to the importance of workers' education, and she wanted to take the idea further and create a "school of unionism" for women, an idea she'd borrowed from France, where similar institutions operated for garment workers. Its mission would be to help women become "better qualified to go forward in the labor movement" without instruction or leadership from men. In her view, the goal of unionism was to "combine for the benefit of all"; therefore, such a school would advance not only the labor movement's goals but also Poyntz's personal socialist goals: namely, the unity of the working classes against the ruling classes. Poyntz believed that education programs were vital for women workers, who were especially vulnerable and disempowered. She and others involved in workers' education paid particular attention to this population's "special needs and desires" and saw improving their lot as essential to the "personal and political liberation of the working class." In other words, Poyntz wanted to train young women to take on leadership roles themselves. As the historian Susan Wong notes, Poyntz's emphasis on workers' education highlights a shift in the idea of unionism. For men, union activity was often strictly political, but Poyntz recognized that women were interested in having a union that was more than just "a rallying point for economic justice." They wanted it to feel like a community where they could "learn, meet friends and have fun," all of which would increase their allegiance.[23]

Poyntz knew she needed to provide a place that not only offered women an education but also gave them a place to find "Joy in life." Her first steps toward a school of unionism began with a group of young immigrant women who were scattered among rooms they'd rented from strangers. Poyntz suggested that they organize a larger group to rent an entire house, where they would only have to answer to one another. This rental home was known as Unity House. Eventually, the union itself created a second Unity House, a rental in the Catskill Mountains, where women workers could go on retreat to learn, socialize, and find "spiritual inspiration." The Catskill house was under the direction of Marie B. MacDonald, an ILGWU leader and a close friend of Poyntz's.[24]

Because the women workers did not want to leave that experience "behind in the mountains," a permanent Unity Center was created in 1917.[25] The ILGWU rented an abandoned school building on East Twentieth Street, which became the union's locus. Shop meetings were held there, often "as many as twenty in an evening." The center contained a cooperative cafeteria and two gymnasiums that were used for meetings, lectures, dances, and physical training. The union brought in a nurse from the Joint Board of Sanitary Control who offered "physical and medical advice" several evenings a week. Labor education was a major focus: the center offered classes on labor problems and the history of the labor movement in both English and Yiddish. Poyntz hoped to add a library with books on "social and economic questions" and for "literary pursuits." The Unity Center was so popular that in its first six weeks of operation "10,000 different individuals" attended "350 shop meetings," and another 7,000 attended concerts, lectures, and more. Poyntz described it as a "home" for workers—a "clean, well-ventilated" place with "cheer and familiar faces," unlike the dirty "ill-ventilated" rooms above saloons where members of other unions were often forced to hold meetings. For Poyntz, the most important thing about the Unity Center was that it offered the "possibility of growth and development of the body and mind" for both individuals and the "collective organization."[26]

Still, it was challenging to foster labor education while creating working-class solidarity. The problem was that education supposedly gave workers "class mobility"—that is, a route out of the working class—but organizers also wanted to use education to help workers become aware of themselves *as* workers. In addition, trainers such as Poyntz, who had often come out of the middle class, valued "knowledge for the sake of knowledge," which was a "bourgeois educational tenet." Their solution was to focus on "knowledge as power" and emphasize its ability to create a "new and better social order." In an article in *Life and Labor,* Poyntz wrote that teachers in the workers' classes used direct, clear language and introduced concepts simply. She assured readers that these programs were not meant to train a worker "away from his class."[27]

Many of the ILGWU's membership and leadership were socialists, and they believed that unionism's goal was "the rebuilding of society." In their eyes, workers' education was one element in the realization of that goal. Within this congenial atmosphere, Poyntz began to develop her socialist worldview around class solidarity and unity, which included a focus on women's issues. In June 1916, she became the editor of Local 25's magazine, the *Message.* The union used the magazine to communicate with members and increase their connection and commitment to the labor movement, but it also politicized them on other issues. In a 1918 article titled "The Feminist Revolution," Poyntz argued that wartime gains, including higher wages for women, needed to continue into the postwar era. She wrote that the great victory to come out of the war was women's economic independence; a woman was no longer a "mere parasite, [an] appendage" of her male relations. Women could now challenge both men and the state, particularly in regard to being wives and mothers. They could refuse to produce cannon fodder for the next capitalist war. Poyntz insisted that part-time workers should receive double wages, which would prevent women from continuing to be a dependent class. The state should guarantee a standard of living and protect the wages and health of its workers, particularly vulnerable women workers, as it had during wartime.[28]

In other *Message* articles, Poyntz argued that the right to vote would empower women workers specifically. She was wary of upper- and middle-class suffragists, who, she claimed, wanted the vote only in order to have access to the tools of economic oppression that their husbands, brothers, and fathers were already using. She saw such democratic sentiments as vaguely philanthropic rather than genuinely committed to reform. But for working women and men, the vote was a weapon they could wield to "influence the high cost of living, [and] the price of food and clothes," as well as demand improved housing, a better police force, and higher wages. Not only could the vote "force" the state to listen to their needs and fulfill their demands, but it would also help women work toward a "Socialist state."[29]

While they certainly could fight for economic justice, women also needed maternity leave. Poor women needed financial assistance for themselves and their children as well as access to medical care and health advice. Poyntz understood that the work of parenting fell primarily to women; thus, their children's needs were wrapped up in their own. She argued that, with the vote, women could help improve schools, provide lunches for poor children, and create cooperative kitchens and warehouses in tenement neighborhoods. Importantly, they could also address the blight of prostitution, an institution that victimized them. Poyntz was not addressing prostitution as a moral issue; rather, she believed that women must protect themselves from sexual exploitation—from becoming mere "articles of commerce and objects of degradation." One way to do that was to ensure that their wages were commensurate with men's.[30]

One of Poyntz's articles on suffrage focused on the state legislature's vote on extending the franchise to New York women. The following week's editorial celebrated passage of that law. For Poyntz, this was a victory for women and for workers more generally. She argued that workers had now moved from "mere talk" to "action," which promised a better future for all. The union sponsored a suffrage jubilee to celebrate and to rouse working-class women to do the work required to make the vote meaningful. The jubilee announcement noted that upper- and middle-class women were already mobilizing and educating their ranks about the duties of citizenship and emphasized that the union, too, had to take up the challenge.[31]

Poyntz's time in the ILGWU led her down an increasingly radical path, as evidenced by her growing commitment to suffrage as a tool for working women's emancipation. She met many people in the union who became important friends and confidantes for the rest of her life. Among them was Elias Lieberman, who served on the ILGWU's Committee of Education while she was the education director. He was a frequent contributor to the *Message* under her editorship. She also became close to Marie MacDonald of the Catskill Unity House.

During these years, Poyntz met a Russian man named Schachno Epstein who worked for the *Gerechtigkeit,* the ILGWU's Jewish newspaper. After her disappearance some friends claimed that the two had been "intimate friends" during their time in the union; others believed there was a romantic connection, though at this time she was still married to Glaser. In 1917, Epstein, inspired by the Bolsheviks' revolutionary fervor, returned to his home country. In 1928, he was accused of being a Trotskyite, but he ingratiated himself with the Communist Party and eventually earned favor. In 1933, the OGPU sent Epstein back to the United States under the pseudonym Joseph Berson, but he stayed for only two or three years. In 1937, he was in the United States again, where he was seen in in Poyntz's company. He left the country shortly after she went missing, leading many of her friends to believe that he had probably been her abductor.[32]

Communism

Many of the ILGWU leaders and members were moderate socialists, but Poyntz was moving toward the party's left wing. In 1917, after a series of tense debates among socialists in the union, Poyntz resigned from her position as union educator. She stayed on as editor of the *Message* until January 1919, when it was folded into the ILGWU's larger newspaper.[33]

By the time of her resignation, Europe had been embroiled in war for two years, and the United States was about to join the conflict. The Bolshevik uprising in Russia was inspiring many radical socialists, though not all approved of its tactics. Poyntz was certainly influenced by events in Russia; but even before the revolution, her radicalism was inspired by that country's radicals.[34]

One of her closest friends in the Socialist Party was Ludwig Lore, the editor of *Volkszeitung,* a German socialist daily published in New York City. Lore was the leader of the German language branch of the party, and through him Poyntz met a number of leading Russian radicals. In 1915 and 1916, he arranged a U.S. speaking tour for the Russian feminist Alexandra Kollontay. Kollontay impressed Poyntz with her ability to combine socialism and feminism. Among socialists and later among the communists who subscribed to Marxist tenets, this link could be controversial, given that many radicals rejected feminism as bourgeois. Some believed that focusing on women's rights ignored class oppression and the economic conditions that created inequality. But Kollontay argued that women's rights could not wait for the revolution because women were suffering now from huge pay differentials, limited job opportunities, sexual harassment, and limited access to birth control. Kollontay's political work, coupled with her insistence that personal issues were political, inspired Poyntz to devote more time to socialism. Through Lore, she also met the Bolshevik leaders Leon Trotsky and Nikolai Bukharin, who were staying in New York as representatives of the Socialist Party's Russian federation. (Both returned to Russia at the outbreak of the revolution.)[35]

World War I revealed divisions among socialists around the world. Even before the war, as tensions increased in Europe, many socialists believed that the only way to avoid the impending conflict would be to overthrow their countries' governments. But in Germany, Belgium, and

France, Social Democrats and socialists in parliament voted in favor of war, which frustrated and stymied American socialists. When the United States entered the fray in 1917, the American party released an official platform opposing the war. As a result, the government evoked the Sedition Act and blocked mailing privileges for some of the party's publications. At the same time, the party's left wing was emboldened, and it began creating foreign language federations such as the one Lore controlled.[36] The Bolshevik uprising fueled these divisions. In many countries, socialism was a moderate movement, one that sought reforms rather than revolution. These moderates were alarmed by Bolshevik communism and the dictatorship of the proletariat.

For Poyntz, socialism was directly linked to labor issues. In a 1919 article in the *Nation,* she wrote about the working-class unrest that was so visible in the United States after the war. During the war, she said, an "industrial truce" had allowed wartime production to continue unhindered by labor unrest. But after the armistice, a need for higher wages and better hours led to an "industrial outbreak unparalleled in virulence and extent." Poyntz blamed the unrest on industrial leaders, who despite the "quarter of a million workers" involved in labor disputes nationwide and the "unemployment affecting another quarter of a million," were clinging to their wartime advantages. She spoke of the garment industry, where "collective bargaining" had been terminated, thus ending a long period of industrial peace. For Poyntz, collective bargaining was key to maintaining the "equal distribution of work during the slack season" and eliminating the "right of free discharge" that allowed employers to terminate employees at will. Workers had gained both of these assurances during wartime collective bargaining agreements.[37] Now they had to fight for them again. Poyntz had little patience with the industrial giants whom so many people saw as capable leaders but who pushed their own agendas for personal and financial gain.

Although Poyntz was beginning to identify with the radical left, she and Lore were still devoted to a moderate socialism that viewed the state as the institution best able to create change for the working classes.[38] Now they and others found themselves in the unenviable position of having to choose sides in a divided party. In 1919, Vladimir Lenin invited "revolutionaries all over the world," to join the Communist International

(Comintern), his proposed replacement for the international Socialist Party. Meanwhile, the left-wing faction of the American party was agitating for a larger percentage of the party's substantial resources. The language federations and the Michigan Socialist Party decided to splinter off from the socialists and create a Communist Party (CP). Both groups planned conventions in Chicago on September 1. John Reed and Benjamin Gitlow were the only big left-wing names who persisted in trying to take over the Socialist Party. When they and the rest of their caucus were kicked out of the party's 1919 convention, they decided to form their own organization, which they called the Communist Labor Party (CLP). The CP attempted, unsuccessfully, to persuade CLP members to join them.[39]

While the socialist right and left wings were splintering and arguing, Poyntz and Lore remained part of another, more obscure centrist faction that tied itself to neither the right nor the left. Both admired the Bolsheviks, and both hoped to keep the Socialist Party intact, making changes from within to align it with the Comintern. But eventually, as debate among the American socialists became more intense, the centrists were forced to take a stand: they left the Socialist Party and formed the Workers' Council, a "radical offshoot" linked to the Comintern.[40] In 1921, the CP merged with the Workers' Council to create the Worker's Party of America (WPA). Lore and Poyntz were leaders within the council, which was apparently held in some esteem as it had five representatives (among them Lore) on the WPA's central executive committee. In 1925, the WPA changed its name to the Workers' (Communist) Party of America and, in 1929, to the Communist Party USA (CPUSA).[41]

During this period, Poyntz's personal life was as tumultuous as her political life was. Her marriage was in a constant state of flux as she and Glaser repeatedly separated and reunited. Meanwhile, her growing radicalism had estranged her from her mother and her sister, who were living more conventional lives. On May 16, 1911, her younger sister, Eulalie, age nineteen, had married Raymond McClelland, the son of Alice Points's roommate at Oberlin College. At the time of their marriage, Eulalie was attending Oberlin, and Raymond was a recent graduate of Winona Agricultural College in Ohio. The McClellands settled on a farm in Knox, Ohio, where they brought up four children.[42] Eulalie later said that she and her mother had disapproved of Poyntz's politics and that Poyntz did not communicate with either of them very often. The sisters last saw each other in 1926 at their parents' funerals: their mother's in February, their father's in April. Eulalie learned about her sister's disappearance from a newspaper article.[43]

In 1924, the year her marriage to Glaser finally ended, Poyntz became embroiled in a long-brewing leadership conflict within the WPA. It came to a head at a plenary session in Chicago, which Poyntz was attending as a representative of Lore's faction. Two other factions, led by William Z. Foster and Charles Ruthenberg, were also vying for party leadership. The conflict was linked to questions about the party's level of involvement in mainstream politics. At this time, the communist-led Trade Union Education League, under Foster's aegis, had been making headway within some American Federation of Labor (AFL) unions. Now those unions wanted to publicly back Robert LaFollette's progressive candidacy in the 1924 presidential election. Foster, however, did not "seek a leading role in a mass political movement." At the plenary session, Ruthenberg's faction argued in favor of becoming involved in LaFollette's campaign, but Foster's faction "carried the day" by allying with Lore's, "the most leftist of the three" and the one least interested in participating in mainstream politics.[44] This alliance did not end the conflict as Foster's faction in fact wanted to get involved with the campaign, just not in a leadership role.

In addition to this internal strife, events in the Soviet Union were influencing the direction of the WPA. Lenin died in January 1924, leading to internal battles over control of the Communist Party. Trotsky was pitted against Grigorii Zinoviev, Lev Kamenev, and Josef Stalin. Like Lenin, all were committed to the dictatorship of the proletariat, violence to effect "revolutionary transformation," the one-party state, "concessions to peasants and oppressed nationalities," Marxism, and the "inevitability of world revolution." Trotsky differed from the others because he wanted to "expand state planning, accelerate industrialization and instigate revolution in Europe." Kamenev, Zinoviev, and Bukharin each hoped to be Lenin's successor. Though they were worried about Stalin, they allied with him out of a greater fear of Trotsky.[45]

This was a pivotal moment in the future of Soviet and American communism. Trotsky's conflict with the Bolshevik leadership—and later, with Stalin—compromised his position and eventually led to his exile and assassination. The Bolsheviks saw him as arrogant and believed that socialism could be introduced in Russia faster than Lenin's timeline had proposed. Already, by 1922, Lenin had been suspicious of Trotsky and had turned to Stalin and his allies. That honeymoon between Lenin and Stalin was brief, and Lenin eventually turned back to Trotsky as the "lesser of two evils" to help him reverse the Politburo policies favored by Stalin, Kamenev, and Zinoviev. From his sick bed, he had attempted to prevent Stalin's ascendancy to power, but a major stroke silenced him.[46]

In May 1924, Foster traveled to Moscow with John Pepper, a Ruthenberg ally, and Moissaye Olgin, a "Lore ally." Their intent was to seek Soviet guidance in solving the WPA's internal conflict. As answer, Trotsky and the Comintern denounced the Americans' support for LaFollette's campaign. The Comintern also denounced Lore because his "leftist position" resembled Trotsky's. Thus, at the 1925 WPA convention in Chicago, Foster's caucus allied with Ruthenberg's caucus, and they moved to expel Lore. Many in Lore's ranks immediately abandoned him, including Olgin. Poyntz remained the only person willing to stand up for her old friend, which put her into a dangerous position with the WPA's Central Executive Committee (CEC).[47]

Poyntz's commitment to Lore led to questions about her loyalty to the party. In response, she went on the offensive and refused to back down. The CEC was not impressed. On May 26, 1925, it released "Statement Regarding Comrade Juliet Stuart Poyntz," which eventually made its way to Moscow and the Comintern. It began by claiming that Poyntz had been a "militant figure" within the Lore group since its beginning. The committee accused her of "opportunist policies" that were on prominent display at the convention and an "irresponsible attitude" since then. The CEC condemned her attempts to reconcile herself to the party as "right deviations," noting that she had not changed her ideology or admitted that she had been wrong. According to the "Statement," she was the kind of "dilettante intellectual" who is "a problem in the Communist Party."[48] The "Statement" noted that Poyntz had recently created a workers' school in the WPA, similar to the workers' education programs she had created for the ILGWU. In that role, it claimed, she had rejected the "Comintern conception of communist education" in favor of her own. She was accused of using "factional discrimination" in the hiring of teachers and thus making the school the "factional machine for the right wing." She had appointed Lore to teach about the Comintern despite his "serious misconception[s]" on the topic. The CEC accused her of sabotaging the efforts of the WPA's New York branch to bolshevize the school and of resigning her position at the school rather than conform.[49]

Perhaps her greatest crime was in not denouncing Trotsky. According to the CEC, this lapse had fostered distrust toward the Leninist branch of the party (which was how Stalin and his allies were identifying themselves). The party took particular issue with a statement Poyntz had sent to the CEC on May 12, which was not conciliatory. In it, she wrote that she aligned herself with the Foster-Lore majority in spite of its "syndicalist right-wing tendencies." She also backed the CEC's opposition to the LaFollette campaign. Poyntz did not denounce Lore, instead reminding the leadership that he had voted with the majority "90%" of the time. She argued that his faction was "more Marxian and more Communist" than the majority was. And she took issue with the party's management of organizing among garment workers and other needlework trades, calling its policies "right-wing deviations." But because she was a "disciplined Communist," she said she would postpone those criticisms until future meetings. Her attack on the party line and her refusal to apologize or back down from her position was a bold move in an organization in which people were expelled for less. But Poyntz believed she was right. She ended her statement by demanding the opportunity to answer the CEC's accusations in person and asking the committee majority to "refrain from ventilating these serious and entirely false" charges against her.[50]

Lore was not allowed to defend himself and was permanently expelled from the WPA, but on May 13 Poyntz answered the charges in a speech before the CEC at the WPA's fourth convention in Chicago. Years later, in his 1940 book *I Confess,* Gitlow, by then a vehement anti-communist, described her at that meeting. At the time she was in her thirties, of "American stock," and "rather tall, rather fleshy, rather good-looking." Gitlow said that she had an aristocratic bearing but was not snobbish and thus was popular with the party's rank-and-file. She was the "outstanding woman in the Party," both "headstrong and ambitious," and her address to the party leadership was "highly dramatic in [its] delivery." Notably,

Gitlow wrote that she had no equal regarding the factional disputes but was a poor organizer and had only a superficial knowledge of the "underlying philosophy" of the movement. This was an astounding claim about a well-educated woman who had devoted her entire adult life to Marxism, one that reflected Gitlow's sexist prejudices rather than Poyntz's abilities. Other accounts contradict such assertions.[51]

In her speech, Poyntz reiterated much of what she had written in her statement. She added she had remained part of the Foster-Lore faction after they had combined into one and that she was still committed to working with Foster. Yet she also argued that Foster was the person who had organized the Lore group by drawing in its members at the previous party convention. Whenever Foster or his allies James Cannon and Alexander Bittelman were in New York, she said, they met at Lore's *Volkszeitung* offices. She said that Foster was enthusiastic about the alliance with Lore and sought to maintain it. In other words, Poyntz simultaneously denied the existence of a separate Lore group and claimed that Foster had sought alliances with it.[52]

Poyntz reiterated that the Lore group was the left wing of the party and that its goal was to seek "INDEPENDENT POLITICAL ACTION." But because the faction also sought to maintain its alliance with the Foster group, it was not promoting its own thesis. Poyntz took serious offense at being labeled right wing and said that she had always been a member of the left. She claimed she had the "highest respect for" her good friend and "comrade" Lore. She described him as a "football" in the party's factional fights, but made it clear that she was not loyal to any one of these groups but to the Comintern as a whole, which she supported "organizationally and ideologically." Finally, she restated her support for the "old guard of the Russian Communist Party against Trotsky."[53]

According to Gitlow, Poyntz's "venom and tenacity" were unstoppable during this meeting; he called her a "spitfire." His descriptions of the listeners' reactions are amusing, though the falsehoods in his books make their accuracy questionable. He said that Foster and his faction squirmed and "fumed at her sallies." William Dunne, known as Wild Bill, "shouted and yelled derisively" at her, while Cannon muttered curses "under his breath." Foster paced throughout her speech and yelled, "It's a damn lie," whenever her accusations "hurt most." Gitlow, who was in the Ruthenberg faction at the time, "listened with glee" and "roared with laughter" at the others' discomfort. He recalled these events many years after he had left the party, but his memory of Poyntz's forcefulness aligns with how others also described her.[54] Clearly, she was not afraid to challenge the male leadership of the party or the official party line.

The WPA's factional disputes continued throughout the 1920s, and the ongoing power struggle in the Soviet Union kept spilling over into the American party. But Poyntz was not expelled, thanks to the intervention of her friend Jack Stachel, then the head of the New York branch, as well as her own concessions to the Comintern and her denunciation of Trotsky. Though she also had to denounce Lore, she covered "her capitulation" by vehemently attacking the Foster faction. Her involvement in these disputes seems to have had no long-term effect on her position in the party, In fact, she became a rising star. In 1928, Poyntz was named the head of its women's committee, appointed at the Sixth World Comintern Congress in Moscow. That same year she ran for New York attorney general on the Communist Party ticket. She lost the election but soon picked up a nickname: "the Joan of Arc of the Communist movement."[55] During one campaign spot she warned her audience not to trust the reformism of the capitalists and socialists. Only the Communist Party, she said, was devoted to ending racism and sexism; only the destruction of capitalism could make African Americans and women free.[56]

By 1927, Stalin's faction had taken power in the Soviet Union, and he had expelled not only Trotsky but also his former allies Kamenev and Zinoviev from the party. The latter apologized and sought reinstatement, which Stalin approved after they "recanted their opinions." Trotsky, however, refused to recant and was exiled to Alma-Ata along with his family and others who had refused to bend to Stalin's will. In January 1929, Trotsky was deported from the Soviet Union. But Stalin was not finished with him. He continued to accuse Trotsky of spying and claimed that critics of his policies were aligned with the exile. Stalin's ruthlessness came to a head during the show trials and purges of the 1930s. Few were safe from accusations of Trotskyism, but those who, like Poyntz, had been accused of being allied with Trotsky before the purges were particularly vulnerable. Both Kamenev and Zinoviev were executed during those years, and Trotsky was assassinated in Mexico in 1940.[57]

For the moment, however, Poyntz's leadership and influence within the party seemed to be secure. By 1929, she was serving as the national secretary of the International Labor Defense (ILD), the American wing of the Comintern's Red Aid Network, created in 1925 to provide legal assistance to "class war prisoners" (though not everyone with that label was a communist). Poyntz headed the ILD during the famous 1929 Gastonia textile strike, organized through the National Textile Workers Union (NTWU). Founded in 1928, the NTWU was among the first of the dual unions, which were responses to a Moscow directive to avoid forming separate communist unions. Rather, the CPUSA (as the WPA was now known) was instructed to work with those that were already part of established umbrella associations such as the Industrial Workers of the World (IWW) and the AFL.[58]

In March, the NTWU sent Fred Beal to Gastonia, North Carolina, to organize workers at the Loray Textile Mill. Headed by Beal, the workers, then went on strike in April.[59] The Loray millworkers, and other textile workers who went on strike in North Carolina that year, had a long list of grievances. These included low wages and long hours: a sixty-hour work week was common in the mills. Efficiency systems put into place by millowners made those long hours even more arduous, requiring fewer workers to watch more looms and move at a faster pace. In most mill families, wives and children older than age fourteen had to go to work because the wages were so low. Low wages also meant less money for food. Millworkers survived on "grits, field peas, beans, bread, corn meal, and 'fat back'—a salt, fat pork." There were few, if any, fresh vegetables in their diets; as a result, pellagra (the result of a niacin deficiency) plagued the milltowns. In 1929 there was a 50 percent increase in pellagra-related deaths in North Carolina alone. The Loray millworkers were further burdened by a cut in hours, which meant less income to bring home. The striking workers were met with "state pressure and vigilante violence," so the CPUSA sent in party members to assist. Local police and the press were not happy about the arrival of these communist outsiders. In an editorial, the *Charlotte News* described the them as "atheists, home-wreckers, church-destroyers, and society-rapists." A Nashville newspaper claimed that all of the mill workers had been content until communists arrived to make trouble. Police harassed both strikers and organizers. In one incident, an armed battle broke out after the police tried to break up the strikers' tent colony. During the gun fight, Orvill Aderholt, the chief of police, was killed. Union leaders and strikers, including Beal, were arrested and charged with murder.[60]

Poyntz headed to Gastonia to help with the legal defense.[61] She and Alfred Wagenknecht, of the Worker's International Relief Society, arrived in town on June 9, 1929. By that time, seventy striking women and men had been arrested for Aderholt's murder, and four other officers and a civilian had been wounded during "strike disturbances."[62] Of the original seventy defendants, sixteen were eventually indicted and put on trial for murder and conspiracy. Fred Beal was among them, as was Vera Buch, an NTWU strike leader.

Because of heightened feelings against the strikers in Gastonia, the defendants secured a change of venue, and the trial was held in Mecklenburg County. Poyntz declared that case would go down in "the history of the labor struggles in America" alongside the Sacco-Vanzetti case. She was intent on making sure that the defendants would be tried not just in the courtroom but "by the mass action of the American Working-Class."[63] At this time, Poyntz was "at the height of her public career in the Party," and the forceful style she had honed as a suffrage organizer was now on full display. She often clashed with colleagues, and many did not take kindly to her manner. Buch thought Poyntz might have been a double agent. Tom Jimison, the defendants' lawyer, described her as "utterly unscrupulous." In his view, she was so devoted to communist revolution that she was willing to let the "Gastonia defendants 'go to the electric chair as martyrs in the class struggle.'" Despite this distrust, Poyntz continued to organize the defense, both in and out of the courtroom. She spoke publicly about the injustice of admitting the defendants' radical beliefs as trial evidence. When one defendant's lack of religious belief was brought up in court, Poyntz derided the session as a "heresy trial . . . conducted in the medieval spirit of entrenched autocracy."[64]

During her time in Gastonia, Poyntz was arrested, and a reporter for the ILD newspaper the *Labor Defender* wrote that she gave the police a "bad half hour." It was not her first arrest: the year before, she had been arrested in Boston for calling President Calvin Coolidge "an errand boy of the capitalist system."[65] But Gastonia, during and after the trials, was a powder keg; and everyone who worked for the defendants was a police target. Her colleague Wagenknecht, along with her friend Paul Crouch, a representative of the ILD's youth section, were under surveillance "from the time they entered the city."[66]

A mistrial was declared in August. Before the second trial began in Mecklenberg County, the ILD and the lawyers managed to get the charges dropped against nine of the original defendants. At the second trial, the prosecution focused on the remaining defendants' communist beliefs, even asking Beal on the stand if "he advocated the overthrow of the government of the United States." The jury found all seven of the defendants guilty, and the judge sentenced them to long prison terms. But those questions about political beliefs, along with others about religious affiliation, became the basis for appeals. In the meantime, five of the seven jumped bond and fled, including Beal, who went to the Soviet Union.[67]

The Gastonia affair became a propaganda tool for the CPUSA. Poyntz and the ILD used it to draw attention to working-class labor and legal struggles and to highlight the reactions of the powerful to workers' demands for economic rights.[68] As a leading spokesperson for the party, Poyntz received considerable attention in the press. But law enforcement and intelligence sources were also keeping an eye on her. The Canadian police tracked her when she traveled to Toronto as part of a movement to save Sacco and Vanzetti. In 1922, officials in the U.S. State Department noted that she was in Berlin and in contact with Dutch communists. By 1930, when she attended the Comintern's Sixth World Congress in Moscow, the State Department was calling her a "prominent American Communist."[69] Despite this surveillance, Poyntz remained active and visible in the party, probably unaware that international intelligence organizations were watching her so closely.

Even as Poyntz climbed the communist ladder, she continued to work for women's rights. In 1928, she chaired a socialist-founded International Woman's Day celebration. In her speech, she declared that women around the world were "shaking off ancient shackles and prejudices," to push for their own rights. She claimed, however, that only Soviet women were truly "able to develop their own destiny and future" because they had access to "better working conditions, higher wages, and better schools." For communists, the Soviet Union was proof that revolution could end women's oppression and thus eliminate the need for bourgeois feminism.[70] Many CPUSA members liked to compare American conditions to those in the Soviet Union, and Poyntz's particular focus was on women's issues. She often emphasized that, while Soviet women flourished, American women faced poverty and harassment. In 1929, as chair of the fifth New York Working Women's Federation, she spoke of the need to stop the factory speedups that made work conditions more difficult and dangerous. Her focus on working women was important in a party that often did not clearly differentiate between labor problems that affected women in particular versus those that affected all workers. Poyntz and other women in the CPUSA had to push the leadership to acknowledge that difference in its policy approaches and in its campaigns and agendas.[71]

During the Great Depression, party organizers focused much of their work on worsening labor conditions. But the growth of fascism in Europe during the early 1930s was also worrying leftists. Party leaders recognized that the fascists were targeting left-wing organizations such as labor unions as well as socialists, Social Democrats, and communists. Others in the party worried about fascism's effect on the personal liberty of women and people of color. Thus, even while Poyntz was working as a public figure for the CPUSA, the party may have been grooming her for the underground. One hint is that her name use became more fluid than ever during these years. When Poyntz received her new citizenship papers in 1924, she did so under her married name, Juliet Stuart Glaser. Those papers were not among her effects after she disappeared. However, friends did find another naturalization form, this one dated 1932, listing her name as Juliet Stuert Glaser, although the signature under the photograph read Julia Stewart Glaser. Was Poyntz able to use a sexist law to her advantage and create another identity for herself? Somehow the Immigration and Naturalization Services did not pick up on the error, and Poyntz was able to get a passport in the name of Julia S. Glaser.[72]

Poyntz, no longer married and with no family obligations, may have been the perfect candidate to work in the underground, but she remained a visible party figure until 1934. One of her last public events was a dramatic face-off with New York City's mayor, Fiorello LaGuardia. Early that year, LaGuardia had asked the state legislature to give him sweeping powers to reorganize the city government. The bill he proposed (which had a two-year lifespan) gave him the power to control all public compensation, including pay freezes, and the power to create or dissolve government agencies at his discretion. LaGuardia claimed these drastic measures would help him solve the city's extreme economic problems, but they also gave him unprecedented control over city government.[73]

On January 3, LaGuardia was riding to work in his limousine when he was accosted by a band of protestors led by Poyntz. She and a number of unemployed women confronted the mayor about his "bulldozing tactics." Later, LaGuardia claimed that he knew Poyntz, thus confirming her prestige within the party, and he publicly declared that he would "put her to work if she actually wants a job." He told the other women protesters to get jobs shoveling snow, and an article in the *Daily Worker* accused him of insulting them in other ways. Perhaps the most memorable part of the incident is the photograph that accompanied the *New York Times* article. In it, LaGuardia and Poyntz are face to face. He is surrounded by large masculine figures, she by a smaller group of women. In this way, the situation seems emblematic of a confrontation between workers and bosses. But Poyntz towers over the other women, and she is pointing directly at the mayor. The powerful image speaks to her aggressive style and her air of authority. These qualities may have been exactly what made her so valuable to the Soviets.[74]

CHAPTER THREE

THE ANARCHIST

Juliet Stuart Poyntz's disappearance was reported in the *New York World-Telegram* on Friday, December 17, 1937, seven months after she went missing. The reporter who revealed it, Arthur Irwin, wrote that Poyntz had fallen into "disfavor" with the CPUSA leadership and was engaged in a "fight against the Nazi government" for her deceased husband's estate. Irwin suggested two potential motives for her mysterious disappearance and two enemies—the Soviets and the Nazis—who might have wanted Poyntz out of the way.[1] He noted that, only a week before, an American named Mrs. Donald L. Robinson had gone missing in Moscow after reporting her husband's disappearance to American embassy officials. While Irwin wondered if Nazis could have also been involved, other members of the press were suggesting that the three American citizens had been caught up in Stalin's political purges.[2]

The timing of these disappearances may have been coincidental, but to the reading public and to some anti-Stalinist observers they would be forever linked. The anarchist Carlo Tresca immediately connected them and zeroed in on the CPUSA and its Soviet counterpart as the culprits. His evidence was Poyntz herself, who, he claimed, had admitted to him only weeks before her disappearance that she wanted to leave the party. Though they had ideological differences, Tresca and Poyntz were long-time friends; and as a known anti-Stalinist, he feared that their friendship and their alleged conversation about her Soviet handlers might have created trouble for her. For several years, Tresca made loud and persistent accusations against the communists, accusing them of conspiring to kill Poyntz, though there was no actual evidence that she was dead. In early February 1938, he held a press conference in which he accused the Soviets of orchestrating both her disappearance and the Robinsons' arrest as well as the likely murder of Donald Robinson. He published articles in Italian- and English-language newspapers outlining what he believed had happened and named several party members that he said were responsible for her abduction. He harassed public officials to make sure they were investigating the CPUSA and the Soviets, publicly accusing them of not doing enough. He laid out these theories before a grand jury. In short, Tresca was a nuisance; and when, in 1943, he was gunned down on a New York City street, many of his allies believed that his accusations against the Soviets and the CPUSA had gotten him killed.

Even before Poyntz and the Robinsons (later identified as Arthur and Ruth Rubens) went missing, Tresca was in the habit of accusing the CPUSA of various misdeeds, without evidence and with an abundance of speculation. The FBI had serious doubts about the information he was giving them. Tresca was disappointed in communism and horrified by Stalin's leadership, and he had come to believe that the great Soviet experiment was a terrorist threat. He also believed the CPUSA was complicit in that threat. His accusations in the Robinson-Rubens and Poyntz cases opened the door to an increasingly vocal anti-Stalinist cohort on the American left. Over the next eighty years, the theory he outlined—that she had been abducted and either murdered or taken to a gulag because of the disillusionment she had revealed only to him—was repeated, with few variations, by anti-Stalinists, anti-communists, journalists, conservatives, and others.

Radical anti-Stalinism such as Tresca's eventually transformed into anti-communism as activists began to couple their anti-Stalinism with a wholesale rejection of Marxism. Tresca did not survive long enough to see anti-communism come to fruition as a dominant ideology in American domestic and foreign policy, but his dogged investigations into Poyntz's disappearance kept her at the forefront of the minds of those who constructed that policy. What he could not have anticipated was that his vocal anti-Stalinism would also lay a foundation for undermining the American left and the principles of class solidarity and anti-capitalism to which he had devoted his life.

Carlo Tresca

Carlo Tresca was born on March 9, 1879, in Sulmona, Italy. Today his bust, inscribed "Carlo Tresca: Socialist Exile, Martyr of Italy," is publicly displayed in the center of the city. Tresca's mother had hoped he would become a priest, but he rejected that idea out of hand, instead opting to attend technical school. According to his biographer, Nunzio Pernicone, Tresca's radicalism began with the growing anti-clericalism in Italy. Those on the left saw the Catholic church as a barrier to their hopes for a liberal and secular Italian state. By the late 1890s, the teenaged Tresca was attending lectures at the local chapter of the Partito Socialista Italiano (PSI). For him, socialism's appeal would always be more "visceral than intellectual." He was far more interested in action than in abstract "orthodoxy". Over his father's objections, Tresca joined the PSI and began organizing Sulmona's workers, attending rallies, and giving speeches. He quickly became a "full-fledged agitator." He started working as a journalist for the socialist weekly *Il Germe,* eventually becoming its editor-in-chief. He also wrote for PSI's *L'Avvenire,* and in 1904 published an article accusing the Italian government of using military force against Italian workers. Though he had already been arrested, the article now made him a special target of the police.[3]

In 1904, a libel suit was brought as a result of Tresca's *L'Avvenire* article. Facing prison time, he decided to emigrate to the United States to join his older brother, Ettore, who had left Italy the year before. Tresca traveled first to a colony of Italian socialist exiles in Switzerland. There he met a "young socialist firebrand" named Benito Mussolini. Even the action-loving Tresca was too conservative for Mussolini. As he saw Tresca off on the train, he predicted that the United States would transform him into a "true revolutionary comrade." After Mussolini converted to fascism and became a dictator, Tresca would send him a telegram every year "reminding him of his prediction." But their political sympathies were no longer aligned. Eventually, Tresca became an outspoken critic of fascism and particularly of Mussolini.[4]

In the United States, Tresca made his way into American radical circles. Meanwhile, his politics were evolving. Once a revolutionary socialist, he now saw himself as an anarcho-syndicalist, advocating the destruction of capitalism and in favor of a worker-led state. According to Pernicone, this shift was the result of three factors. The first was ideological. In Italy, revolutionary syndicalism had evolved from Marxist doctrine and the PSI. Its American version was the IWW in which Tresca would eventually work. The second was Tresca's dislike of strict organizational rules. He was unable to commit to any doctrine that limited individual action and free thought. The third was his "propensity for direct action." As always, Tresca was uninterested in intellectual debates but wanted to be directly involved in strikes and other actions.[5]

Tresca remained an independent radical anarchist. He chose to work with the CPUSA in its early years because he considered it to be a revolutionary organization. Yet as early as August 1921 he was expressing disappointment in the Soviets. After sailors in the port city of Kronstadt revolted against the Bolshevik government and were crushed by Soviet forces, Tresca was convinced that the Bolshevik revolution had been a failure. In the 1921 May Day issue of *Il Martello*, Tresca's Italian-language newspaper, he invited the Russian anarchist Peter Kropotkin to write about Bolshevik oppression. By the summer of 1922, Tresca was "lament[ing] the end of the revolution" as long as the Bolsheviks remained in power. Yet in Pernicone's view, Tresca was essentially nonsectarian and, in his early years, resisted being labeled. For a time, he did not wholeheartedly condemn all communists, especially those who followed Trotsky. Because he was vehemently anti-fascist, he continued to cooperate with communists on anti-fascist campaigns. He soon became known as the "deus ex machina of anti-fascism," and *Il Martello* was banned in Italy.[6]

Tresca and Poyntz met in 1916 when she was working for the ILGWU. At this time, Poyntz was concentrating her efforts on the "socially disinherited," particularly laborers in sweatshops. The pair shared this interest, but they also began collaborating on anti-fascist campaigns. In 1925, Poyntz attended a meeting that Tresca had organized to protest Mussolini's role in Giacomo Matteotti's murder. Matteotti was the leader of the Italian Unitary Socialist Party, who in 1922 had accused the fascists of using intimidation and violence to win that year's elections and was demanding that the results be nullified. On June 10, 1924, a group of Blackshirts kidnapped and killed Matteotti; his body was found later that summer. Tresca immediately blamed Mussolini for the murder, and his fellow anti-fascists echoed his accusations.[7]

By the 1930s, ideological schisms within the CPUSA and its dismissal of other left-wing groups as social fascists was frustrating Tresca's cooperation with the communists. He believed that the CPUSA was standing in the way of a true united front against fascism and in 1931 declared that "with the Muscovites no understanding is possible."[8] By now, Tresca was an aggressive critic of Stalinism and the Soviet Union, joining the ranks of a growing anti-Stalinist left. Events in the Soviet Union increased his distrust of "Stalinists," a term he also used to described CPUSA members—and one that they rejected. Though he and Poyntz remained friends, he could not separate rank-and-file party members from the larger Soviet machine and developed a myopic focus on all party members as Stalinist collaborators.

During the Great Terror (1936–38), the Soviet leadership, under Stalin's direction, began purging so-called enemies of the state, with the goal of discrediting Stalin's critics, especially Trotsky.[9] During public show trials, former colleagues were forced to confess "to the existence of grandiose" conspiracies aimed at overthrowing Stalin. They were given scripted statements outlining their guilt and made to read them.[10] According to the historian, Vadim Rogovin, the trials were intended to offer solid evidence that such plots existed; without them "the mass terror could not have been carried out."[11] Though the courts failed to present any physical evidence and some of the scripted "confessions" could be easily disproved, the condemned were convicted and immediately executed. Among them were the former Bolshevik leaders L. B. Kamenev, Grigorii Zinoviev, Georgi Pyatakov, and Nikolai Bukharin. Others, accused of being accomplices, were imprisoned, tortured, or killed. In this period, 750,000 people were executed, and twice that many were sent to prisons or camps.[12]

Anti-Stalinists in the United States rallied around Trotsky, who provided "a ready-made critique of Stalinism cast in Marxist terms." For them, following Trotsky did not require an abandonment of "socialist thought." Thus, even though Tresca had by now severed his ties with the communists, he maintained his links to "prominent Trotskyites." He joined the American Committee for the Defense of Leon Trotsky, a group that the communists abhorred. In 1937, the committee, chaired by John Dewey, organized a commission of inquiry (the Dewey Commission) into the charges against Trotsky. Commission members, including Tresca, traveled to Mexico to hear Trotsky respond to the charges. The hearings brought together a diverse group of left-wing activists who found common ground in their dislike of Stalin, and eventually the committee "bec[a]me part of the radical opposition to Stalin."[13]

Figure 3. Herbert Solow with Leon Trotsky during a trip with the Dewey Commission to Mexico, 1937. Herbert Solow Papers, Hoover Institution Archives, Stanford University.

In December 1937, its commission released its findings and declared Trotsky not guilty. Trotsky himself later wrote to Tresca, thanking him for his involvement, expressing his "deepest esteem," and calling him "every inch a fighter."[14]

Anti-Stalinists were increasingly concerned as it became clear that the Great Terror was not confined to the Soviet Union. On June 20, 1937, Alexander Barmine, a Soviet chargé d'affaires at the Athens's embassy, disappeared. Weeks earlier, he had been recalled to Moscow but refused to board the ship on which he was ordered to return.[15] Barmine, as it turned out, was lucky: he was warned by his would-be assassin Walter Krivitsky.[16] He later reappeared in Paris and by 1940 had moved to New York City, where he supplied the FBI with information on Stalin's purges. Krivitsky himself defected to the United States after he, too, defied a recall order to Moscow.[17] Ignace Reiss, an agent for the Soviet secret police stationed in Paris, dared to send a letter to the central committee denouncing Stalin and announcing his own defection. On September 4, 1937, his "well-dressed corpse" was found outside Lausanne, Switzerland, with a Czech passport and an "unused rail ticket to France." In 1938, Rudolf Klement, a German who was working to build "an anti-Stalinist counterinsurgency" as part of Trotsky's fourth international, went missing in France. A headless corpse was later found in the Seine River. Though a positive identification was never made, many suspected it was Klement. In 1938, Lev Sedov, Trotsky's eldest son, was allegedly murdered while recovering from an appendectomy in Paris.[18]

It was during the Spanish Civil War (1936–39) that many nonaffiliated leftists abandoned communism and the Soviet Union for good. Most democratic governments were ignoring Spain's great anti-fascist struggle. As Germany and Italy supplied aid, weapons, and troops to Francisco Franco's fascist insurgents, the Soviet Union was the only major world power to provide (limited) aid to the Spanish Republicans. A number of international brigades sent volunteers to Spain from various countries in support of the Republicans. While most brigadists were communists, some did represent other left-wing groups. The Workers' Party of Marxist Unification (POUM), a leading Marxist organization independent of both Moscow and Trotsky, was among them. Because POUM was loudly critical of the show trials, Stalin wanted to crush it, and his agents diligently complied. By 1937, hundreds of POUM leaders in Spain were arrested. The Soviet interior ministry imported their "methods of torture, forced confession, and mass shootings" into Spain, and numbers of brigadists were kidnapped and murdered.[19] Although the bodies were piling up, it seemed as if nothing could placate Stalin's paranoia.

Tresca had a personal interest in the Soviet purges in Spain. His friend Camillo Berneri, a fellow Italian anarchist, was among those who were murdered, and Tresca came to believe that George Mink, a known Soviet agent, had engineered Berneri's death. The former head of the CPUSA's seaman's organization on the New York City waterfront, Mink was the chief of Soviet police in Spain during the civil war, which meant he likely oversaw the liquidation of POUM members and Tresca's friend. He also served as a link between the CPUSA and the Soviet Union, cementing Tresca's belief that the American party was complicit.[20] Much later, it was rumored that Mink was involved in the plot to assassinate Trotsky, and Tresca believed he was also a reason for Poyntz's eventual disillusionment with the Soviet Union. In short, Tresca's distrust of the Soviets was personal. He took every opportunity to attack the CPUSA, he published "shocking exposés" of their violence, and he annoyed fellow anarchists by willingly informing on communists to the FBI.[21]

The Robinson-Rubens and Poyntz Connection

Donald Robinson disappeared from the National Hotel in Moscow on December 2, 1937. His wife disappeared on December 10 after she reported her husband's arrest to American embassy officials. Reportedly, the couple was in Moscow to celebrate the twentieth anniversary of the Bolshevik revolution. But according to embassy officials, by December 11 their belongings had been cleared out of their hotel room and another guest was already checked in. The embassy had no access to the Robinsons' passports because it was Soviet policy to confiscate passports during the country's lengthy registration process. Before her own disappearance, Mrs. Robinson had told American embassy officials that hotel employees were claiming that her husband had been taken to the hospital because of pneumonia. The hotel denied those claims to embassy officials. Those officials reminded the Soviets that agreements between the countries gave them seventy-two hours to report an American citizen's arrest.[22]

Irwin's article on Poyntz's disappearance suggested "several curious parallels" between Poyntz's disappearance and the Robinsons'. By now the U.S. State Department suspected that the Robinsons were former communists who had fallen out of favor with the CPUSA over Trotsky. They were also reportedly traveling with false passports. Mrs. Robinson was quickly located in Lublanka Prison, making CPUSA membership the only real parallel with Poyntz. U.S. officials knew very little about

Mr. Robinson, but friends and family later reported that Mrs. Robinson was a devoted radical. Without evidence, Tresca believed that Poyntz's involvement with the Lore controversy and allegations that the Robinsons were also Trotskyites were important clues as to why the Soviets had sought to eliminate them all.[23]

The exact date of Poyntz's disappearance remains uncertain. According to Irwin, she had made an appointment with a friend on June 3, 1937, but failed to appear. Her attorney, Elias Lieberman, claimed that on June 5 she had received a call at her lodging that prompted her to leave and that she was never seen again. Friends believed that she may have gone into seclusion to work on something she was writing. But after not receiving her rent payment for several weeks, the boarding house manager contacted Marie MacDonald, Poyntz's emergency contact, and MacDonald contacted Lieberman. Because of the sensitive nature of Poyntz's work, the two believed that alerting the police might put her into even more danger, so they put off reporting her disappearance.[24]

According to Lieberman, he began his own investigation into Poyntz's disappearance; only after he exhausted his avenues did he formally report it to the police. MacDonald said that Lieberman went to the police at her urging.[25] The FBI, however, noted that Mr. Thackerberry at the boarding house told a detective friend that Poyntz had vanished and thus became "instrumental" in Lieberman's "decision to inform the police."[26] It may have been mere coincidence that she was reported missing just as the Robinsons actually went missing, but for both the press and Tresca the cases were immediately linked.[27]

The police report described Poyntz as between forty-nine and fifty-two years of age. She was listed as five foot, six inches tall and weighing 160 pounds. It noted that she had an ulcerated red mark on the bridge of her nose, which was likely from lupus, a fatal rheumatoid illness that was not well understood in 1937. Friends believed that she had every intention of returning to her room since she had filled a prescription on June 4. In the room they found a Macy's receipt for a recently purchased book, "two trunks, handbags," and manuscripts. She had apparently bought moth balls, an indication that she was planning to store her winter garments. Her passport and citizenship papers were in the room, and no money had been withdrawn from her bank account. In fact, she was short of funds, and her attorney was waiting for her to sign litigation papers so that she could secure more money.[28] Poyntz allegedly had appointments scheduled with "the attorney, friends, a warehouseman, a doctor, a druggist, [and] a hairdresser."[29] According to Tresca, her friends and Lieberman all agreed that she had not committed suicide and was not an amnesiac but "the victim of involuntary detention, if not murder." Tresca called her the "victim of political crime."[30]

The police officially described Poyntz as "one of the ten principal Communist Leaders in the United States." That statement promptly appeared in newspaper accounts of her disappearance and was used as a way to link her to the Robinsons. Yet even though she was reported as missing in December 1937, the police did not begin investigating her disappearance until January 11, 1938, when Lieberman specifically asked them to do so. Tresca accused the police of a "long delay." He was concerned that, as a communist, Poyntz was not a priority and that police may have had little interest in locating her. Eventually, they checked "morgues, hospitals, and asylums," using clues given by Poyntz's dentist, and took other "steps usual in missing person's cases." They came up with nothing. The FBI listed her as a missing person but, according to Tresca, undertook no criminal investigation.[31]

Some media outlets began to speculate on what could have happened to her. One reporter suggested that Mr. Robinson was Poyntz in disguise, and the *Daily Mirror* claimed she was part of a "suicide club" of volunteer spies who took the "chances of death" with the "dread OGPU." Friends dismissed the idea that she might have killed herself, saying that she had been highly energetic, though slightly anxious, in the days before she went missing. All indications were that she had been taken involuntarily.[32]

In Tresca's view, the "Stalinist Party" response to Poyntz's disappearance was disturbing and odd. He noted that party members were, in general, "quick to protest almost anything" but now were suspiciously quiet about the disappearance of a woman who had been, at one time, a leading figure among them. A CPUSA spokesman, H. C. Adamson, released a "puzzling" statement after press inquiries, stating that the party had no record of "the woman" as a member and had had "no knowledge of her whereabouts for ten years."[33] The *Daily Worker* reiterated Adamson's claim. C. A. Hathaway, the editor of the *Daily Worker* and a member of the central committee, added that she had held no position on the party's leading committees since 1928 and was thus inconsequential in party circles. Hathaway reported that there had been no bad blood between Poyntz and the party; therefore, it could have no knowledge of the reasons for her disappearance.[34]

On December 24, 1937, the FBI received an anonymous tip asserting that there was "good reason" to believe that the Robinson and Poyntz cases were linked to the "operations of the Russian Secret Service" within the United States. The tipster had it on "good authority" that the Drama Travel League, an organization linked to the Robinsons, was also working with a steamship agency. Presumably this implied that the league could help get the Robinsons to the USSR or help the Soviets take Poyntz out of the country. The tipster concluded that anyone associated with the Robinsons could be "valuable" in tracking down this "sinister instrument of foreign power." The FBI's director, J. Edgar Hoover, forwarded the letter to Secretary of State Cordell Hull, along with a tip from a Mr. Selwyn Harris of New Orleans, who had seen the Robinsons' photograph in the paper and claimed that he recognized them as "persons" he'd been acquainted with in Barcelona in 1935. By the end of the month, the State Department was suspecting that Mr. and Mrs. Donald L. Robinson were really Adolph Arnold Rubens and Alma Marie Rubens, called Ruth by family and friends.[35]

On February 14, 1938, Tresca held a press conference and released a public statement declaring that the link between the Robinson-Rubens case and Poyntz's disappearance was being "glossed over." He claimed that the Robinson-Rubens's case was part of a larger conspiracy based in Moscow to "smear opponents of Stalin's regime" such as Trotsky and legitimize Stalin's purge of his enemies. Tresca met with Francis Mahoney, the acting chief of the U.S. attorney's office, to answer questions about his accusations. He told Mahoney that the Robinsons and Poyntz had been caught in a "frame-up" to "incriminate American Trotskyists." He said that the Robinson-Rubens were being held in the USSR as suspected spies, and Tresca believed that this was part of Stalin's larger plot to eliminate enemies, including Trotsky himself. Tresca's accusations appeared in several newspapers and earned him a subpoena to appear before a grand jury investigating the case.[36]

The accusations against the Robinson-Rubens had been, Tresca believed, trumped up to discredit and eventually eliminate them. But as authorities investigated further, they learned that the couple may not have been as innocent as Tresca believed they were. Inquiries revealed that they had obtained the Robinsons' passports using fraudulent documentation, a forged birth certificate, and stolen naturalization papers. The pair sailed to Europe under their Rubens's names but then used their false passports to enter the Soviet Union.[37]

Investigations into the couple brought up many questions about their political affiliation and, in the case of Mr. Rubens, his identity. Adolph Arnold Rubens claimed in his passport paperwork to be the son of a naturalized American citizen named Christian Rudewitz who had been accused by Russian leaders in 1906 of murdering czarist sympathizers. Rudewitz was never extradited to Russia, and acquaintances claimed that he had never had a son named Adolph or Arnold. Officials also learned that Mr. Rubens had managed to get three passports—one in his Rubens name, the others in the names of Mr. and Mrs. Donald L. Robinson—using a contract (a politician's word for a favor) with Albert Marinelli, a Tammany leader. The contract allowed Rubens to get the passports without appearing in person. Discovery of these favors led to a federal grand jury investigation into a "passport ring" that was found to be issuing a number of passports of dubious legality.[38]

Meanwhile, after confirming that Ruth Rubens was a citizen, State Department officials demanded that the Soviets offer information about her whereabouts. The Soviets did confirm that both she and her husband were being held on suspicion of espionage; but when the American embassy in Moscow tried to arrange an interview with Ruth, it was denied. On February 2, 1938, the *Daily Mirror* published a report alleging (incorrectly) that Mrs. Rubens had been shot and killed in Lublanka Prison and that Mr. Rubens had escaped. This may have prompted the Soviets to finally agree to allow Loy Henderson, American chargé d'affaires in Moscow, to visit Mrs. Rubens on February 6. By this point both Rubens had spent two months in Soviet prison. The Soviets, however, kept delaying the interview until it was finally arranged for February 10. At the meeting, Ruth Rubens said very little about her arrest because the Soviet officials seated with her would not allow her to discuss details. All she revealed was that her husband had indeed illegally obtained their passports and that she wanted no further assistance from the American embassy.[39]

On February 22, Tresca appeared before the federal grand jury investigating the Robinson-Rubens arrests. He testified for more than two hours, listing fifteen witnesses who could "cast light" on the Poyntz and Robinson-Rubens mysteries.[40] In a typed statement to the "Gentleman of the Federal grand jury," he tried to prove that the Robinson-Rubens were Stalinists. The applications for the false Robinson passports had an address for a home that housed CPUSA members, and the individual whom the Robinson-Rubens had used to obtain the passports was Arthur Sharfin, a "member of the Communist Party." The passports were "received, accepted, and signed for" by the wife of Dr. Solon Bernstein, William Z. Foster's physician. Foster was chair of the CPUSA and the International Workers Order, a communist-linked organization. Though the evidence was circumstantial, it seemed to point toward the conclusion that the Robinson-Rubens were communists.[41]

Tresca speculated before the grand jury that Poyntz's disappearance might have been linked to her ability to shed light on the Robinson-Rubens case, given that both she and Mr. Rubens were clearly OGPU agents. Tresca then claimed that he had been told that Schachno Epstein, the person responsible for killing Ignace Reiss in Switzerland, had also "engineered" Poyntz's kidnapping. He said that in the late 1920s, thinking Tresca was a communist sympathizer, Epstein had asked for his help in getting a fraudulent passport. Tresca had refused, and Epstein soon returned to Russia. Meanwhile, both Tresca and Poyntz had become disillusioned with the USSR, which made Poyntz dangerous to the Soviets because of her knowledge of the underground. Tresca also pointed out that Mr. Rubens had allegedly worked for the German consulate. Poyntz, too, had had connections to the consulate via her now deceased husband, and she had made frequent visits there during litigation over his estate. Tresca believed that Poyntz could have known precisely what Rubens was doing for the Soviets in the United States. He closed by telling the grand jury that he felt obligated to testify because of his affection for Poyntz and because of their twenty-year friendship.[42]

Tresca's testimony was based on circumstantial evidence that was impossible to prove, such as his claims that Epstein had asked him for an illegal passport and that Poyntz had told him that she wanted to leave the party. While few anti-Stalinists challenged his accusations, the CPUSA firmly denounced them. After Tresca's press conference on February 10, the *Daily Worker* claimed that a "stool-pigeon" was concocting a "cock-and-bull" story about the Soviets having an "American Woman" kidnapped in the United States. The article stated that even Poyntz's lawyer called the claims too "imaginary" for belief. (Tresca found it interesting that the *Daily Worker* would not use Poyntz's name in the article.) The article went on to denounce his red baiting as a "left-wing plus" tactic that was being used to destroy the anti-fascist united front.[43] A February 14 article cited three "leading" Italian anti-fascists who dismissed Tresca as a "discredited," "disgruntled," washed-up, wanna-be radical who edited an "obscure" newspaper. The communist Pietro Allegro accused him of siding with the "Trotzkyites" and claimed that he was "politically dead." Giralelmo Valenti, a socialist, believed that Tresca was lashing out because he was isolated and no longer a leader of the "masses." Vito Marcantonio, a well-known socialist congressman from New York, stated that Tresca had been discredited in the eyes of the state's Italian community and was a stooge for "reactionary forces." Yet as the historian Judy Kutulas argues, the CPUSA did itself no favors in ignoring Stalin's purges. Despite the questionable credibility of Tresca's accusations, the party's silence on Stalin's terror fed into anti-Stalinist speculation about its complicity.[44]

The party was also intent on distancing itself from the Robinson-Rubens controversy, and it did so by deflecting the blame for the couple's disappearance onto the "Trotzkyite anti-Soviet conspiracy." The *Daily Worker* reported on December 17, 1937, that the Soviets were convinced that the Robinsons were Trotskyites and that the American press was sensationalizing the incident, an accusation the party repeated so often that it came to mean nothing. All evidence suggested that Mr. Rubens was probably working for the Soviets and was not a "Trotzkyite." By parroting the Soviet line, the CPUSA failed to distance itself from Stalin, a stance that disturbed a number of its members.[45]

Eventually, the grand jury investigating the passport ring heard witnesses claim that Mr. Rubens had crossed into Czechoslovakia and Austria forty-five times between July 1935 and November 1936, thus casting doubt on the assertion that the Robinson-Rubens were Trotskyites. It seemed more likely that Mr. Rubens was working as a Soviet spy, trying to pinpoint Nazi motives in the years before the Germans conquered those territories. It also emerged that a friend of the couple had been entrusted with money for Mrs. Rubens's daughter from a previous marriage, in the event that something should happen to the couple overseas. This indicated to many, including Tresca, that they were not planning to return.[46]

Another important feature of the Robinson-Rubens and Poyntz disappearances was the gendered construction of victimization. The newspapers' single-minded focus on Mrs. Rubens's looks illustrates the prewar era's preoccupation with the appearance of female spies. Articles quoted witnesses in Moscow who described her as an "attractive female of youthful American appearance," reportedly seen weeping because of her husband's prolonged absence. Always, the emphasis was on her appearance, not her husband's, and the descriptions were very specific. She was described as "slim, very cultured, gracious, a woman of refinement"; later as "thin and finely drawn and of the Duchess of Windsor type."[47] In her study of media depictions of female spies during the Cold War, Kathryn Olmsted confirms this obsession with physical attractiveness. The difference was that, during the Cold War years, such women were painted as sinister femme fatales, not as sympathetic victims.[48] Thus, prewar descriptions of Mrs. Rubens humanized her. Articles included details of a car accident that had left her scarred. They emphasized that she was a good mother, though in reality she had left her daughter behind with no apparent intention of returning. She was married to a husband described in positive masculine terms as a man with a career in publishing, a "conservative businessman," a "capitalist in every way."[49] Likewise, descriptions of Poyntz insisted that she had been "living in fear" for at least two years before she went missing. Irwin and other journalists highlighted her friends' concerns that she had been harmed, probably by the persistent male with the "Teutonic voice" who was always "impatient" with those who answered the telephone. The caller's aggressive behavior and his deep voice were used as proof that Poyntz's communist attacker was a dangerous masculine threat.[50] Both the newspapers and individuals such as Tresca humanized the Robinson-Rubens and Poyntz in order to underline Soviet brutality. Anti-Stalinists of the period focused their attacks on Stalin and the Soviet apparatus, not on communists and communism.

Tresca did not limit his activities to press conferences and grand jury testimony. He wrote articles about Poyntz in various left-wing publications, where he accused the communists, and later the Nazis, of killing her. In one article he wrote that, in 1934, Poyntz had "entered on the course which led to her undoing," moving into the Soviet underground and using her married name, Juliet Glaser, to conceal her work. Tresca acknowledged that, before 1939, "Kremlin policy" was not yet "pro-Hitler" and that Poyntz's work in anti-German espionage was still essential. Her job was to recruit German students, others with connections in Germany, and American anti-Nazis for espionage in Berlin; and she used the International House at Columbia University as a center for recruitment.[51] According to Tresca, she would approach the German students who lived there and discuss the problems in Hitler's Germany; from there she would convince them that they had to get involved to help stop fascism. In 1935, she held a Christmas party to introduce the students to "cultivated American Communists" and used her communist allies to turn the students against Hitler and eventually enlist them in "secret work" for the "international anti-Nazi movement." The goal was to get them to return to Germany and work with the "underground military espionage machine" run by Walter Krivitsky.[52]

Tresca believed that Poyntz's communist commitment began to unravel in 1936. He said she told him that she had been in Moscow with George Mink during the show trials. What she saw there disillusioned her, and she was resolved to break away from the underground apparatus. Tresca believed that her growing disgust was known to the "Stalinists" and that they had reason to fear her because she might "disclose secret matters."[53] Tresca also announced that he had identified another link between her and the Robinson-Rubens, one suggesting that her disappearance had been "essential to the handling" of the couple's situation. He noted that Poyntz had a German husband with links to the German consulate and argued that she may have met the Robinson-Rubens there as they were in the process of obtaining illegal passports. Anything she might have been able to "confess" about their activities at the consulate would have been damaging for the Soviets. Unless the Soviets had successfully taken her to Moscow, he claimed, they would have needed to kill her.[54]

Tresca's belief in Poyntz's disillusionment was sincere, as was his distress about her, but his claims raise questions. If she had really told him about her disillusionment in the summer of 1937, why didn't he report her subsequent disappearance? If they were close friends, why didn't he know she had vanished until her disappearance was announced in the press in the winter of 1937? If she had told him she was in danger, why didn't he check on her well-being? Why would the Robinson-Rubens or Poyntz need German papers at the consulate if they were recruiting German nationals? Yet despite the gaping holes in Tresca's theory, the anti-Stalinists were convinced.

As I have mentioned, Tresca accused Schachno Epstein of having "valuable information" about Poyntz's disappearance. This was the same Epstein with whom Poyntz had worked in the ILGWU. According to Tresca, in late 1936 Epstein traveled to Paris and found a job with a liberal newspaper; he was then admitted into the Association of Foreign Press Correspondents. Journalism was Epstein's cover. In Paris, he worked with a Soviet agent named Spiegelglass who ran the "political murder corporation" responsible for Reiss's murder and the attempts on Krivitsky and Barmine. Spiegelglass gave Epstein instructions to eliminate Poyntz, and in early 1937 he traveled to New York, ignoring former acquaintances and even denying his identity to one "old friend" who met him on the street.[55] That spring, Epstein and Poyntz were allegedly seen together on numerous occasions, and Tresca argued that he was probably the man who had telephoned her at the boardinghouse "daily at eleven" because the caller had a "deep voice" like "Epstein had." On Monday, May 31, Poyntz telephoned a man she was attempting to recruit. This man, according to Tresca, said she behaved in a "hysterical manner" and declared that she needed to see him "soon." Days later she vanished. Epstein left New York on August 12 aboard the *Queen Mary,* where an old acquaintance from the ILGWU spotted him. Epstein told his friend that he had been in New York to renew his citizenship. Neither Epstein's name nor that of Joseph Berson (his OGPU name) was listed on the passenger manifest. However, a Samuel Stone did appear on the manifest; Tresca claimed that this "Stone" was using a forged American passport and that the FBI wanted to question Epstein about it.[56]

Tresca speculated that Epstein had used his past troubles with the party to ease Poyntz's fears and make her believe that he, too, was disillusioned with Stalin. Perhaps he allowed himself to be seen publicly with her in order gain her confidence. Was it Epstein's intent to kill her? Not necessarily: Tresca believed it was just as likely that she had been taken back to the Soviet Union. He said that a former Soviet spy had once told him that, "to stop a cat's squeals, skull-smashing is superfluous." Indeed, several Soviet thugs in Paris had been convicted of kidnapping "an opponent" and putting him on a Soviet freighter. In June 1937, the Soviet freighter *Chelyuskinetz* had left New York bound for the USSR; Tresca wondered if Poyntz could have been on board.[57]

Tresca found it curious that seven months had elapsed between Poyntz's disappearance and the filing of a missing person's report and that this filing had happened only because her landlord had mentioned her disappearance to a police officer. He believed that Lieberman had not bothered to go to the police until after the media had revealed the disappearance, contrary to the lawyer's own claims. He pointed out that the FBI were not investigating the case and that the New York city and state police were treating it rather "casually." Convinced that federal kidnapping laws had been violated and that a "political crime" had occurred, Tresca called out the American Civil Liberties Union and the liberal press for failing to draw attention to the infringement of Poyntz's civil liberties. He was convinced that his theories were right because no one other than the communists was challenging him.[58]

With the help of Herbert Solow, Tresca spent the next several years continuing his investigation into Poyntz's disappearance. He was a perpetual thorn in the side of the CPUSA, accusing it again and again of participating in Stalin's terrors. A full year after his friend's disappearance was first reported, Tresca wrote to Vito Marcantonio, then the president of the ILD, Poyntz's former employer. The ILD claimed to have an interest in political disappearances, and Tresca urged Marcantonio (who disavowed any link between the ILD and the CPUSA) to look into her case. Tresca offered to share "important data" with him in order to bring about an "effective investigation." Marcantonio responded by stating that he had forwarded the letter to New York's district attorney, an indication that he would not otherwise get involved.[59] In January 1939, the assistant district attorney asked Tresca to speak to him about any "possible crime committed," but no indictments emerged.[60]

By 1940, the fascists were encroaching across Europe and Asia, and Tresca was increasingly convinced that the communists and the fascists had become the world's two greatest evils. After the signing of the 1939 Nazi-Soviet pact, he began claiming, with no apparent evidence, that the Nazi and Soviet undergrounds were in league. In an unpublished article titled "The Communazi Lady Vanishes," he suggested that even before signing of the pact the "Moscow and Berlin spy agencies" had been linked, and he stated that as early as 1934 Hitler had intended to cement such an agreement. Tresca believed that the link between the two underground spy networks was Poyntz herself and said that working with Nazi spies in the United States was an important part of her work.[61] The goal was to get them to act as double agents to supply the Soviets with information on Nazi Germany. This was the "sole maxim of espionage": to convince individuals to work against the apparatus they were working for. Therefore, he said, the German and Soviet undergrounds were constantly trying to penetrate one another. Tresca wrote that Poyntz was in contact with the Nazi underground through her husband's links at the German consulate. He named two women, Hedwig and Rita, who were active in the German-American bund and worked at the consulate. He believed they were Poyntz's Nazi contacts but did not cite his source for that information.[62]

Yet evidence in fact suggests that Poyntz feared the Germans rather than collaborated with them. In 1936, she and Lieberman attended a meeting at the German consulate, where they tried to obtain a widow's allowance from her husband's estate. Though some of her effects had been found with Glaser's, the German attorneys opposed her request. During the meeting a woman allegedly representing Glaser's sister came into the room; she claimed to have worked with Glaser at the consulate and said that he had never mentioned being married. Poyntz was convinced that this woman was a Gestapo agent who was using the opportunity to get a description of Poyntz. Days after the meeting, she told Lieberman that individuals had been trying to make appointments with her; she suspected they were Gestapo agents. Fearing that they knew she was working in the anti-Nazi underground, she decided to move out of her current lodging.[63]

In the winter of 1936, Poyntz was in France. From there, she wrote to Lieberman, giving him permission to take control of her possessions should anything happen to her. He found her letter troubling. Upon her return, she learned that her request for a widow's allowance had been approved. Lieberman told her that her deceased husband would have been entitled to some of his father's substantial fortune. Now, because the Glaser family had acknowledged the marriage, she, too, could make a claim. Initially Poyntz decided not to pursue this litigation. But in May 1937, she asked Lieberman to try to secure as much money as he could from the Glaser family. She told him that she intended to take an extended trip and would require the funds. Lieberman claimed he ran into Poyntz on Sunday May 30, 1937, days before her disappearance, and told her she needed to come to his office to sign some paperwork. He never saw or heard from her again.[64]

Evidence of Poyntz's fear of Gestapo agents is based on the testimony of only one eyewitness, and Tresca thought his theory was sound. He pointed to CPUSA's attempts to distance itself from her as evidence that the communists had "guilty knowledge" about her. Tresca believed that no criminal investigation was conducted because Poyntz was not a missing person but the victim of "involuntary detention" or murder. In his opinion, clues to what had happened could be found the years before 1937.[65] The source for much of Tresca's information was his friend Solow, and a great deal of that was based on conjecture and hearsay. He also saw himself as a danger: he worried that if any communists had seen her with him, that alone could have endangered her life. For Tresca, the most damning evidence of communist involvement was the party's silence about the case. Until the end of his own life, he would regularly ask, "Where is Juliet Stuart Poyntz?"[66]

Tresca's Assassination

Tresca's fate will forever be entwined with Poyntz's. On February 11, 1943, he was gunned down in the street outside his *Il Martello* offices in New York City. The killer was never publicly identified. Days later police were investigating three different theories, some of which had been supplied by Tresca's friends: the first was that it was a political assassination; the second, that an "Italian fifth column" had eliminated him before he could expose its motives; the third, that it was motivated by personal issues. Giuseppe Calabi, Tresca's friend, was the only witness. According to him, the killer's precision suggested that he was a professional assassin.[67]

Tresca had made many political enemies as a "freelance of radicalism." Though his friends agreed that his murder had been "politically motivated," some, such as the labor leader Arturo Giovannitti, blamed the "long arm of Mussolini," while others pointed at the communists. In March 1943, a group of them created the Tresca Memorial Committee in response to what they saw as a slow official investigation. By October 1945, the committee had produced a pamphlet highlighting theories about his murder.[68] The pamphlet described Tresca as an "implacable enemy of the Stalinists" who had accused them of killing Berneri, Trotsky, and Reiss, among others. It cited his grand jury testimony, when he accused the communists of being involved in Poyntz's disappearance. It noted that he had called a former friend, the communist Carlos Contraras, a "commandant of spies, thieves, and assassins." The pamphlet declared that Tresca had warned the Mazzini Society, an Italian-American organization opposed to dictatorship in all forms, that the CPUSA was trying infiltrate it. He had claimed that, if communists were to join the society, non-communists could expect to be "shot in the back of the head"—as Tresca was.[69]

The committee noted some threats that communists had made against Tresca. In February 1938, as he was loudly blaming the Stalinists for Poyntz's disappearance and testifying before the federal grand jury, the Italian National Commission of the Communist Party issued a statement claiming that he was blocking the organizations' ability to construct a united anti-fascist front. The commission issued a "fraternal appeal" to all militants to stand together against fascism and said that Tresca needed to understand that "police informers will no longer be tolerated in the political and labor movement." Tresca perceived the statement as a clear threat: that arming an assassin was not necessary if one could simply "inflame the mind of a fanatic."[70]

Still, as Pernicone argues, the communists were not stupid. Though they found Tresca annoying, they did not assassinate him. By 1943, there were many others on the left who opposed allowing communists into organizations such as the Mazzini Society. The Soviet Union was too distracted by the war to bother about Tresca. The police identified the likely killer, a gang member named Carmine Galante, but lacked enough evidence to indict him, and the case remains officially unsolved. Nonetheless, people continued to suspect the communists and treated Tresca's accusations against them, particularly those regarding Poyntz's disappearance, as a motive for murder.[71]

Today, it is not clear how close Tresca and Poyntz really were. In his 1938 statement to the grand jury, he claimed that, "however mistaken" her political beliefs might have been, she was always "sincere and self-sacrificing." In general, his ire against the CPUSA did not differentiate between leaders and rank-and-file members, but somehow Poyntz was an exception. For her sake, Tresca made a nuisance of himself and in the process acquired a lot of enemies. Until his own violent death, he would not let anyone forget Juliet Stuart Poyntz.[72]

CHAPTER FOUR

THE INTELLECTUAL AND THE FEDS

It was the journalist Herbert Solow who spent the most time investigating Juliet Stuart Poyntz's disappearance. Solow was a leftist who dabbled in Marxism and Trotskyism in the 1930s. Like his friend Carlo Tresca, he grew disillusioned and became a vocal anti-Stalinist, writing articles for the *New Leader* and other left-wing publications accusing Stalin and the CPUSA of various misdeeds. When Poyntz went missing, Solow was convinced that the American party had collaborated with the Soviets to kill her. Using his left-wing contacts, including former communists, he pieced together information about Poyntz's years in the Soviet underground.

The Poyntz case had a significant impact on Solow's evolution from anti-Stalinist to anti-communist. Like many other anti-Stalinists, he came to believe that Stalin was not solely to blame for the deviance in the Soviet system; rather, communism itself was corrosive. This belief became a hallmark assumption during the Cold War years, proof that even before World War II the anti-Stalinist left was shifting toward the anti-communist right. In Solow's view, Soviet communism was inherently violent, as evidenced by the Great Terror and Poyntz's suspected murder. Like Tresca, he presumed, without evidence, that she had been killed; and in his post-1937 attacks on communists, he repeatedly invoked her alleged murder.

Given the FBI's dogged pursuit of communists after World War II, its prewar indifference to the Poyntz case is confounding. When Poyntz went missing, Solow did what the FBI did not: he began an intense investigation into her life in the Soviet underground, searching for evidence of what had happened to her and for proof of Tresca's claims that the CPUSA was complicit in the Great Terror (a link he never made). He was concerned about the FBI's apparent lack of interest in her case, and he was right to be concerned. Before the Cold War, the agency seemed unwilling to expend energy on a missing communist. Only after World War II, when anti-communism became an American obsession and politicians and law enforcement were conspiring to make communism illegal, did Poyntz's disappearance mean anything to the FBI. Still, the agency made no effort to find her; it simply gathered information about her for use in its ongoing war against communism.

Herbert Solow

Herbert Solow was born in Manhattan in 1903, the son of Leon J. Solow, a dentist and Russian émigré, and Rosalie Wasserman. During high school, he "attended religious classes" and "may have been bar Mitzvahed." But as an adult, he did not show much interest in his parents' Judaism. He attended Columbia College, graduating in 1924 with a dual degree in history and literature, and remained there for an additional year to study journalism. At Columbia, he met Lionel Trilling, Meyer Shapiro, and Clifton Fadiman, future members of a cohort known as the New York intellectuals, leftist thinkers who were firmly anti-Stalinist and eventually became anti-communist. He also befriended Whittaker Chambers, a "campus rebel," another person who would influence his shift to anti-communism. According to Judy Kutulas, the New York intellectuals have come to dominate anti-Stalinist histories (at the expense of others, such as Tresca, who helped define radical anti-Stalinism), along with outspoken anti-communist conservatives such as Chambers, who cut their teeth in the Communist Party.[1]

Along with Trilling, Solow gravitated toward a Jewish radical magazine known as the *Menorah Journal,* which featured left-leaning Jewish intellectuals in debates about Zionism, communism, and Stalinism. Though Solow became its editor, he, unlike many of his peers at the journal, never had much interest in his own Jewishness. Instead, he wrote angry denunciations of Zionism. Colleagues claimed that, at this time, he was "in the sphere of influence of the Communist International" especially around issues of colonialism, and he saw the Zionist push for a Jewish state as an expression of imperialism.[2]

As a young college graduate, Solow was enthralled by the Communist Party's anti-imperialism, though he never became a card-carrying member. He defended his friend Sidney Hook at a *Menorah Journal* conference when Hook spoke up for the Palestinian Arabs. In 1929, Solow traveled to Palestine, then under British mandate, to attend the Sixteenth Zionist Congress. Upon his return, he described attitudes in Jewish Palestine as "chauvinism of the most repulsive kind." He was inflamed about its "unacceptable policy toward Arabs" and said that some Jews in Palestine behaved "like the worst anti-Semites in America." Solow's anti-Zionist articles caused so much tension at the *Menorah Journal* that he resigned his editorship in 1931.[3] That same year he looked up his old Columbia classmate Whittaker Chambers, then the editor of *New Masses,* a CPUSA magazine. Knowing that Solow was involved in several student-led communist movements and had written favorable articles about them for the *Nation,* Chambers asked him to contribute articles to the magazine.[4]

As the Great Depression threatened capitalist institutions and fascism began to spread across Europe, Solow was drawn to Marxism. During his brief period as a Marxist, he called himself a "full-blown Professional Revolutionist" and demanded that his wife decorate their apartment with red curtains. Yet he did not approach the party with "prostrate awe."[5] Rather, in an affidavit written years later, he described his flirtation with the communists as naïve and ill-informed. In his words, he became "briefly" and "somewhat fuzzily leftist." In this way he was like many in the early 1930s who were concerned about the rise of fascism and its threat to civil liberties.[6]

During the summer of 1932, Solow traveled to the Soviet Union and was "appalled by the experience" and the conditions there. He then traveled to Turkey to meet with the exiled Trotsky, who confirmed for him that Soviet socialism was not living up to the propaganda. After returning to the United States, Solow tried to draw communist intellectuals toward Trotskyism. Yet he later maintained that, while he respected Trotsky, he had always disagreed with his view that Soviet Russia could be reformed and the revolution saved. Trotskyite politics were, Solow claimed, "undemocratic and immoral."[7]

By the late 1930s, when the Robinson-Rubens and Poyntz disappearances became public, Solow was entrenched in the anti-Stalinist left. There was no organizational structure among the anti-Stalinists. For some, such as Tresca and Solow, their independence from group politics was a "point of pride." Others were drawn to the WPA and the Socialist Party.[8] The historian Terry Cooney describes the anti-Stalinists as a "small" but "troublesome minority." The scholar Neil Jumonville suggests that, for many, their independence from "zealous, fanatical, or messianic mindsets" was central to their self-definition as intellectuals. A quest for an "independent radical tradition" had led them to embrace "anti-Stalinist socialism."[9]

Like Tresca, Solow joined the American Committee for the Defense of Leon Trotsky and traveled to Mexico in April 1937 to take part in hearings about the ousted Soviet leader. Solow's job on the Dewey Commission was to organize the Americans involved in the hearings, make "legal and technical arrangements," and serve as the primary contact with the committee's New York office. Despite disagreements, Solow was, in the end, instrumental to its success. After further hearings in New York and Paris in December 1937, the commission released its verdict, finding Trotsky not guilty of the crimes Stalin accused him of committing. The result did not endear either Solow or the other commission members to the CPUSA.[10] The party condemned the Trotsky hearings and the commission members, who, in turn, claimed that the party had tried to thwart their attempts to bring witnesses and observers to Mexico.[11] Anti-Stalinists accused the CPUSA of blind allegiance to Stalin and the Soviet Union, despite the show trials and the purges.

After the Dewey Commission released its report, Solow turned his attention to the Robinson-Rubens and Poyntz cases. Here again, he pointed to one culprit: Stalin and his crusade to eliminate his enemies. As he immersed himself in the cases, his anti-Stalinism slowly "detached from his socialist and anti-capitalist views," and he began a gradual move toward anti-communism.[12] While Tresca was publicly blaming the CPUSA and the Soviets for Poyntz's disappearance, Solow was publishing a number of articles in the *New Leader* and the *New York Sun* outlining his suspicions and the connections he saw between the Robinson-Rubens and Poyntz disappearances. His investigation was detailed and meticulous: he collected considerable information on the background of all three and contacted former communists and friends in the left to gather material. Like Tresca, he was convinced that the Soviets and the CPUSA were guilty of whatever had happened to Poyntz. Though his conclusions rested on conjecture and conspiracy and though he failed to discover the truth, he did pursue her case more thoroughly than anyone else.

Solow's articles openly challenged the CPUSA, arguing that, despite the party's widely circulated claims, the Robinson-Rubens pair were Stalinists, not Trotskyite spies. He urged the State Department to intervene in the "[O]GPU crime[s]" involving both the couple and Poyntz. Solow traced Mr. Rubens's passport papers and unearthed the story (detailed in chapter three) that his real name was Arthur Rudewitz, that he was son of a naturalized citizen named Christian Rudewitz, and that he was thus an American citizen. For his part, Christian Rudewitz disavowed the relationship, claiming that his citizenship papers had been stolen years earlier and that he had no knowledge of any Arthur Rubens. Tresca reported that several of Rudewitz's friends corroborated that claim, though some of his neighbors reported that his farmhouse had been used for "mysterious meetings." In writing about the situation, Solow did not speculate on what those meetings might have entailed.[13]

Some of Solow's contacts were former members of the CPUSA's central committee. In their view, Rubens had all the markings of a spy operating in the United States. He was "well-supplied" with funds from unknown sources, he had "motor cars" and "servants," and he was funding a literary magazine, though he himself was not a writer. He changed his address frequently, and his neighbors claimed that he behaved "mysteriously." He traveled frequently to Europe and was recently in Mexico, where Trotsky was exiled. He and his wife leased an apartment and paid three months' rent in advance in order to cover their disappearance for at least ninety days.[14] Solow learned that the pair had crossed into the Soviet Union in October with the full knowledge of the Soviets. They had registered under the name of Robinson at the Moscow National Hotel; yet according to Solow, in July the Soviets had barred any Americans named Robinson from entering the country. He concluded that this meant they were co-conspirators in their own arrest.[15]

Solow's articles followed the press's typical gendered mannerisms. He repeatedly referred to Ruth Rubens as an "American girl" or a "Philadelphia and Long Island girl," though she had been married twice and had a seven-year-old daughter. He claimed that, when Loy Henderson, a foreign service officer with the State Department, was finally able to speak to her, OGPU agents limited what she was able to say.[16] He depicted her as naïve, as having simply followed her husband's plan, and thus as not responsible for her own behavior. According to Solow, after Ruth's first interview with Henderson, OGPU agents retrained her because she was unable to get her story straight. He suggested that she had been caught up in something her husband had planned but had not shared with her.[17] Solow's descriptions made Ruth seem like someone with no sense of what was happening to her, a woman who had abandoned her only child to follow her husband into the unknown. He infantilized her, transformed her into an unwitting victim, characterized her as unable to make choices or decisions. He erased all trace of her role in the CPUSA or in Moscow. Yet one of Solow's informants, the former communist Melach Epstein, had confirmed through his CPUSA contacts that she was active in party units and that her husband was a known OGPU agent.[18]

Why had the Robinson-Rubens knowingly put themselves into danger by traveling to the Soviet Union and registering under a suspicious name at a time when others were "confessing" to their alleged crimes and being publicly executed? Their actions made little sense, but Solow offered two possible explanations. Perhaps they had a fanatical, almost religious "devotion to Stalin." Or perhaps the alternative was more "certainly and immediately dangerous." The OGPU was known to have abducted other individuals overseas, and Solow wondered if Poyntz's disappearance had convinced the couple that their only choice was to play a part in Stalin's larger plans. He suspected that Mr. Rubens was wishing he had chosen the path that Poyntz had chosen: of trying to find his way out of the OGPU, despite the risk.[19]

In February or March 1938, Solow sent his *New York Sun* articles to the FBI and later followed up with a phone call to the agency. He continued to press the FBI about what, if anything, it was doing to investigate Poyntz's disappearance. On one occasion, he was told that, because no law had been violated within the "federal jurisdiction of the FBI," no investigation was underway. On another, J. Edgar Hoover informed him that the bureau had no file under the name Juliet Stuart Poyntz.[20] These responses were not entirely honest. Though the FBI was not actively investigating Poyntz's case, it had opened a file on her in early 1938, which included Solow's *New York Sun* articles and a March letter to Hoover outlining Solow's phone conversation with an agent. According to the agent, Solow had claimed that the Robinson-Rubens passport fraud case had been fabricated and that the couple would confess to being spies. He also said that he could produce eyewitnesses who would swear that Poyntz had been in the USSR in 1936 and had been seen in the company of the Soviet operative Shachno Epstein, whom both Tresca and Solow believed had engineered her kidnapping or murder.[21]

The agent dismissed Solow's story as inconsistent, telling Hoover that Solow had said that Poyntz was in the USSR in 1936 in the company of George Mink, had disappeared to work in the Soviet underground, and then "redisappear[ed]" in June 1937 in New York. However, the agent clearly misunderstood Solow's timeline, not realizing that Poyntz's initial disappearance was in fact a trip she had taken to Moscow (where her movements could not be traced) and from which she had returned. Additionally, he noted that before her "redisappearance" Epstein was seen in her company and that he left on the *Queen Mary*, registered under another name, after Poyntz went missing. The agent's memo, flawed as it was, gave Hoover the impression that Solow was unreliable.[22]

Both Solow and the FBI wondered if Poyntz had been murdered in the United States rather than spirited to the Soviet Union. Solow looked into the discovery of a woman's headless corpse that turned up on March 10, 1938, in Niagara, New York. No identification was made. Over the years, other unclaimed women's bodies turned up, and some speculated they could have been Poyntz, but none was ever positively identified. Despite these dead ends, Tresca and Solow remained seriously concerned that Poyntz may have been murdered. The FBI was not equally concerned, only following up on inquiries from state and local agencies that were trying to identify unclaimed dead women.[23] As late as 1949, Colonel Herbert Barnes of the Delaware State Highway Department, contacted Hoover after hearing the former communist Paul Crouch's testimony before the House Un-American Activities Committee (HUAC) in which he claimed that Poyntz had been killed and her "body thrown in the East River in New York [City]." Barnes told Hoover that on June 21, 1937, the Delaware state police had recovered the body of an unidentified woman in the Delaware River, and he wanted to find out if it could been Poyntz.

The coroner's report had found no water in the woman's lungs and said that she had been dead for approximately two days before she had been found. But in 1937, there had been no missing persons' reports that matched the description of the woman.[24]

In his 1949 letter, Barnes included autopsy photographs and a description that clearly did not match Poyntz's. The woman in the river had been white, approximately sixty-five to seventy years old, five foot, four inches tall, and 120 pounds. After describing her clothing in detail, Barnes noted as "peculiarities" that the woman's toes had all been taped for corns. He made no mention of an "ulcerated red mark" on the bridge of her nose, peculiar to Poyntz's medical diagnosis of lupus. Poyntz also had false upper and lower teeth, which were not mentioned in this autopsy report. The woman in the river was almost twenty years older than Poyntz was, a good two inches shorter, and twenty to forty pounds lighter. After learning that the Delaware police still had the woman's fingerprints on file, the FBI asked its Boston field office to obtain Poyntz's prints so they could be compared. The hope was that Poyntz's 1928 arrest in Boston had yielded a fingerprint record, but the field office could not locate one and thus could not confirm any connection between the body and Poyntz.[25]

As the FBI reacted sporadically to requests, Solow worked to uncover some of Poyntz's activities in the days before she went missing. He learned that Marie MacDonald had had dinner with Poyntz on May 30, 1937, a few days before her disappearance. MacDonald gave him a list of Poyntz's friends, including Sophie Thiess, who was responsible for packing up the rest of her "partly packed" belongings.[26] In his notes, Solow wrote that he had spoken with all of Poyntz's known friends and that none had seen or heard from her since June 5. She had had dinner with a Mrs. G on May 29 and had phoned the piano teachers Marcel M. Bold and Julienne (last name unknown) that same day. She had ordered a prescription on June 3 but had never returned to pick it up.[27]

Solow's newspaper articles drew attention to his investigation into Poyntz's disappearance, and in February 1938 he received a letter from the former communist Joseph Zack, whose real name was Joseph Zack Kornfeder. A founding member of the Communist Party, Kornfeder had been a devoted comrade. He spent three years at the Moscow Lenin School training in "the various methods of political warfare" and rose to the rank of Comintern delegate for South America. In 1934, however, he left the party and moved into anti-communism sooner than most anti-Stalinists did. He testified in 1939 before HUAC's predecessor, the Dies Committee, and after the war he appeared before HUAC.[28]

In his letter, Kornfeder praised Solow for taking the initiative on Poyntz's disappearance, claiming that the CPUSA's disavowal of her was disingenuous. He attributed both Poyntz's and the Robinson-Rubens's disappearances to the Soviet secret police and expressed astonishment over the audacity of kidnapping an American citizen on foreign soil. He said that the usual Soviet modus operandi had been to lure people back to Moscow "voluntarily," where they were kept in some "far corner of the Soviet Empire" as "guests." Kornfeder claimed to have known Poyntz "quite well" and said that she had worked under "his direction on some occasions." He knew that she was a "GPU" agent and said that she had been privy to all the extralegal activities of that organization. Still, she was no "real GPU material"; rather, her "inclination to adventureship" made her "do it out of principle." (With this statement, Kornfeder became yet another figure who belittled Poyntz's years of devoted communist activity as mere adventurousness.) Kornfeder emphasized his role as a former "high functioning" member of the party and fingered Max Bedacht, the president of the International Worker's Organization (IWO), as the GPU's "high contact man" in New York—that is, the go-between with Moscow. Members of this GPU center would transport kidnapped Russians back to the Soviet Union using Russian ships; Kornfeder claimed that the center also directed all of the party's secret work in the United States. He told Solow that solving the Poyntz case would require going after the GPU and said he doubted that anyone would be willing to do so, though he did offer his aid. A copy of Kornfeder's letter is in the FBI's Poyntz file—a sign that the bureau was at least somewhat curious about her fate.[29]

Perhaps Solow's greatest investigative coup was locating Mark Graubard, whom Poyntz had recruited into the Soviet secret apparatus. During a February 1938 interview at Graubard's home in Worcester, Massachusetts, Solow learned how and with whom Poyntz had operated in the underground. By this time, Graubard had distanced himself from the Soviet underground, fearing that he, too, would be caught up in the purges. He was nervous about allowing his name to be used in any of Solow's articles in case it might damage his chances of getting a "university job or research [position]." He willingly shared details but on the strict condition that Solow would never use his name in anything he published or reveal him as a source before a grand jury. Graubard said he would refuse to testify; yet already he sounded like an anti-communist, despairing that Poyntz had been "deluded" by a philosophy that was "to blame for most of our political troubles."[30]

Solow assured Graubard that he had "no cause to fear for his discretion" and promised to avoid compromising him or his work. Solow believed that, by this time, Poyntz was "beyond embarrassment," though there was a chance she was still alive and being held by the Soviets. He told Graubard that exposing her disappearance would be ammunition against both "Hitler and Stalin." He also framed his own and Poyntz's underground activities as anti-fascist and argued that his investigation would "affirm" that commitment. Solow's emphasis on Poyntz as an anti-fascist made her seem idealistic and hopeful, an anti-communist stereotype affirming that women were more vulnerable than men to communist propaganda.[31]

Graubard told Solow that he had met Poyntz in 1935. She was introduced to him as Juliet Glazer, and he later learned she was Juliet Stuart Poyntz, a former communist leader. At the time, he was a member of the party and doing graduate work at Columbia. Poyntz told him that she had "retired from public political work" and was now engaged in secret anti-Nazi opposition. She asked him to introduce her to foreign students at Columbia who would be able to do underground work in their home countries. Graubard was led to believe that this work would be "directed against Hitler for the benefit of the German masses." He managed to recruit a "Polish girl," who at the time of his interview with Solow was still working in Poland in the underground.[32]

Through Poyntz, Graubard met a man named Phillips who might have been Polish but claimed he was a naturalized American of "Yugoslav, Russian, and Polish extraction." He had an American passport that he had obtained illegally using the birth certificate of a Wisconsin-born man named Moren. In 1936, Graubard landed a job with a travel agency to lead a group of tourists through Russia. Phillips instructed him to stay overseas and settle in Switzerland. He was to get a job in industry and locate contacts in Germany. In February 1936, Graubard settled in Zurich and got a job at a laboratory. In October, Phillips instructed him to travel to Munich to visit a friend, a "former Social-Democrat," and convince that friend to quit his existing job, get one in a factory, and help in the underground. Graubard's friend refused. Shortly afterward Graubard traveled to Paris to pick up his wife. There he met Phillips, who gave him $200 after Graubard complained about a lack of funds.[33]

By February 1937, Graubard had finished his lab experiments and was out of money. He had not heard from Poyntz and Phillips for some time, and he feared that both had been caught up in the purges. In his interview, he told Solow that he did not like or trust Phillips and wanted to "break all connections with underground work." He left Zurich for Paris, where he received a telegram from a man named Danny. Danny had meant to get in touch with Graubard in Zurich, but the contact was delayed because he had been in a hospital in Berlin. Now he was trying to give Graubard a week-old letter from Phillips written from Moscow. Danny encouraged Graubard to stay in Europe and continue to make contacts in Germany, but by now Graubard was afraid for his safety and eager to cut ties with the Soviets.[34]

Graubard told Solow that he avoided Poyntz after his return to New York. He worried that she might be in trouble and did not want to "embarrass her." He later ran into party acquaintances who claimed she had missed appointments with each of them. Graubard read of her disappearance in the newspaper and asked some party members what they knew about it. They claimed that she had been killed by the Nazis. Solow asked Graubard to contact a lawyer friend of his with connections to the CPUSA to confirm this news. According to this lawyer, some of those connections had seen Poyntz after the date of her supposed disappearance; they said she had gone off on "party work" and was not dead after all. Neither Solow nor Graubard had much confidence in those claims.[35]

Graubard told Solow that he later found out that Phillips was a Russian general. He said that Phillips and the other Soviet agents drank excessively, threw money around, and sexually assaulted women. An account by Elizabeth Bentley confirms that Phillips was well known for harassing the women that Poyntz recruited, though Solow believed she had no knowledge of this. Graubard described a conversation in which he asked Phillips about his behavior. The agent claimed he was "testing their character" and said that "in Russia [Graubard] would be shot for talking like that." When Graubard suggested that Poyntz would not approve of his actions, Phillips dismissed her as an "office boy" who was not in a position to challenge him.[36]

One of the more mysterious characters in Graubard's story was a woman named Lena who had worked with Poyntz and Phillips. Graubard described her as a Slav, a "very nice person" who was an "inspector or chief" in the underground. She also went by the name Miss West and had a passport under the name of Anson or Hanson. Graubard met her through Poyntz while he was still in the United States. Lena was living at the boardinghouse where Poyntz also lived; Solow speculated that this was so she could keep an eye on Poyntz. Graubard met Lena once in Zurich, in November 1936, after he decided to leave the underground. He described the meeting as "pointless," but she did inform him that Poyntz had been in Moscow to see a parade on November 7. As Solow would learn, she was an important figure in Poyntz's recruiting efforts.[37]

Graubard also helped Poyntz try to recruit the journalist William Harlan Hale. Hale's father had been a press correspondent in Germany, and the son had contacts there. In June 1936, Graubard visited Hale in Woodstock, New York, to briefly discuss the possibility of working in the German underground. Days later, Graubard left for Europe, and he told Solow that he never knew if Hale had been successfully recruited. Solow discovered that Poyntz subsequently met with Hale through another mutual contact, Helene Galois, who arranged a dinner party so that the two could be introduced. Later Poyntz and Lena met with Hale together. Lena was introduced as Miss West, and Hale described her as a "beautiful, blond" Russian.[38]

Hale told Solow that Lena had a large amount of cash and was prepared to give it to him so he could leave immediately for Germany. He was supposed to travel from Germany to Switzerland and wait until he received orders from Lena, but he kept deferring the trip, insisting on his need for more details about the work. At some point Hale met Phillips, whom he knew as "the General." Later he met Poyntz by chance on the street. She again urged him to accept the job, but he continued to demand more information, which Poyntz was unwilling to provide. Hale decided not to become involved and instead traveled to the West Indies. In late

May or early June 1937, a nervous and excited Poyntz phoned him. She insisted on seeing him, though he reiterated that he was not interested in working in the underground. Nevertheless, Poyntz said she would be in touch in three or four days. He never saw or heard from her again. Later that year he read about her disappearance in the newspaper.[39]

Solow never knew that years later, after World War II, an FBI informant named Mr. Narceny told the New York bureau office that a former OGPU spy named Edna Shultz had linked Lena to Poyntz's disappearance. According to him, on June 3, 1937, Lena had invited Poyntz to a party in Brooklyn. Poyntz became intoxicated, and George Mink left the party with her, taking her to a Soviet ship docked at a Brooklyn pier. The ship set sail the next day, bound for Leningrad. On arrival, Poyntz was taken to a jail in Moscow, where Shultz was asked to interview her. Shultz claimed that Poyntz had resigned from the party and had joined a group of intellectuals in New York who had "started vigorous anti-Stalin propaganda." This was not the only version of Narceny's story. In another, Lena's party was in a restaurant and Shultz conducted her interview in January 1938, which suggests that Poyntz was imprisoned for seven months. In both versions, Shultz alleged that Poyntz was executed a few weeks after the interview. Narceny's was the first of many informant stories, all with different details and perpetrators. Yet it is remarkably close to Tresca's and Solow's accusations that Mink kidnapped Poyntz and took her to the Soviet Union. Perhaps even the party faithful were influenced by their publicity. Or perhaps the story was true but never revealed because the FBI could not confirm it with Shultz.[40]

Narceny's tip did make the FBI curious about Lena. In 1953, the bureau located Amy MacMaster, one of Poyntz's friends, who related an unusual story about Lena. By now it was clear that she went by many names. To MacMaster, she was Mary Delmar, though her passport said Ruth Brataslowsky. Others knew her as Tina or Rywka Brokowicz. It was usual for workers in the Soviet underground to have a number of names and to travel with different passports, but Lena's case was excessive. Eventually the bureau came to believe that all of these names referred to the same woman because she was identified as missing an index finger. Agents concluded that she was Poyntz's "superior" in the underground and that their relationship was not friendly.[41]

MacMaster told the FBI that she had known Poyntz since 1924. Poyntz had often used MacMaster's apartment and at one point stayed there for an entire summer while MacMaster was away. In 1936, Poyntz asked if MacMaster would visit her friend Mary Delmar (Lena) in the hospital. Delmar seemed to be having a crisis. She'd left a train station in Denholm, Pennsylvania, wearing only pajamas. She was found crouching in the corner of a barn, and the farm's owners let her stay with them until June of that year, when she shot herself in the head. Delmar managed to survive the gunshot wound but was hospitalized for a lengthy stay in nearby Lewistown as a suicide risk. This had not been her first attempt: while living in Chicago, she had jumped out of a window. Although Delmar told hospital staff that she had amnesia, they did not believe her. Instead, something made them suspect she was "communistic." A staff member named Dr. J. Brown claimed that she had "no use for the rich" and said he did not believe the "girl was entirely sane."[42]

Poyntz paid MacMaster $25 per week to watch Lena and arranged with a lawyer to have Lena released into MacMaster's custody. On one occasion Poyntz went with her to visit Lena in the hospital. When Lena saw Poyntz, she flew "into a fit of rage"; MacMaster was not sure if her reaction was fear or anger. Poyntz claimed that the suicide attempt was the result of a thwarted love affair, but MacMaster believed that it might have had something to do with Poyntz. She recalled another incident, when she and Poyntz went to claim Lena's suitcase, which Lena had left behind at a train station in New Jersey. Poyntz immediately searched the suitcase. This mysterious behavior suggests that Lena and Poyntz's relationship was tenuous at best. Perhaps Lena really did have a role in her disappearance.[43]

Poyntz asked MacMaster to travel with Lena to Paris to ensure that she arrived safely, and she managed to get another couple, the Littinskys, to escort them to France. As instructed, MacMaster left Lena in the care of the Littinskys, and after three days in Paris she returned to the United States. She knew there was an arrangement between the Littinskys and some Poles who would pick up Lena but claimed she did not know the details. She told the FBI that, after that trip in 1936, she never saw or heard from Lena or the Littinskys again.[44] The Littinskys denied they were communists, telling the FBI that Poyntz had bullied them into helping and that they did not know what happened to Lena after she left them.

Despite its mysteries, this story proves that Poyntz was a forceful personality who could somehow convince, even force, three people to transport a Soviet spy for her. It also suggests that she did not have a good relationship with some of her colleagues in the underground. If the FBI had taken Solow more seriously, he could have told them that Graubard met Lena only two months after this trip, at a meeting he described as "pointless."[45]

The Photograph

In late November 1939, Solow returned to Worcester to clear up some details with Graubard. This time he had a photograph, given to him by a man named Turrou, which he thought might depict Poyntz and Phillips. Graubard identified both of them in the picture, as well as Mink and a Nazi underground agent named Griebl. Solow believed that the Soviet and Nazi undergrounds had had a "moment of cooperation" before the signing of the Nazi-Soviet pact in 1939, during which they traded "negligible" information. The honeymoon was brief, but the photograph might implicate Poyntz and other Soviet operatives in a plot with the Nazis—exactly what Tresca had suggested in "The Communazi Lady Vanishes." Solow's information on this connection came from a "source" he believed to be "informed and reliable." This source claimed that the underground contact had been made by a commercial attaché at the German consulate in New York: Dr. Frederick Franz Ludwig Glaser, Poyntz's ex-husband. Did Poyntz know something about "Soviet counter-espionage" in the Gestapo that would have made her dangerous to the Soviets?[46]

The photograph was Solow's only evidence tying Poyntz to the Soviet and Nazi undergrounds. It was also problematic. Though Graubard confirmed that both Phillips and Poyntz were in the photo, he felt that Poyntz looked "very young" compared to how he remembered her. He suggested that Solow show it to Ludwig Lore, who had been close to her. Lore positively identified Mink but denied that the woman was Poyntz. Nor could Hale identify Poyntz in the picture. A State Department employee named A. J. Nicholas claimed that the photograph had been "touched up considerably" and said that the woman pictured was "considerably younger than Miss Poyntz." (Nicholas's connection with Poyntz is not clear in his correspondence with Solow.)[47]

Figure 4. George Mink, lying down; Juliet Stuart Poyntz, right. Herbert Solow Papers, Hoover Institution Archives, Stanford University.

Once again, Solow and the FBI separately obtained details that clarified part of the story, but neither was privy to the other's information. For years, Tresca and Solow had sought a link between Poyntz and the German consulate, but they could not definitively find one. In 1944, the FBI interviewed Gertrude Loescher Hirsch, who had served as secretary to the commercial attaché at the German consulate in New York between 1924 and 1938. She told the FBI that Glaser had been a close personal friend and said that when Poyntz came forward in 1936 to claim her husband's estate, bringing proof that she was his widow, "everyone was surprised" to learn that he was married. Poyntz and Glaser were already estranged by the time he began to work at the consulate—though Hirsch clarified that technically he did not work for the consulate but as a "freelance economist" for the German section of the Associated Press. For the consulate he provided updates on the German steel industry. When Poyntz came forward, Hirsch contacted Glaser's sister in Germany, who also expressed surprise. It is likely that Hirsch was the woman who entered the room when Poyntz was speaking to consulate lawyers, the woman whom she believed was a Gestapo agent trying to get a description of her. According to Hirsch, Glaser was a known socialist without a particularly important role at the consulate; there would have been no reason for the Nazi underground to trust him.[48] The FBI's interview with Hirsch suggests that in 1935 any connection between Poyntz and Glaser would have meant nothing since he was not a central consulate figure.

The source of the photograph was also problematic. Solow described Turrou as a "peculiar man," a naturalized American with "obscure nationality" who claimed three mothers on "three continents." While working with the American Relief Administration in Moscow under General William Haskell, State Department officials questioned his loyalty and called him a "liar." According to Solow, he "presumably" obtained the photograph from the Nazi agent Griebl who appeared in it. Turrou's reputation was so shady that Solow believed he would never be called as a "rebuttal witness" because he was a "perjurer or worse." Turrou was a disgraced FBI agent who resigned from the bureau in 1938 and tried to sell a story to the press about his time in German counterintelligence. He was officially censured by President Roosevelt.[49] The photograph was shaky evidence from the first and appeared to contradict Solow's and Tresca's claims about Nazi and Soviet cooperation. The FBI did not take this line of inquiry seriously and never investigated it.

Solow's Journalism

Solow learned a great deal about the Soviet underground because a former spy, identified as "Karl" in his notes, was feeding him information. Karl was likely Whittaker Chambers, Solow's old college friend. In 1938, the year Chambers broke with the Communist Party, Karl and Solow spoke frequently. The information he gave Solow is identical to information that Chambers later included in a lengthy affidavit on secrets from the underground. Karl indicated that Poyntz's entire apparatus had been liquidated by the Soviets. He told Solow that Phillips was killed first, then Poyntz, and Mr. Rubens shortly thereafter. He shared a rumor that Poyntz had been murdered and buried in New York and that the investigation into her death had been quashed in the Department of Justice by a Communist Party operative who was working there. He did not offer any evidence for this.[50]

In Solow's view, these tales of intrigue and back stabbing made it clear that the Stalinists could not be trusted, that they were pawns of the Soviets. His article "Stalin's Spy Scare—American Edition" uses Poyntz's disappearance as a way to define the Soviet terror. As a "back-sliding" Stalinist, he wrote, she had faced the harshest penalty. She "knew too much" so she received "the highest form of social sanction"—a Soviet euphemism for death. Directly linking Poyntz's disappearance to the show trials, Solow claimed that Soviet methods of torture and murder had been used on her in the United States, just as they were being used on the ousted Bolshevik leaders. He quoted former Soviet journalist Karl Radek: "whoever had the slightest rift with the party may be tomorrow a traitor."[51]

In June 1938, Solow published "Missing a Year! Where Is Julia Poyntz?" in the *New Leader,* marking the one-year anniversary of Poyntz's disappearance and revealing some of the details he had collected about the case. He confirmed that, in 1934, Poyntz had begun recruiting for the Comintern and that, in 1936, she had traveled to Moscow several times with Mink, using the name Mrs. Glaser. In May 1937, she had told her old friend Carlo Tresca that she "could no longer approve of things under the Stalin regime in Russia" and that she was going to leave party work. Tresca believed that her new stance on the Soviets was "well-known" among American Communists, making her a "marked person." Solow noted that party rules prohibited relationships with individuals whom the party had labeled "an enemy." Thus, her friendship with Tresca, a well-known critic "on par with the Trotskyites," in the eyes of the Stalinists, "would be regarded as treason." In an early draft of the article, Solow had written that a New York City detective believed that Poyntz had been "drifting from the CP" when she went missing. The published article largely repeated many of Tresca's claims, including the accusation that Schachno Epstein was responsible for her disappearance and that he had been seen on a ship heading for the Soviet Union during the summer Poyntz had disappeared.[52]

In an unpublished manuscript, Solow took aim at Poyntz's attorney, Elias Lieberman, claiming that he had not behaved like an "active searcher." Solow pointed out that Lieberman had not wanted to reveal the disappearance to the press or the public and only reported Poyntz missing after the news appeared in the papers. He subsequently told reporters that he had come to believe that she had gone missing involuntarily. Solow accused the CPUSA of pressuring Lieberman to denounce Tresca and said that Lieberman had made no statements discrediting the party. He believed that the lawyer was lending "aid and comfort" to the perpetrators and denounced his "complicity in the fate" of his client. Later, however, Solow learned that Lieberman had a sister living in the Soviet Union. He may have remained silent in order to protect her.[53]

The FBI also did some investigation into Lieberman. Agents learned that he had once been associated with the National Committee of the International Juridical Association, a communist-linked group, according to the New York field office. But the bureau received confirmation from three individuals that Lieberman was not a communist. When an agent spoke with him, he was "quite cooperative," and said that he had met Poyntz while both were associated with the ILGWU. The two remained friends for years, he said, and she would come to him whenever she "was in any trouble." Lieberman told the agent that he had kept her disappearance to himself for so long because he had been "quite attracted to her," citing the "brilliance of her mind and the force of her personality." He felt it would be "indiscreet to initiate a search" with the New York City police because she was linked to the CPUSA and the OGPU. He worried that law enforcement would be "'dogging' her footsteps." When the agent showed Lieberman the passport photo of Samuel Stone (see chapter three), he identified him as Schachno Epstein, confirming at least one of Tresca's and Solow's suspicions. Lieberman claimed that Epstein's son came to his office after seeing newspaper articles that attached his father's name to the disappearance. He denied that his father had had anything to do with it.[54]

Throughout the war years and beyond, Solow continued to write about and investigate Poyntz's disappearance and eventually Tresca's assassination. Though the Soviets had become American allies, and anti-communism was less fashionable, Solow never wavered in his attacks. For instance, even as others on the Tresca Memorial Committee began to consider different culprits in Tresca's murder, Solow continued to blame the communists.

In notes on the murder, he claimed that communists had hated Tresca because he had a "broad reputation" in the American trade union movement and was a "bitter and bitterly hated enemy" of the party.[55]

In 1945, Solow worked with Eleazar Lipsky, an assistant district attorney for New York City, during the investigation into Tresca's murder. He supplied Lipsky with a list of people with possible information about the assassination and in return asked Lipsky to help him obtain a transcript of the surrogate court hearings in which Poyntz's sister, Eulalie McClelland, asked to have her declared dead. With Elias Lieberman's help, McClelland's suit had been successful. After Poyntz was declared legally dead, she claimed her $14,000 estate from the Glaser family. Solow reminded Lipsky that Poyntz's disappearance had been directly related to Tresca's death, and he hoped the hearing transcripts might reveal more information. However, there is no indication that he obtained them.[56]

In 1953, Solow wrote to Judge Joseph M. Proskauer, the head of the New York State Commission, about political murders in the state. He claimed that in the previous ten years there had been at least two political murders and a possible third—Poyntz's. Solow briefly described the likely death of Poyntz and the murder of Tresca and mentioned the more recent murder of Joseph Scottoriggio, "no one in particular," who was killed on Election Day in 1946, allegedly for trying to challenge fraudulent votes cast for Vito Marcantonio. Solow believed that law enforcement was reluctant to pursue these cases and told the judge that "informed private citizens" would be willing to help him investigate.[57]

Solow's search for answers continued throughout the war years and beyond. When his old college classmate Whittaker Chambers defected from the underground in 1938, Solow saw an opportunity to learn more about life for Americans working as Soviet agents. Throughout the early Cold War years, Solow would rely on information from Chambers to try and solve the puzzle of the Poyntz disappearance and its possible connections to the Robinson Rubens case. Meanwhile, his investigation would further fuel his transition from anti-Stalinism to anticommunism.

CHAPTER FIVE

THE WITNESS

On the night of February 1, 1938, Whittaker Chambers showed up at Herbert Solow's doorstep with a man named Mike Intrator. It was a cold, snowy night, and Chambers looked unfriendly, with his collar up and hat pulled down. Solow had had a falling out with Chambers three years before and was not eager to speak to either of them. Knowing Chambers had been in the Soviet underground for the past few years made his company even less welcome. Solow did agree to talk with them, primarily for the sake of their old friendship, but he was unwilling to let the pair in; they had to go somewhere else. Solow put on his overcoat. Then, remembering a scene from a movie he had recently watched, he grabbed a pipe and put it into his pocket. Holding the hidden pipe like a revolver, he pointed it at the startled men and told them to start moving. Keeping his "gun" on them, Solow forced them down the street to a restaurant. Once there, he looked directly at Chambers and demanded, "Do you have anything to do with the liquidation of Poyntz?" Chambers immediately denied responsibility, but Solow noted that he made no objection to the word *liquidation.* Perhaps Chambers had at least "heard her screams" in his imagination.[1]

Like many others with insider knowledge about the communist underground, Chambers was frightened by the Soviet purges and wanted to break away. Now he was turning to his old college friend Solow with a plea for help. Although Chambers later became a virulent and public anti-communist, he avoided public attention during the war years. His fear of falling prey to the Soviets, as he assumed Poyntz had done, kept him in the shadows. The historian Alan Wald has described Solow as a "behind-the-scenes" person, who never received the open "renown" of people such as Chambers, but he was influential among those who knew him. In these early years, Chambers became an important anonymous source for Solow. Eventually, Chambers did speak to legal authorities, but he stayed quiet during the years before and during the war, when the

Soviets and the United States were allies. Only later were the American people and the security services ready to take his allegations seriously.[2]

Chambers is a transitional figure between the anti-Stalinists and later anti-communists. As the historian Ellen Schrecker writes, repression of communists and the CPUSA required Cold War policymakers and elites to convince the American public that communism was a Soviet conspiracy "so bad" that it had to be "driven" out of the United States. This, she argues, was not a natural process but involved the "well-coordinated" activities of the anti-communist network, which included political parties, criminal proceedings, legislative hearings, and "intellectual conversions" such as Solow's and Tresca's. This aggressive approach blunted any "nuanced and realistic picture" of American communism and communists. Many of the stereotypes that emerged about communists were easy to sell because they were based on actual communist behavior as purveyed by careerist anti-communists such as Chambers. The most sensational of these stories involved Poyntz's disappearance and her assumed murder by Soviet authorities.[3] Chambers told Solow that he believed Poyntz's disappearance marked the beginning of the Great Terror, and in his 1952 book *Witness* he claimed that the case had motivated his final break with communism.[4]

Whittaker Chambers

Whittaker Chambers was born Jay Vivian Chambers on April Fool's Day in 1901, the son of Jay and Laha Chambers. As a student at Columbia University, he met Solow and quickly made a reputation for himself as a writer. By the end of his sophomore year he was elected editor-in-chief of the college newspaper, the *Morningside,* but almost immediately created a controversy with an article he wrote satirizing Jesus Christ. After some faculty members and students called for his expulsion, Chambers decided to take a break from school in 1923 and traveled to Europe with friends. Upon his return to the United States, he re-enrolled at Columbia, intending to pursue a degree in history. For a time he became interested in Fabian socialism, but neither it nor school life could hold his attention. Before the end of the semester, he had stopped attending classes.[5]

In 1924, he stumbled onto Vladimir Lenin's "The Soviets at Work," the transcript of a 1918 speech about "[a] day in the life of a local soviet." The piece, as Chambers recalled in *Witness,* was not abstract Marxist theory but had the "reek of life." What impressed him most was that it represented socialism "in practice": the "thing itself" and "how it worked." From this introduction he moved on to other writings that argued that "terror and dictatorship are justified" in order to maintain the socialist state. Gradually, he warmed to the idea that terror could be a part of "socialist policy" because it would be a way to guarantee the success of the revolution. Chambers "faced the necessity to act" and approached a former classmate about joining the CPUSA. In 1925, he became a card-carrying member of the party, inspired to join by his new belief in the need for violence—or at least this is what he claimed years later, when his anti-communist career was thriving.[6]

Chambers noted in *Witness* that he saw Poyntz at his first-ever party meeting. He remembered hearing much broken English there because many of the attendees were not native-born. Whether this memory was true or not, Chambers was playing on a Cold War trope that framed foreigners as responsible for the communist threat and radical ideas as imported. He described the conversation at this meeting as hyperbolic and aggressive: "No matter" what a speaker was talking about, it was delivered "as ferociously and rudely as possible." At some point (he could not recall the particular context), Poyntz stood up and accused someone of being a liar. This, he wrote, was his first encounter with the "Midwestern American and Barnard graduate" whose murder "by the Russian secret police" made a "deep impression" on him during his own defection.[7]

Solow and Chambers lost touch for a few years after college but reconnected in 1931, when Solow was still interested in Marxist politics. They met several times, along with Mike Intrator and his wife, Grace Lumpkin, to discuss communism. Intrator was a Lovestoneite—a follower of Jay Lovestone, once the general secretary of the CPUSA, who was expelled in 1929 when he sided with Bukharin, the last "major obstacle to Stalin's consolidation of power." The party had condemned Lovestone and his followers; and at the time Chambers and Solow reconnected, Chambers was in "some trouble" over his associations with them. He eventually reconciled with the party leadership and was assigned to edit the CPUSA journal *New Masses.* Solow wrote a few articles for Chambers but signed them under the name Henry Storm as he was not "wholly in agreement" with the CPUSA.[8]

Solow and Chambers met often during 1933, the year that Chambers and his wife, Esther, had their first child. During this period Chambers also left *New Masses* and told Solow he would be doing "confidential" work for the party. He said he was no longer in the CPUSA but was now a member of the Soviet party. After Chambers entered the underground, Solow noticed that his behavior became increasingly odd. On one occasion he asked Solow to enter his apartment before him because he was afraid of opposition spies. The two began to spend less time together, partly because Solow was "fed up with [Chambers's] smug devotion to the Moscow regime."[9] By 1934, Solow's growing anti-Stalinism had created a rift between the two. They had several unpleasant arguments, and Solow, in anger, called Chambers a Stalinist, which party members viewed as an insult. During a visit to their friend Adelaide Walker, who was in the hospital after having a baby, their discussion turned to politics. Both Solow and Walker told Chambers they believed that the CPUSA had helped Hitler come to power in order to force the French into a pact with the Soviets. This led to an argument in which "hot words were exchanged." Outside the hospital Solow called Chambers a "revolting cynic" and told him that he wanted nothing to do with him. The two did not see each other again until 1938.[10]

Leaving the Party

In the fall of 1937, Solow heard from a friend that Chambers was getting fed up with the party. Solow was not sympathetic: he was angry that the communists seemed to be standing by while blood was being spilled in Stalin's purges. Then Chambers and Intrator showed up at Solow's apartment. Solow wrote about the incident several times. In one version, he was home alone and did not want to meet with the pair by himself. In another, he was with a group of friends and decided to take the two elsewhere. The dummy-gun variation was the most dramatic. But in every version, Poyntz was an ominous presence, haunting Chambers's movements in the days, weeks, and months surrounding his defection from the Soviet underground. It was her disappearance that had prompted him to seek out his old friend in the first place.[11]

In a version of this story written fifteen years after the incident, Solow claimed he was frightened to see Chambers on his doorstep. In February 1938, he and Tresca had been printing article after article on the doings of the communist underground. While Tresca was primarily concerned with Poyntz, Solow was plying his trade as a "whodunnit journalist on the left front." Their public accusations could "have worried the whole underground." Solow recalled that it was ten o'clock at night when Chambers and Intrator knocked on his door. As soon as he knew who they were, his "heart began to thump." Chambers was burly, but Intrator was even "huskier" and this made Solow nervous. What did they want with him? Why couldn't he have just reported on sports or education? Why did he have to be such a "wise guy"?[12]

Once they reached the restaurant, Chambers asked Solow if he and Tresca were "using a rifle or a shotgun." Solow understood this question (or invented it for dramatic purposes) as referring to Chambers's concern that Tresca might name him to the grand jury—that is, accuse him of being involved in Poyntz's disappearance, or able to "cast light on it," or able to give the jury "every important Communist name." In return, Solow asked if Chambers had been involved in Poyntz's liquidation. Chambers denied any involvement and brushed aside Tresca's theories about what had happened to her and the Robinson-Rubens—though years later he repeated Tresca's exact story. Solow noted that Chambers had not contested his use of the word *liquidated,* which indicated that Poyntz's fate had been sealed. The Soviets might have intended to use her death as a warning to others: if they betrayed the Soviets, their end would be the same. This could explain Chambers's fear about being named before the grand jury. At the restaurant, Solow continued to press Chambers about Poyntz, asking if he knew anything about her disappearance. Chambers continued to deny any knowledge of it. Solow then told him that he and Tresca were planning to "use a rifle": to name everyone whom they believed had been associated with her disappearance, except for Chambers. He assured Chambers that his name had never occurred to either of them; in fact, he was not sure Tresca even knew Chambers. But Solow now recognized that Chambers had been shaken by Poyntz's disappearance, and he took the opportunity to encourage him to break ties with the CPUSA. Chambers was noncommittal. They parted amicably, with the intention of meeting again in the future.[13]

Months later, Solow wanted to confirm some of the information he had since gathered about Poyntz and the Robinson-Rubens, but he did not know how to get in touch with Chambers. In articles he was publishing in *the New Leader* (originally under the name Junius), he tried to get Chambers's attention by including anagrams of his friend's name: W. C. Hambers, Walter Hambers. The hint did not work, and Solow was forced to wait for Chambers to seek him out.[14] By the time he did, late in the spring of 1938, the news was filled with discussions of Ignace Reiss's murder, Poyntz's disappearance, and the Robinson-Rubens's imprisonment. Solow warned Chambers to be careful, counseling him to leave an affidavit with a friend to be used as leverage against the Communist Party. Chambers did agree to write the affidavit. For the moment, however, he refused to go public about the Soviet spy network. Though he told Solow that he had made that decision primarily to protect himself and his family, he was undoubtedly also concerned that his activities could lead to his arrest for espionage.[15]

Despite his fears, Chambers did speak privately with Solow about the people with whom he was involved in the underground, confirming that a number of them were frightened by the purges and beginning to distance themselves from the Soviets. Solow was primarily interested in learning more about Poyntz and the Robinson-Rubens couple. Poyntz's underground career had started shortly after Chambers's, and he told Solow that her disappearance had been a major catalyst in his own defection, though he had had no personal contact with her in the underground.[16] He believed that the OGPU had killed her but did not seem to know this for sure. He did confirm that Poyntz had worked with a woman he knew as Tina—known to others as Lena, Mary Delmar, Ruth Brataslowsky, and Miss West. Solow noted that Chambers seemed frightened by the mention of Tina's name.[17]

Though Chambers did not have much to share about Poyntz at this time, he seemed to know quite a lot about the Robinson-Rubens affair. He wrote a long, detailed account of the situation that became a primary source for Solow's articles on the case. Titled "The Faking of Americans," the document focused mostly on Mr. Rubens, who had been Chambers's colleague in the underground. Though Chambers wanted to publish it, Solow argued against this because there was no way to independently verify anything in it. According to Chambers's account, Rubens was a Latvian who had worked at the Washington. D.C., navy yard. Chambers said he often went to the Stockholm Restaurant in New York with a member of the CPUSA Politburo. Rubens may have had a brother who was also in the OGPU and another serving in the Latvian army. His assignment in the United States was to obtain fake passports, and he frequently used material from the genealogical division of the New York Public Library as biographical information for them.[18]

Chambers wrote that Rubens belonged to the "Praetorian Guard of the Bolshevik Party," which Chambers associated with Latvians or Letts. The two became acquainted in 1932, when Rubens was transferred to the American branch of the Soviet secret service. He had been demoted to the American branch from the more prestigious German branch because of a stupid blunder: he had exposed another underground agent in an incident involving his false-passport work. Rumanians in Germany were required to get their passports stamped at the Rumanian consulate once every six months. To avoid this hassle, Rubens had given the agent two official stamps that he'd obtained. This lazy maneuver immediately came to the attention of the German authorities, and Rubens was exiled to the United States.[19]

Rubens was known to American communists as Richard, to the Soviets as Ewald. His assignment in the United States was to create or collect one hundred "boots" (passports) per month. Rubens became an American citizen by using the naturalization papers of Christian Rudewitz. Chambers explained that this gambit had now become part of the passport racket: the naturalization papers of individuals who had claimed children were used to gain citizenship for people posing as those children. Of course, this only worked if the actual children were dead. Therefore, Rudewitz himself must have been involved in helping Rubens get his citizenship, presumably after his own son had died. Rubens later legally changed his name from Rudewitz to Rubens. Despite Rudewitz's denials that Rubens was his son, authorities later discovered that he had cashed a money order from Ruth Rubens.[20]

Rubens led a careless and lavish lifestyle; Chambers claimed that, like "most Soviet job-holders," he was fond of "good living." He and Ruth stayed in an expensive onboard suite when they sailed to Russia. On a visit to England, he leased a summer home near Kew Gardens and an "apartment at London Terrace." He was a member of an American yacht club and owned or leased a launch. According to Chambers, the Soviets had a special interest in "motor-boating," so Rubens's was not extraordinary. As evidence, Chambers pointed to General Alexander Kutepov's abduction in Paris in 1930 and Poyntz's in New York City, both of which may have involved boats. (In 1930, to suppress documents that allegedly challenged his leadership, Stalin had ordered the OGPU to kidnap Kutepov, a former czarist living in exile in France. Kutepov was brought back to the USSR, put on trial, and forced to "confess" to fabricating the documents.) Yet Chambers's information was not wholly reliable. For instance, while both Tresca and Solow continued to posit that Poyntz had been carried off to the Soviet Union, not killed on American soil, Chambers eventually abandoned that theory in *Witness*, suggesting that his assumption that Poyntz was dead was what Ellen Schrecker refers to as yet another "obviously fictionalized" Cold War account of her disappearance.[21] Clearly, the news stories that were circulating about the Poyntz and Robinson-Rubens cases had as much influence on Chambers as his own experience in the underground did. He revealed nothing new about Poyntz, and even some of his information about Rubens (such as his involvement with the passport ring and the participation of Christian Rudewitz) was already publicly available.[22]

Chambers did not particularly like either Rubens or his wife, and he assumed that Rubens behaved badly to Ruth during the affair. After the two married in May 1935, she became involved in her husband's work. Chambers was unkind in his descriptions of her, regularly referring to her as a "plump young woman," "Unmistakably American," who "apparently had a high school education." His physical description was a far cry from the evidence of her passport photo as well as from the newspapers accounts of a beautiful young woman of the "Duchess of Windsor type." He did soften his rhetoric when describing her as a victim of the Soviets and her husband. Chambers wrote that the American embassy had heard about a "frightened American girl" at the Hotel National in Moscow whose husband had gone missing. Ruth was twenty-nine years old in December 1937, when she and her husband were arrested and detained—most certainly not a "girl"—yet both Solow and Chambers depicted her as such. Their language erased her culpability; she was instead portrayed as merely following her husband's directions.[23] Chambers alleged that Rubens, known for his mistakes, made a truly terrible one when he came to the USSR: against orders he had brought his wife. Chambers believed this was an attempt to protect himself, and it backfired. It also ruined the Soviets' plans to have her "just disappear" and "dragged ten years of espionage" into the open by revealing the passport racket.[24]

But it was not Rubens's laziness that led to his arrest nor his carelessness in the service. Chambers claimed that the "immediate cause" was his personal relationship with the executed General Viovt Putna. This, for Chambers, was the real connection between the Robinson-Rubens and Poyntz. All three had had personal relationships with Putna; and when he was liquidated, his associates were endangered. No one outside of the underground would have seen this connection, and Chambers did not offer any proof.[25] What is known is that Putna, a Latvian like Rubens, was the Soviet military attaché in London, and Poyntz spent significant amounts of time overseas. In August 1936, Putna was recalled to Moscow and arrested on charges that he and others were plotting against Stalin. This "plot," according to the historian Robert Thurston may have motivated Stalin to hold his first show trials. Putna had been part of the Trotskyist opposition before Trotsky's exile, and he admitted to being part of "Trotskyst-Zinovievist centers" within the military. A show trial defendant declared that Putna was active in "terrorist work." After his arrest, the general began to name others who were involved in the plot against Stalin, and at least one former NKVD member has claimed that this plot actually existed. Thurston believes that Putna was "probably guilty of treason." He was eventually put on trial, found guilty, sentenced to death, and executed on the same day as his sentence, a week after Poyntz went missing.[26]

Chambers closed his written account with a speculation about another connection between Poyntz and the Robinson-Rubens, one that both Tresca and Solow believed in: that the three were involved in an arrangement between the German and the Soviet military intelligence services.

After the Robinson-Rubens case and Poyntz's disappearance were revealed in the press, Gunther Rumrich, a Nazi spy, helped American authorities uncover a Nazi spy ring in the United States. This was the case that the disgraced FBI agent Turrou worked on. Solow speculated that the Soviets had manufactured this situation to draw attention away from the Robinson-Rubens arrests and Poyntz's liquidation. The link between the two underground apparatuses, Chambers believed, ran through the German consulate in New York and was organized by Poyntz's estranged husband. What did Poyntz know about potential links between the Soviet Union and Germany that made her elimination necessary? This supposition closely resembled Tresca's and Solow's previous hypotheses. Because he had already admitted to not knowing Poyntz in the underground and could offer nothing to support this claim, Chambers was most likely repeating assumptions that were already circulating. But Chambers did believe her liquidation was the "first step to the developments of the Purge."[27]

In 1938, Chambers placed Poyntz's suspected murder at the center of his own fears about communism, an assertion he would repeat later. But the statements he made in his early years out of the underground were often contradicted by those he made later during the Cold War. For instance, in 1938, he claimed that the purges showed "how far Communism had died out among Communists," writing that many who returned to the Soviet Union simply hoped that this would allow them to enjoy a "unique and exalted position above the law," in "comfort and affluence," as recompense for the sacrifices they had made in the underground. In other words, communism still meant something to him; he recognized that affluence and status were not in line with communist theory. In these early years, Chambers was still evolving his belief that communism was violent. Fourteen years later, when *Witness* was published, he was sure that it was violent—or at least he was committed to convincing the American public that it was.[28]

Solow later determined that Rubens's real name was Fritz Braun. A member of Rudewitz's family had identified him, claiming that he was a Latvian working for the Russian government. The Braun family had been close to the Rudewitz family in Russia. Solow also followed up on Ruth, who spent eighteen months in prison. Upon her release she pleaded guilty to entering the USSR with fabricated documents, but her sentence was considered time served. Ruth reportedly saw her husband twice after their imprisonment, the last time a year before her release. She told her mother and stepfather (who were in contact with Solow) that she believed he was dead and said that he had been a "fascist spy." She did not indicate that she had any intention of returning to the United States. In November 1939, Ruth Rubens renounced her American citizenship, allegedly to avoid a charge of passport fraud in the United States, which carried the threat of a two-year prison sentence. She officially became a Soviet citizen and settled in Ukraine, a sign that she would not be returning for her then nine-year-old daughter because Soviet citizens were not allowed to travel outside the country without clearance. At a court appearance, Ruth had asked for information about her husband, and the court refused to offer any. His fate remains unknown. Solow and Chambers were convinced that he was certainly purged.[29]

When Chambers approached Solow at the time of his defection, he had hoped to use Solow to get him into contact with U.S. government officials who would allow him to talk directly to President Franklin Roosevelt. He wanted to share his information about the Soviet underground with the FBI, but only through someone in government who could guarantee his immunity from espionage charges. Instead, he spent most of 1938 in hiding. Chambers did save documents he had collected during his time in the underground as a way to create some leverage with the Communist Party. He threatened to release them to "American authorities" if "he or his family were harmed."[30] But he did not "publicly renounce" the party, deciding it was best to stay quiet for the moment and avoid implicating himself.[31]

Chambers changed his mind after the signing of the Nazi-Soviet pact in 1939. Now he was convinced that war was on the horizon and that the Soviet Union would be a Nazi ally. That alliance would put "Soviet supporters in conflict with American national policy." His friend and confidant, the journalist Isaac Don Levine, managed to arrange a meeting between Chambers and Assistant Secretary of State Adolf Berle on September 2, 1939. Chambers gave Berle a list of individuals who were working in the federal government as espionage agents. As he left the meeting, Berle was already on the phone. Chambers believed he must have been calling the White House, given the excitement in his voice.[32]

The historians Harvey Klehr and John Earl Haynes describe Chambers's defection and his eventual confession to the authorities as a "missed opportunity" for American internal security apparatuses. As it turned out, Chambers was wrong about who Berle was calling; it took years before his meeting notes would see the light of day, even though he had labeled them "Underground Espionage Agent," indicating he must have known how serious the matter was. Chambers had given Berle "a large part" of the "CPUSA-GRU network" that was operating in Washington, D.C. If he had shared that information with intelligence services, they might have used it to shut down spy networks operating in the United States. But the FBI only learned of Berle's interview with Chambers in 1943, and only then obtained his notes. Even at this point the bureau did little with the information before Elizabeth Bentley came forward in 1945. Not until 1948, when Chambers was subpoenaed to testify, did his information become public. It launched him on his public career as an anti-communist, a full ten years after his defection.[33]

One of the individuals whom Chambers accused was Alger Hiss, a "prominent member of the Washington Foreign Policy establishment." Between 1948, when Chambers first testified against Hiss, and 1950, when Hiss was found guilty of perjury, the accusation made headlines and gained Chambers "lurid and stunning" notoriety. The trial captivated the nation and "divided Harry S. Truman and J. Edgar Hoover." In 1950, Chambers began writing what would eventually become *Witness.* Along with the Hiss case, the book solidified his reputation as a vehement anti-communist and right-wing hero.[34]

In the book, Chambers said that he decided to make his break with the CPUSA because he had realized that communism was evil. There was no doubt that Stalin was a bad character, he wrote, but "his personal perversion" was not the "point." Communism merely acted through Stalin, who was its "logical manifestation." He carried communism to its "inevitable development" as the "greatest of fascist forms." Chambers claimed that he came to this realization when he broke with the CPUSA in 1938, an assertion that his affidavit that year contradicts. In truth, his realization reflected the atmosphere of the 1950s, when politicians and conservatives were trying to sway American opinions about communism.[35] As the historian Matthew Dunne writes, arguments against communism during the Cold War were based on "vague assertions" and "vague rhetoric." The ideology was treated as both "diffuse" and "omnipresent." Your neighbor or your children's teachers could be communists. Not knowing was partly what made communism threatening because it meant that everyone was susceptible to brainwashing. When Chambers wrote that he fell prey despite his iron will and his critical mind, he was warning the American public that the manipulations of communism endangered the entire country.[36]

In *Witness,* Chambers repeated his earlier assertion that Poyntz's disappearance had motivated him to make his final break with the Communist Party. He wrote that he began contemplating his defection in 1937, the "year of the long knives." In that year, he said, more and more people were deserting from the party, and the OGPU was cutting down "more fugitives in their flight" than it ever had before. Chambers believed that agents would attempt to kill him—which he described as the "wet" method, in the jargon of the underground. Still, there was always the possibility they would use the "dry" method—kidnap him and bring him to the Soviet Union. He believed that the OGPU had used the "wet" method on Poyntz, and this filled him with fear for himself and his family.[37]

Chambers wrote that he was aware of others who had made the move to leave the underground; but like Poyntz, they were rarely successful. He said that many of those who were killed or kidnapped had made a big mistake before their defection: namely, they had told someone in the underground about their plans to leave. Chambers emphasized that no one in the underground could be trusted. Thus, defection meant "utter loneliness" for the defector, and some were drawn back into the underground because of that isolation. He believed that this was how Poyntz and Reiss had been trapped.[38]

Chambers claimed in *Witness* that Reiss's murder had "moved" him "deeply. Reiss had bravely and publicly broken with Stalin to denounce the purges, but Chambers argued that "defiance [was] not enough." One needed cunning to "fight cunning," and Reiss was not smart enough to stay alive. He wrote that Poyntz's "murder [also] touched me closely," though he did not know that her "underground apparatus" even existed until after her disappearance, which makes his 1938 claims difficult to believe. In *Witness,* however, he continued to emphasize the impact her liquidation had had on him. If an American citizen in the United States could be so easily dispatched, how could he and his family be safe? Chambers decided it was time to leave. He wrote that he was convinced that Poyntz had managed to desert in 1937, a signal that she had made a break with communism. This is an important point to stress because Chambers was using his book as a way to redeem himself: to own up to his mistakes and plead for forgiveness. Even if it was not clear that Poyntz did defect, she was no longer around to contest his claim.[39]

Chambers wrote that she had been living in a New York hotel, which she left one evening, "with the light burning and a page of unfinished handwriting on the table." She meant to come back but "was never seen again." It was known, he said, that she was going to meet a "Communist friend" in Central Park, which was not far from her "hotel." But this friend had "decoyed" her there as "part of a G.P.U. trap." It is not clear how Chambers, all these years later, was able acquire this so-called information—material that he had apparently not possessed when he was first talking to Solow. Yet in *Witness,* he claimed that, once Poyntz was in the park, she was "pushed into an automobile"; then "two men drove her off" and "coldly murdered" her.[40]

In his memoir, Chambers noted an important difference between Poyntz and himself: unlike her, he had never been a Trotskyite and had never challenged the party line, so he was "affected but not endangered" by the earlier conflicts in the party over Trotsky. In some places he suggests that the risks of being a defector were enhanced by any link, past or present, to Trotsky. Chambers wrote that he had studied the mistakes of defectors such as Reiss and had learned how to be more cunning than the communists were.[41]

In his account of her alleged abduction, Chambers's descriptions of Poyntz gender her as a victim but also buttress his own redemption narrative. He wrote that he felt "sickened" in a "physical way" at the thought of this "intensely feminine woman" being murdered by Soviet men. He described her as "heavy-set" and "dark" yet also "softly feminine." Echoing the newspaper descriptions of Ruth Rubens's girlishness, his language suggested that Poyntz, as a fragile female, could not be blamed for the actions that led to her death.[42] He also reminded his readers that women often could not handle the responsibilities thrust upon them. Like many "Communist bureaucrats," Poyntz had become "absurdly imperious" and "mysterious." But this authority was too heavy, and she began to sag "self-consciously under the weight of so much secret authority and knowledge." Chambers did not have to directly say that women could not handle positions of authority; his 1950s reading audience would have understood his inference. He told his readers that Poyntz's fate haunted him, that he "could always see her in [his] mind's eye." In other words, communism was particularly evil because it easily trapped the most vulnerable.[43]

In *Witness,* Chambers recalled speaking to Boris Bykov, his Soviet handler, about Poyntz when they discussed the liquidation of the Bolshevik Leo Kamenev during the show trials. Bykov usually discussed Stalin's victims with "malicious splutter," but he had admired Kamenev and mentioned him with regret. Chambers took the opportunity to ask, "Where is Juliet Poyntz?" Bykov claimed that the OGPU had undoubtedly "murdered the defenseless woman"; "gayly," he told Chambers that she was "gone with the wind." Chambers's description of Bykov's flippancy emphasized both Soviet callousness and Poyntz's vulnerability.[44] His approach makes it easy to forget that Poyntz worked in the underground for many years as a communist spy—that she was exactly the kind of person he was otherwise relentlessly exposing. But if she could be forgiven—and who wouldn't forgive a defenseless woman who needed the protection of home and domesticity?—then so could he.[45]

In *Witness,* Chambers was displaying a battle between good and evil, one that he also framed as a religious battle. The historian Jonathan Herzog has credited him with influencing and perpetuating the belief that communism was more than economic theory; it was also a "religious system." This is why, for some Americans, fighting the Cold War "took on the sense of religious urgency." Herzog calls *Witness* one of the "strangest" and "most celebrated" of conversion narratives, "a story about faith" in which Chambers, "after stumbling in the darkness for years, . . . finally saw the light." Like other former communists, he belonged to the "broad category of Cold War converts" who were outspoken about their religious renewal and conversion. But he went further, claiming that religious people "could not be Communists" and "irreligious" people could not be Americans. He totally repudiated his communist past.[46] This was why he saw Poyntz's story as so unfortunate: allegedly in the midst of her own awakening, she became a casualty in a religious war.

Sidney Hook, a self-proclaimed Democratic socialist and anti-communist, believed that *Witness* was one of the "most significant autobiographies" of the twentieth century. In a *New York Times* book review, he urged readers to approach it without "partisanship"—as the review did not. Hook's article ignored his own investment in anti-communism. In his opinion, no "reasonable person" could deny the book's truth, which he said Chambers made clear in "overwhelming detail." Hook wrote that Chambers had "long since" atoned for his sins in the "conspiratorial apparatus," enduring harassment from Hiss supporters and arguments that anti-anti-communism was blind to "political realities" and overly emotional. His primary issue with the book related to Chambers's tendency to interpret his own experience instead of just presenting the "facts."[47]

Chambers's testimony and his book helped craft public perceptions about communists and communism, and the Communist Party was not very amused. By the time *Witness* was published in 1952, its leadership had been embroiled in numerous legal cases. Between 1949 and 1958 several of them had been charged under the 1940 Smith Act, which made it illegal to support or belong to an organization that advocated the violent overthrow of the U.S. government. According to Schrecker, the trials that arose from the Smith Act were essential to the anti-communist crusades because they linked communism to criminality, dehumanized individual communists, and "turned them into crooks." By the end of the 1940s, nearly anything a communist did "could be the pretext for a criminal prosecution."[48] The party responded by labeling Chambers and other ex-communist witnesses as stool pigeons, FBI lackies, and opportunists. In a review of *Witness* in the *Daily Worker,* Robert Friedman called the book an 808-page alibi with two purposes: to demonstrate Chambers's greed and his hatred of the working class and to paint himself as a devout, repentant Christian rather than a "police-informer." Friedman emphasized that Chambers was making a career out of informing and that one of his goals was to link the New Deal to the Soviet Union. He articulated a fear that did indeed come to pass as a result of the anti-communist hearings and trials: that Americans would not engage in "democratic struggles for their rights" for fear that they would be called "liberal[s]" or "progressive[s]" and be accused of communism. Friedman also explicitly linked anti-communism to racism, noting that Chambers described John Rankin, a congressman from Mississippi who was a notorious racist and anti-Semite, as a "friendly and gracious man" and characterized future president Richard Nixon, who talked of "colored maids" and congratulated himself for eating dinner with a Black woman, as a "long-suffering patriot."[49]

In July 1952, the *Daily Worker* published a letter that the Christian pacifist and labor activist Grace Hutchins had written to Random House, the publisher of *Witness*, challenging Chambers's written claims that she had threatened his life. Hutchins called this claim totally false and in total contradiction to her "philosophy of life." The CPUSA, which relished pointing out inconsistencies in anti-communist witness testimony and publications, argued that Hutchins's claim was particularly troubling. Though she had been linked to the Socialist and Communist parties for decades, she had a long history of working in Christian institutions, and her letter took strong issue with Chambers's claims to piety.[50]

Legacies

By 1945, while Chambers was acting as a professional witness, Solow had accepted a job with *Fortune* magazine. For some, this signaled his complete abandonment of socialist values. Though he continued to take unpopular positions, his career and his controversies became "less exciting," hampered by "considerable conservatism" at the Luce Corporation, which owned the magazine. According to Wald, Solow had by this time lost sympathy for Trotskyism, but he was concerned that America's "security structures" were becoming more rigid in protecting themselves from Soviet sympathizers. Although Solow supported Dwight D. Eisenhower's 1952 candidacy for president and regularly spoke with FBI agents who were seeking information on radicals, he was "at times skeptical of the[ir] motives and level of sophistication."[51]

In 1961, Chambers died of a heart attack at the age of sixty. Solow died on Thanksgiving Day in 1964 at the age of sixty-one. Both left a mixed legacy whose value depended on where one stood on the issue of the Cold War trials. After the Vietnam War cast doubt on America's Cold War containment policy, Hiss found some support for his claim that

Chambers had falsely accused him. While some historians have concluded that Hiss was in fact guilty, that has not quieted the controversy. In the end, Chambers's reputation will forever be mired in the controversy and doubts that emerged from the Hiss case.[52]

Solow's legacy is equally complex. Though he and many of his colleagues were anti-Stalinist in the 1930s, this common lineage did not mean that, as anti-communists. they all shared the same ideas during the Cold War. Wald argues that Solow in particular suffered so many personal and political blows as an anti-Stalinist that the parts of his personality "that drove him to the left . . . rapidly and militantly" might have also "accentuated his conservative drift to the right." In other words, his investigations into the Poyntz and the Robinson-Rubens cases and the loss of Tresca and Trotsky may have made his personal brand of anti-communism especially severe and unforgiving.[53]

CHAPTER SIX

THE INFORMERS

In 1962, a law professor named Herbert Packer published *Ex-Communist Witnesses,* his analysis of the public testimony that had "obsessed" the American public since the end of World War II. His primary goal was to examine how the congressional and judicial institutions "at our disposal" were "eliciting and testing the information about Communist penetration in the United States." Packer was interested in the role that former communists were playing in "legislative investigation, court trial[s]," and administrative proceedings.[1] His concern was that "literally scores of ex-Communist witnesses" had testified before "official tribunals," yet their stories were piecemeal. One witness might begin a story; another might finish it or even contradict it. Sometimes witnesses simply repeated what others had said. Sometimes they told entirely new stories, adding a "new chapter to the history of Communist penetration." But with each new witness there arose "contradictions, inconsistencies, and gaps."[2]

In his book, Packer chose to analyze only four witnesses, but they were of central importance to these government-sponsored "fact-finding missions." He chose Whittaker Chambers and Elizabeth Bentley because their stories of "espionage carried on by clandestine Communists" had "captured the public imagination to a greater degree than any other aspect of the Communist problem." He also chose John Lautner, less well known but a far more prolific testifier, who had spoken publicly between 1932 and 1950 and had acted as the chief witness "in every Smith Act case" since leaving the CPUSA. The final witness under study was Louis Budenz, a former editor of the *Daily Worker,* who was a "leading interpreter" of communism during his testimonies and a "prolific source of accusations" against prominent individual communists.[3] For Packer, these four witnesses proved that the CPUSA was devoted to the "principles of Marxism-Leninism" and the ideal of worldwide revolution under the direction of "the Party apparatus in the Soviet Union." What was less clear from their testimonies was whether every individual the witnesses accused had in fact engaged in espionage against the United States or even was a communist at all. While the witnesses seemed to prove their own involvement in the party, their accusations against others were doubtful. Nonetheless, they were a major influence on public opinion during the Cold War.[4]

Witness accusations certainly captured the American imagination during these years, but contradictions among testimonies and general public fatigue led a number of observers to question the witnesses' veracity. Many Americans had been critical of these ex-communists from the beginning. Still, what they shared during public tribunals was instrumental in creating and reifying American anti-communism. An anti-communist cottage industry emerged from the testimonies as witnesses wrote books and articles and gave lectures about their time in the party or the underground. Poyntz's disappearance was a common denominator in the testimonies and books of the big three—Chambers, Bentley, and Budenz. These former leftists had not only walked away from the party but had done so loudly and with much fanfare. All used Poyntz's suspected murder as a way to demonstrate communism's inherent violence and brutality.

In their testimony and publications, the witnesses described how American communists, including themselves, had become inured to such brutality; and the Poyntz case was a primary example. In 1946, Budenz spoke specifically before HUAC about her disappearance, also writing about the case in his 1947 *This Is My Story*. In 1948, Benjamin Gitlow, once a high-ranking communist leader, published *The Whole of Their Lives* in which he provided astonishing details about Poyntz's murder. In 1949, the ex-communist Paul Crouch wrote a series of articles for the *Miami Daily News* about communist terror and Poyntz's murder. He was later revealed as an enthusiastic perjurer, but not before he helped to inflame anti-communism. All of these accounts alleged that Poyntz was murdered while trying to defect. They seemed to confirm Tresca's initial claims—that a foreign communist power in league with American communists had murdered an American citizen—but their testimony was suspect because it simply mirrored his assumptions. None of the men offered any evidence to prove their allegations, but they did make Poyntz's supposed murder a central part of the anti-communist creed.

Louis Budenz

Budenz structured *This Is My Story* as part autobiography, part religious conversion narrative. As Chambers also did in *Witness*, he described his early religious upbringing, which he rejected when he became a communist, and to which he recommitted when he repudiated the party. At the time of writing, he was, according to his narrative, a fifty-year-old anti-communist Catholic who sought forgiveness.

Budenz was born in Indianapolis in 1891 and grew up less than a mile from his family church. He was raised in a "genuinely Catholic" household and attended Catholic school.[5] As a young man, Budenz was attracted to organized labor, an interest he framed as religiously motivated. He wrote that Catholics in the early twentieth century spoke of the "righteousness" of labor organizing, a stance influenced by the "encyclicals of the thirteenth Leo." Budenz said that he learned about anti-racism from the church and from his devout father, who was friendly with a "mulatto porter" at the bank where he worked. The "sin of segregation," in Budenz's early recollection, was "repulsive to a Catholic" such as his father. Though the book universalized his father's views as those of all of Catholics and claimed that friendship with a person of color was evidence of anti-racism, it also suggested that Budenz's early religious faith was in line with his later radical devotions. This is an interesting claim, considering that the Catholic church was very active in American anti-communism.[6] According to Budenz, he was initially repulsed by socialism because it rejected any "higher moral authority" than the state and thus rejected God. His claim to strict religiosity as a young man makes his radical politics and eventual membership in the CPUSA puzzling. It seems likely that the memoir highlighted his religious devotion to emphasize, for his contemporary readers, the heathen godlessness of communism.

In 1924, Budenz became the editor of *Labor Age*, a radical socialist magazine, and worked there until 1933. The magazine staff eventually joined with the Brookwood Labor College to create the organization Progressive Labor Action (PLA), and Budenz became the secretary. The PLA, which focused on organizing the unemployed, worked with the Communist Party; but in 1934, it merged with a group of Trotskyites. Budenz disapproved of this move. He wrote that he had not wanted to merge with the

Trotskyites because they "advocated the [violent] overthrow" of the U.S. government. He instead believed that socialism could happen peacefully in the United States through a "constitutional amendment." Nonetheless, in 1935, after some thought, he chose to join the CPUSA.[7] This is a surprising admission, considering that the goal of the professional witnesses was to help prove that communists were trying to violently overthrow the U.S. government. Budenz flatly contradicts this in his book.

Like so many others on the left in the 1930s, Budenz was concerned about the rise of Italian and German fascism. The Comintern and its affiliates such as the CPUSA were aggressive in their condemnation of fascism; and when the 1935 Seventh World Congress of the Comintern adapted the Popular Front policy to organize against fascism, Budenz was interested. In his view, it offered a new outlook on America and religion. He saw in anti-fascism a rejection of "antireligious persecution," a fight for freedom that included "freedom of worship." But in later testimony, he said that he learned about the party's "true conspiratorial nature" immediately. He began as a secret member of the "Party of Stalin" and in October 1935 became an "open member" assigned to the staff of the *Daily Worker*. He became managing editor of the paper in 1941.[8]

At the *Daily Worker*, Budenz came into contact with Jacob Golos, the chair of the Soviet party's Control Commission, which was tasked with ensuring that American communists followed the Stalinist line. Through Golos, Budenz met agents who were trying to locate Trotskyites who might be involved in a plot against Stalin. Budenz introduced them to Stalinists who were working to penetrate Trotskyite circles. More importantly, he put Golos in touch with a woman whose name he did not know, and she was eventually involved in Trotsky's assassination. On the whole, however, Budenz seemed to use his role at the paper to evade some of the demands of the underground apparatus, and thus his involvement was tangential.[9]

Budenz began preparing to leave the party in the summer of 1945. He later claimed that he had been disillusioned by the Soviet "enslavement of people," the regime's hostility to religion, and his belief that American communists were "subservient to the Soviet dictatorship." He also wanted to rejoin the Catholic church but felt that he could not reconcile that move with his work in the CPUSA. In the fall, he secured a teaching position at the University of Notre Dame. Then, on October 10, 1945, he knelt before Monsignor Fulton Sheen, a prominent anti-communist priest, at New York City's Saint Patrick's Cathedral and petitioned to rejoin the church. His conversion and his new job marked the end of his CPUSA career, but the party only learned about his defection in the newspaper.[10]

For a year, Budenz chose to remain silent, though he did share some information with the FBI. His main focus was on his new teaching job and his newfound commitment to his faith. But in October 1946, he began his second career, serving as an anti-communist witness in congressional hearings and court proceedings and writing articles and books about his time in the party. He taught courses at prestigious universities such as Fordham and Seton Hall, and he went on the lecture circuit. His anti-communist career was lucrative; in 1953, he claimed that he had earned $70,000 from his activities. The historian Robert Lichtman describes him as the "prototypical excommunist political informer," one who "set the standard" for other informers. Budenz was "ubiquitous" during the McCarthy period, testifying more than thirty times before committees. He gave the FBI the names of hundreds of individuals whom he claimed were "secret" party members, without substantial evidence. The bureau had doubts about his reliability: according to an internal FBI memo, he lied at least seven times before one congressional committee.[11]

On April 3, 1946, Budenz appeared before a HUAC executive session and testified that, in his role as *Daily Worker* editor, he had often asked questions about well-publicized individuals who had gone missing. When he asked certain unnamed sources about Ignace Reiss, he was told that *Daily Worker* staff should keep their mouths shut. The inference was that Soviet agents had killed him. Budenz later inquired about Poyntz's disappearance, claiming he wanted to "hammer [it] home" in his paper. Again he was told to stay silent. Though the party was always willing to denounce an individual as a "liar and thief," it was not willing to discuss disappearances in the press.[12]

Budenz said that the threat of "physical intimidation" or death was always hovering over those who challenged the party from within. People in the "conspiratorial apparatus," such as Reiss and Poyntz, were most at risk. He found it remarkable that Poyntz, an American citizen, had "just walked out of the picture" and vanished. Though he did not go into depth about what he claimed to know as someone in a level of authority, he did emphasize that it was no secret that the party was engaging in such tactics, though nothing was said outright.[13]

As editor, Budenz had to be careful about printing pictures in the *Daily Worker* in case someone shown had been "shot or purged." At one point, he had been about to print a photo of a Soviet general named "Yessof." He showed the picture to William Patterson, a CPUSA leader, who told him he could not print the image. Patterson said that Yessof's whereabouts were unknown: some thought he was in Siberia; others claimed he had gone to Leningrad and then "just walked off the face of the earth." Budenz testified that he had not directly been told by party leadership that Reiss, Poyntz, and Yessof had been liquidated. However, he was sure they had been, given the party's discomfort in discussing them and its refusal to allow mention of them in the party press.[14]

Before HUAC, Budenz testified that the Soviets were directly responsible for the murder of an American citizen, but his claim did not make many waves because the hearings were closed to the public. Later, however, he did tell the press that every member of the CPUSA was a potential Soviet spy and that the American party was a "direct arm of the Soviet Foreign Department" and served a "foreign power." This was a common assertion among anti-communists, who regularly implicated even rank-and-file party members who were working in campaigns against racism, sexism, and economic inequity. It was simpler to dismiss all members as spies and to generalize a link between communism and social justice movements. Budenz claimed that it was communist policy to foment "continuous hostility to the United States" and seek "injury" to the nation. He told the press that the Soviets sought world domination and used "fifth columns" such as the CPUSA to meet that end. Budenz compared Soviet policy to Hitler's. If he was trying to scare war-weary Americans, framing communism as akin to Hitlerism and social change as akin to communism was certainly a way to do it.[15]

Budenz's stories and accusations were not front-page news in 1946; the *New York Times* buried the story about his testimony on page 19. But he continued to speak out. The following year he published *This Is My Story*, dedicated to "Mary Immaculate, Patroness of Our Beloved Land," in which he recounted his years in the CPUSA and reiterated much of his HUAC testimony. By now, relations between the Soviet Union and the United States had begun to sour, and more and more ex-communists were coming forward with tales of Soviet terror. In his memoir, Budenz continued to stress the parallels between Hitlerism and communism, describing membership in the CPUSA as a "mental concentration camp." He suggested that his position as editor of the *Daily Worker* allowed him to see the party's "links to Moscow" and the operations of secret agents in the United States. According to Budenz, the CPUSA was responsible for holding the Soviet line, which meant no internal criticism of the USSR. The Soviets, he said, kept personal records of every CPUSA member and required each to submit a detailed biography listing family members, employment and salary history, arrests, membership in political organizations, and other information. If members took up a new positions in the party, they were required to update their biographies. The records were managed by a control commission in the United States, staffed largely by Soviets with contacts with Moscow agents. No one was allowed to know who was on the commission; members of CPUSA's National Committee voted for them using anonymous ballots that did not reveal candidates' names, only their qualifications. The party used these records to punish any "recalcitrant members."[16] In Budenz's telling, foreigners controlled the fate of those in the American party, including Poyntz, and they were capable of liquidating people on American soil.[17]

Budenz's book described the Soviet underground as especially secretive. In order to protect its spy network, agents operating within it often did not know who else was involved. Budenz wrote about an incident that took place in 1937, when the Poyntz and Robinson-Rubens cases were news. At that time he was living in Chicago and working at the party's *Midwest Daily Record,* which ran a front-page story on Soviet reactions to the Robinson-Rubens case. The article did not seem inflammatory, so Budenz was surprised when leading party members took issue with it. Later, after he returned to New York, he asked "Comrade H," a leader on the CPUSA's Political Committee, why they were angry about the story. Comrade H replied that such publicity "might lead too closely to the Poyntz case," a subject that the party did not want to discuss in its newspapers.[18] When Budenz asked what the Robinson-Rubens case had to do with Poyntz's, Comrade H called Poyntz's case "hot cargo" that could cause serious problems in the underground. He then tried to distract Budenz by making a meaningless joke and changing the subject, but Budenz came to believe that Poyntz had been "liquidated" by the Soviet secret police. His book suggests that, while the party clearly did not want to implicate itself in the American press, members were told indirectly about her murder as a form of intimidation.[19]

Budenz, like other ex-communists, parroted preexisting rumors that the Soviets and the CPUSA were responsible for Poyntz's murder. Yet even as he admitted that she was a prominent CPUSA member who had worked in the underground, he presented her as an innocent bystander within the communist apparatus, an interesting reversal for a man who had made a career out of naming names. His book described her sympathetically as an "American Schoolteacher" who walked into "Nowhere" from the "streets of New York." Certainly, Poyntz had taught, and she had also been a pioneer in labor education, but her time in these fields was brief. Budenz's gendered "schoolteacher" language reified her as a victim, erasing any power or agency she may have had as a communist. He distanced her from communism by emphasizing that she had "begun to differ" with the underground and therefore was on the righteous side in the conflict against communism.[20] This schoolteacher could not be implicated in the Soviets' crimes because she had been injured by their crimes.

The memoir's accusation that the CPUSA had been instrumental in the assassination of Trotsky captured press attention. But those who had been following Poyntz's case were also interested in what Budenz was saying. Herbert Solow, always alert for any mention of Poyntz, noted in the *New Leader* that the book had confirmed many of his and Tresca's accusations, including their argument that Mr. Rubens had been a Soviet agent. Apparently he did not reflect on the fact that Budenz's claims almost exactly matched theirs while also offering no evidence. Though Budenz became the first former communist to publicly offer an answer to the Poyntz mystery, one wonders how much Solow's and Tresca's public writings and testimony had influenced his accusations.[21]

Members of the Tresca Memorial Committee, headed by Norman Thomas, believed that Budenz's book had exonerated Tresca, confirming that he had been right to implicate the Soviets and the CPUSA in Poyntz's disappearance and murder. In their view, Budenz had proven that Soviet "terrorist operations" were extending beyond the USSR's borders into

Europe and the United States. The "threat of political murder" was real, committee members declared, and it was targeting the "working-class opponents of the Stalinist regime." Their wording is interesting, given that some of the signers, among them Thomas and the committee's original convener, John Dewey, were still vocal socialists. Rather than invoke anti-communism, they focused on Stalin as the problem. Clearly, the anti-Stalinism of the 1930s had survived into the 1940s and remained an important part of the nation's growing anti-communist political culture.[22]

The committee formally asked the New York district attorney, Frank Hogan, to open a grand jury investigation into Poyntz's disappearance and Tresca's assassination, in light of this new "evidence." They wanted the office to look into NKVD activities and those of "certain American Communist Party leaders" who might have been complicit in their liquidation. Committee members also wanted to subject Budenz to "official examination" and to any "judicial action" that might be warranted. Although their letter had asked for a meeting with Hogan, members instead spoke with Jacob Grument, an assistant district attorney in the homicide bureau. They pushed him to interview Budenz and other "prominent individuals" who were or had been associated with the CPUSA. Grument decided that his office would "consider a request" to investigate whether or not the NKVD had had a role in the "unsolved slaying of Carlo Tresca" and the disappearance of Poyntz.[23]

A grand jury was convened in June 1947. Budenz took the stand for more than an hour, during which time he claimed he would "amplify . . . statements made" in his book. But when asked if he had any information about Tresca's death, he replied, "That is a case I know the least about." Frustrated, Norman Thomas asked the mayor of New York City to urge the FBI to investigate Tresca's and Poyntz's murders. There is no indication that he did. To the dismay of everyone on the committee, the answers they wanted were never revealed.[24]

Communist Party newspapers printed several articles attacking Budenz's book. In the *Worker*, the reviewer Samuel Sillen placed the memoir within a larger tradition of "unscrupulous appeal[s] to ignorance and bigotry." He saw Budenz's recommitment to Catholicism not as a religious conversion but as a conversion from workers' advocate to workers' enemy. Sillen challenged several of the book's claims, denying that the CPUSA had a religious test and that Budenz had been the party's leading voice for labor. Instead, he wrote, Budenz was merely an "ex" supporter of labor, justice, and communism. He took particular issue with Budenz's claims to religious fidelity, accusing him of simultaneously attacking Baptists and Episcopalians. He also pointed out that Budenz had published attacks on the Catholic church and anti-communism in the *Daily Worker*. In Sillen's view, Budenz was just another "turncoat" against the "progressive and labor movement" on its march toward "socialist freedom."[25]

The Marxist historian James Allen, whom Budenz had attacked in his memoir, wrote a lengthy rebuttal titled "A Puny Soul Seeks Salvation in Fascism." He accused Budenz of "prostituting" his religion in service to anti-communism and argued that the book revealed the fabrications at the heart of the "red scare." Allen poked holes in details that Budenz had included about Allen's travels overseas—for instance, a trip to Mexico that Budenz had dated as 1945, two years before the actual visit. The memoir accused Allen of upholding the Soviet line during an internal party debate, an allegation that the historian decried as hypocrisy. If Budenz was arguing that the entire CPUSA was an "agent of Moscow," then he was undermining his entire thesis by claiming that a single man was responsible. Allen clearly did not have much respect for Budenz, writing that he had turned the editorship of the *Daily Worker* into a figurehead position because of his "ineptitude and poverty of ideas" and his lack of "independent thought" on political issues. Like Sillen, Allen believed that Budenz was allying himself with those who sought to undermine progressive movements and to "arouse hate" against religious and racial minorities, much as Hitler had done.[26]

This Is My Story was published early in the Cold War. Budenz would go on to write other books, but this was the one that focused most on alleged Soviet brutality. Readers responded with anxiety to his and other witnesses' claims about communist terror, yet a certain amount of inductive reasoning was on display in these public allegations and reactions. While Stalin and his ilk were certainly bad, were all American communists really Soviet agents, as Budenz had claimed? First-person witness statements were often taken at face value; they carried a level of authority that few questioned. Yet the FBI doubted that all of Budenz's information was reliable, and Lichtman argues that Budenz's "fail-safe" approach was designed to prevent challenges to his claims. He accused people whose names appeared on organizational letterhead of being "concealed communists," knowing that the label would make his claims almost impossible to prove or disprove. Many people never knew he had named them. Those who did would have had to disprove his allegations, which might have revealed their political sympathies, a liability during the Cold War. Therefore, absence of evidence "tended to prove" his claims to a public willing to believe them.[27]

Some of Budenz's testimony might have been exaggeration or fabrication, but he clung to the notion that his religious faith was the answer to defeating communism. In the year *This Is My Story* was released, he accepted a teaching job at Fordham University. In a public talk there, he "delivered an attack on the Communist fifth column" and told his audience that only the Catholic church could "challenge the slave state" that flourished under Marxist-Leninism. In 1955, he suffered a heart attack and halted his public appearances. Over the next several years his health continued to decline, as did the audience for anti-communist witnesses; but Budenz held firm to his religious and political devotions, continuing to write about them until his death in 1972.[28]

Benjamin Gitlow

Benjamin Gitlow's hostility toward communism was rooted in what he saw as a personal slight from the CPUSA. He had been a founding member of the American party and, as such, was a target during the first red scare in 1919. His arrest and conviction made civil liberties history, and many legal scholars remember his name. Nonetheless, he eventually walked away from the left entirely and became a vocal anti-communist. His version of anti-communism did not have the religious overtones of Budenz's; instead, he believed that communism was akin to Nazism and a fundamental threat to democracy.

Gitlow's parents had been interested in radical politics, including socialism, and their son followed suit, joining the Socialist Party at the age of eighteen. Like so many others in 1917, he saw the Russian Revolution as the realization of socialism, but he also recognized that the goal of "shatter[ing] capitalism" was leading many socialists to place unquestioned faith in the Soviets. As a result, the Bolsheviks were able to make demands on the American Socialist Party that eventually led to its division. Like Poyntz, Gitlow was caught up in the "internecine war" between the right- and leftwing branches of the party, and he later claimed that he had "helped to wreck" it by siding with its left wing.[29]

Gitlow was one of about fourteen writers who co-authored "Left Wing Manifesto," which criticized the "moderate, petit-bourgeois socialism" of some of the older and more conservative members of the Socialist Party. It advocated mass action to challenge capitalism rather than the reform advocated by moderate socialists. The manifesto was introduced at the 1919 socialist conference at which the party split into different factions, including the Workers' Council, Poyntz and Lore's breakaway organization. At this convention Gitlow and his group (among them John Reed, the famed reporter of the Bolshevik Revolution) were expelled. But the manifesto and the conference had even larger consequences for Gitlow.[30] After reading the document, Archibald Stevenson, the special counsel for the Lusk Committee, created by the New York State Legislature to investigate radical activity in New York, believed that it violated the 1902 Criminal Anarchy Act, passed in the wake of President William McKinley's assassination by the "sometime anarchist" Leon Czołgosz. Gitlow had not only co-written the manifesto but, as business manager of the radical magazine *Revolutionary Age,* had been involved in publishing it. He and dozens of others were arrested, though only five went to trial. Gitlow was represented by the progressive attorney Clarence Darrow, who was becoming increasingly concerned about the anti-communist assault on freedom of speech. Despite his lawyer's prowess, Gitlow was found guilty and sentenced to five to ten years of hard labor at Sing Sing Prison. He served two years before he was released, pending appeal.[31]

This case enshrined Gitlow's name in legal history. On appeal, the Supreme Court upheld his conviction on the principle of incorporation, which "appl[ied] the Bill of Rights to the states." Yet the case involved "compelling debate" about the "bad-tendency principle," by which speakers or writers were held responsible for the "probable outcomes" of their words. In other words, Gitlow was declared guilty because the state feared that his words could lead to criminal activity. Justice Oliver Wendell Holmes, joined by Justice Louis Brandeis, wrote a famous dissent, arguing that the manifesto was not advocating the violent overthrow of the U.S. government and that only a small minority of individuals supported the ideas it contained.[32]

After losing his appeal, Gitlow was ordered back to prison but received a pardon from the New York State governor and never finished his sentence. With his legal troubles behind him, he now became an active member of the CPUSA, rising all the way to general secretary. In 1929, he traveled to Moscow with Jay Lovestone and Bert Wolfe to argue before the Comintern for the right of the American party to "choose its own leaders and policies." Gitlow engaged in a direct and heated confrontation with Stalin in favor of the proposal. This led to the Gitlow's expulsion from the CPUSA. Angered by this slight, Gitlow moved from one leftwing organization to another, including back into the Socialist Party. Like Tresca, Solow, and other independent leftists, he watched the Moscow show trials with disgust. His final break with communism and leftwing politics in general came after the 1939 Nazi-Soviet nonaggression pact.[33]

After World War II, Gitlow served as a witness in several hearings and trials against accused communists. Despite having himself faced prosecution and prison for expressing his views, he enthusiastically supported the prosecution of former communists under the Smith Act. Already, by 1939, he was giving "lengthy, voluntary testimony" to the Dies Committee, the precursor of HUAC, though on the eve of war Americans were more focused on the fascist threat than on communism. That same year, he published *I Confess,* a memoir with an "unnecessarily lurid" title, in the opinion of one reviewer.[34] In it Gitlow focused primarily on the party's internecine conflicts in which he and Poyntz took an active part. He described her as a forceful and important communist leader and wrote that her speech before the central executive committee in 1925 had an impact on the party. Poyntz, he said, was the "outstanding woman in the Party," both "headstrong and ambitious." Yet his description of her suggests that he saw her as holding a token position among the largely male leadership. Though she was a "college-bred woman" and knew much about the party's factions, he claimed that she had only a "superficial" knowledge of Marxist-Leninism. Gitlow depicted Poyntz as strong but not that smart, a characterization that the historical record contradicts.

But powerful, independent women were a threat in Cold War America, and Gitlow was known for subscribing to gendered assumptions about women's vulnerability and limited intelligence.[35] Describing the speech in which Poyntz defended herself before the central committee, he recalled the amusement that he and his compatriots felt when she went after their shared enemies. He called her a "spitfire" with unlimited "venom and tenacity." According to his account, William Foster paced while she spoke and occasionally shouted that she was a liar. Foster's allies "squirmed and fumed at her sallies." In Gitlow's view, she "was safe" even while making such waves because she "had eaten the Comintern's humble pie," denouncing Trotsky and distancing herself from Lore.[36]

In the first and second editions of *I Confess* (it was reprinted in 1940), Gitlow did not share much information about Poyntz's disappearance. He did note that, after the Lore debacle, she was forgiven and even became an agent of the "G.P.U." In his telling, she "finally fell into disgrace" (for a reason he failed to provide) and was denounced by a party member named Charles Krumbein as "an agent of the United States Department of Justice." This was the first instance in which any of the Poyntz story narrators named an individual allegedly responsible for publicly denouncing her, and Gitlow failed to explain why. Krumbein himself had been involved in the Soviet underground, but in 1934 he was arrested in the United States and sentenced to prison for using a false passport. He served fifteen months, during which time the Comintern recommended that he be appointed to the CPUSA's Political Bureau. In 1938, he became the American party's national treasurer. It is unclear when he might have denounced Poyntz: for most of the time that she was in the underground, he was in jail or dealing with his own legal issues. Nonetheless, Gitlow claimed that he had alerted the Soviets to her disaffection, and soon thereafter she "disappeared from her living quarters."[37]

In 1948, as former communists such as Budenz were making their accusations public, Gitlow published another book about the CPUSA. In *The Whole of Their Lives,* he reiterated much of what he had written in *I Confess* but offered a "less turgid" account of the squabbles that had plagued the party. According to the reviewer Granville Hicks, himself a former communist turned anti-communist, it was a more up-to-date account of the American communist apparatus. Hicks believed the book had the "earmarks of essential accuracy," yet Gitlow's stories were often outlandish and the author refused to reveal his sources, making its believability suspect. In addition, the book covered years when Gitlow was not in the party and thus casts doubt on its trustworthiness.[38]

Hicks did wonder about some of these claims, including the murder of Poyntz. Perhaps Gitlow was in contact with former communists who knew what had happened. Certainly his new book revealed an astonishing level of detail about Poyntz's death that, if accurate, would prove Tresca's arguments and put the mystery to rest forever. Gitlow again intimated that Krumbein had had some involvement in the case, though his new book now downplayed it. When her disappearance was reported, Krumbein was working as the head of the party's New York district, and he claimed he had never known her. But, in Gitlow's telling, Poyntz and Krumbein worked closely together for years on the district's executive committee. Certainly, she was a regular delegate to all CPUSA conventions between 1926 and 1934, when she went underground; and she was at one time a member of the central executive committee. Gitlow noted that Poyntz was the party's best "woman speaker" and propagandist. Given that she had toured the country as a speaker and organizer and had frequently been nominated by the party to run for office, he found Krumbein's feigned ignorance suspicious. When pressed, Krumbein admitted that she had been a party member but "failed to recall her" because she had dropped out years before. In his 1948 account, Gitlow does not accuse Krumbein of denouncing Poyntz, just of disclaiming any knowledge of her. His about-face is curious. Perhaps he was trying to avoid a libel case. In any case, he no longer implicated Krumbein in her suspected murder.[39]

Still, Gitlow did offer more information about the "very popular" Poyntz. In 1934, he wrote, she went into the underground. As a Soviet agent, she was forbidden "under pain of the severest consequences" to attend public party meetings or associate with party members or friends. According to Gitlow, the OGPU wanted her "badly." Poyntz, he said, was "typically American," attractive, well educated, cultured, "shrewd, [and] alert." She could easily mix with various groups of people. Perhaps most importantly, she had a long history of devotion to Marxism, beginning with her early Socialist Party membership and her union work, and an impressive record of involvement in the CPUSA. In other words, she was a "dependable and courageous communist."[40]

According to Gitlow, Poyntz's assignment in the underground was to gather scientific information in the United States "in the fields of chemistry and physics," which could be of "great importance" to the Soviets.[41] However, this claim contradicts information from those who knew her in the underground and whom she tried to recruit and thus casts doubt on the accuracy of his allegations. Gitlow's timeline also seems suspect. He noted that, in 1934, after Sergei Kirov was assassinated (the event that historians often see as leading to Stalin's purges), the OGPU immediately reorganized itself and Poyntz became disillusioned. Kirov was one of Stalin's friends (if Stalin *had* friends), and his murder was used as a pretense for searching out alleged plots against the Soviet leader. This took place a full three years before Poyntz's friends claimed that she had begun expressing her doubts about communism, long before she went missing.[42] But Gitlow alleged that, during the OGPU reordering, Poyntz and other agents were recalled to Moscow. Here the "American girl" (who was in her late forties at the time) saw things that "knocked the romance" out of communism. His language framed Poyntz as weak and vulnerable and reinforced his claims in *I Confess:* that she was not savvy about the theoretical basis of the movement to which she had devoted her adult life.[43]

While in Moscow, Gitlow wrote, Poyntz participated in interrogations and was herself interrogated. She knew that the people she interrogated were devoted communists, and it was this, Gitlow suggested, that disillusioned her, not the interrogations of show trial defendants, as others had claimed. He wrote that, upon her return from Moscow, she did not want to carry out her orders and spoke "guardedly" about her disillusionment. According to him, she hoped that distance from the OGPU would give her a chance to think her way out of this position, but her fatal mistake was to procrastinate for three years. Somehow rumors reached the OGPU that she was writing about her disillusionment. When confronted, she denied it but said that she might do so in the future. This account is bewildering. Gitlow depicted Poyntz simultaneously as a naïve child unable to realize that her life is in danger and as an agent who knew her life was in danger because she was trying to detach herself from the OGPU. His claim that Poyntz was writing about her disillusionment matches other people's claims about why she was probably killed. But why would she tell the OGPU that she was thinking of revealing everything she knew? That would have been sheer stupidity. Gitlow's purpose for making Poyntz look like a simpleton is unclear, but his gendered language was pointed: Poyntz was not clever enough to realize the danger she was in, yet she still wanted out.[44]

Gitlow's account requires leaps of the imagination at every turn, but at this point in the book he took the narrative to another level, providing details that only the killers could have known. Now, he wrote, the OGPU had to deal with its Poyntz problem, and it decided to liquidate her as "speedily as possible." Three people were chosen to do the job, and Schachno Epstein, allegedly her former lover, was the decoy. Gitlow characterized him as a coward "who cringed" at danger, yet for some reason the OGPU found him valuable and used him "over and over again." Repeating Tresca's claims almost exactly, Gitlow described how Epstein lured Poyntz away from her boardinghouse. Though he wanted no part in her murder, he could not refuse the OGPU, so he telephoned his "former sweetheart" to talk about old times. He asked her to meet at Columbus Circle, and from there they walked into Central Park.[45]

Poyntz, Gitlow wrote, was excited to talk to her old flame but was so wrapped up in her own affairs that she failed to notice how nervous and incoherent he was. If this was true—that she did not notice her friend's odd behavior—then she could not have been a good spy. Gitlow also failed to explain why she would have been excited to talk to someone with links to the underground that she was trying to leave. Nonetheless, in his telling, Epstein took her by the arm and led her to a "large black limousine" that was parked near a sidewalk. When they reached the car, two men jumped out, grabbed Poyntz, shoved her in, and left. Meanwhile, Epstein stood motionless, "looking into space." He then took out a handkerchief and wiped his forehead, before turning and walking away. How could Gitlow have unearthed such details? Epstein was an unlikely source. Why would he have implicated himself in the murder? Perhaps Gitlow was simply dramatizing the situation for his readers. But his accusations were clear and his sources were not.[46]

The book goes on to describe the responses to Poyntz's murder at the next OGPU cell meeting, where there was "laughter and jubilation" as the killers made their report. Once again Gitlow offered no source for these details. He wrote that one killer claimed he had felt sorry for the "poor girl" as she pleaded for her life in the car. She had told them that she was not a traitor, just tired and sick. When they asked why she was writing about the party, she denied the charge, though they claimed to have pages from her manuscript. The killer told his compatriots at the meeting that the once-hardened spy had begged desperately for her life: "I want to live. I promise I will not say a word against the Party or the OGPU. You can trust me; I have proved that time and again." But the OGPU agents coldly murdered her, yet another demonstration of the heartlessness of communism.[47]

According to Gitlow, Poyntz was "afraid to die," and she cried and pleaded "not at all like a communist." His implication is unclear. Were communists supposed to die for the cause? Was her behavior not communist because she was crying? Whatever his point, he clearly was reinforcing the notion that communism was violent and expected violence from its adherents, even when faced with their own death. The killers drove her upstate to Dutchess County, into a wooded area "not far from the Roosevelt estate." Here "the girl" was killed and buried under lime and dirt in a gulley. The three killers heaped "dead leaves and branches" over the grave and stamped them down with their feet. They concluded their report by claiming that Poyntz was "too beautiful" and that it was too "bad we had to kill her." The tale was a horrifying but familiar amalgam of merciless men, a hidden grave, and a beautiful girl, and it emphasized Poyntz's weakness and helplessness.[48] Tresca had repeated the same story often in the prewar years. Gitlow only had to invent the drama and the dialogue.

But Gitlow's story about Poyntz was not done. Lore, her long-time friend and colleague, could not abide what the OGPU had done to her. Though he had long ago been expelled from the party, he retained connections . What they were and how Gitlow knew about them are not mentioned in the book. Gitlow did claim that the OGPU had kept Lore in its clutches because he knew too much, that he had tried and failed to kill himself to break free of the communist grip. After Poyntz's murder, he had reached his limit. Gitlow suggested that Lore had finally found the courage to tell authorities all he knew about the OGPU, but suddenly and without any "previous premonition of illness" he died.[49]

Now the communists were even killing Poyntz's friends! Gitlow continued this tack by suggesting that Tresca might also have been killed by the party, which could not abide his constant "hammer[ing] away." After Tresca attempted to exclude communists from the Mazzini Society and the anti-fascist Italian American Victory Council (claims circulated by the Tresca Memorial Committee), the "time for elimination" had arrived. A man named Charles Pappas bought the "murder car." Pappas, whose identity the police could never trace, may have been a goon for the communist-dominated furriers' union. But, as Gitlow emphasized, communists specialize in unsolvable murders, so Pappas was never found out. Gitlow did not offer any substantive evidence to suggest that the communists had killed Lore or Tresca, or even that Lore was murdered at all. In the end, his allegation that the murderers may have been communists was evidence enough for his Cold War audience. Yet he did not paint either man as a helpless victim, as he did Poyntz. He simply stated that both had been killed by communist assassins.[50]

The Tresca Memorial Committee took notice of the accusations in Gitlow's book and again pushed the FBI and the state of New York to act. On November 15, 1948, Norman Thomas sent a memorandum about Gitlow's disclosures to both FBI Director Hoover and District Attorney Hogan in hopes that the revelations would prompt them to investigate the Tresca and Poyntz cases. In February 1949, Gitlow was questioned by Assistant District Attorney Louis Panucco about the Tresca assassination, but no new investigations or indictments were issued.[51]

In a draft of his book, Gitlow included certain details that did not make it into the book's final version. He claimed that OGPU agents had tried to counsel Poyntz to get back into line and that they had suggested she take a trip to a Crimean spa. (A "trip to the Soviet Union" was code for imprisonment and eventual liquidation.) The agents also reminded her that Bolsheviks had no room for sentiment and were impatient with those who forgot their duty because of "temperamental moods." Scared and aware that she had been threatened, Poyntz returned to her room, pacing up and down while the blood vessels in her head "throbbed." She threw herself on her bed and began sobbing, but eventually an idea came to the "demented woman." She began to destroy every document about her time in the underground. In the draft account, at least one agent objected to her liquidation, suggesting that she could still be useful. He was shouted down, and his comrades dismissed her as a "Trotskyite traitor." It is clear why this part was cut from the final version: it is beyond belief. How could Gitlow know what Poyntz was thinking or doing? His descriptions added drama but also clarified that he had invented the entire episode. It was pure fiction and lent no credibility to his account.[52]

A great deal was edited out of Gitlow's earlier draft, including lengthy descriptions of Epstein as a communist tool and a coward. That draft also included a character named Agent Peterson who was disgusted by his fellow OGPU agents' boasting about Poyntz's murder. In Gitlow's telling, Peterson decided to defect. But instead of being secretive about it, he went directly to his chief and claimed that Poyntz's murder had proven that a "vile and corrupt degeneration" was gripping the agency, and he no longer wanted to be a part. He said that they would not dare to liquidate him because he had written the whole story down and had kept an account of all of his work in the underground. If the Soviets killed him, the information would be leaked and would destroy the Bolsheviks. Was Gitlow suggesting that Peterson was his source? There is no way of knowing. Peterson disappeared from the narrative, and the Poyntz case was "closed."[53]

In his review, Hicks questioned much of what Gitlow had written in *The Whole of Their Lives,* which should have cast doubt on the entire book. But anti-communism was such a powerful force that even obvious exaggerations and lies did not undermine his belief in the text. Other reviewers were less generous. Writing in the January 1948 issue of *Commentary*, an anti-Stalinist magazine, Raymond Rosenthal described the book as a "hodge-podge" of verifiable history mixed with "hearsay tales, [and] radical gossip," all delivered in a tone of indignation. He called Gitlow an "agitator" and said that the book was the result of "hasty improvisation" peppered with "spurts of outrage" and lengthy passages of "exposition." The book, like much of anti-communism, included a few grains of truth and an abundance of fabrication.[54]

Gitlow died in 1965, and today he is remembered more for the Supreme Court case that bears his name and for his leadership in the CPUSA than he is for his work as an anti-communist witness. Yet he spent many years testifying and writing about communists. Perhaps he was motivated by being expelled from the CPUSA, but he also believed that the party had proven that it was not democratic when it removed him for standing up against Stalin. The purges and the Hitler-Stalin pact had driven that belief home for him.[55]

Paul Crouch

Gitlow's book was melodramatic; and if Poyntz's FBI file is any indication, it did not make waves among law enforcement. In contrast, Paul Crouch's articles in the *Miami Daily News* and his testimony before congressional committees attracted a great deal of attention. Crouch, like many ex-communist witnesses, seemed to devote as much energy and passion to anti-communism as he had to communism. His biographer, Gregory Taylor, believes that this "Manichean perspective" and self-righteous confidence often blinded him to other points of view. Though Taylor agrees that Budenz and Chambers also fit this pattern, he argues that Crouch embodied it even more than others did.[56]

Paul Crouch was born on June 24, 1903, in Moravian Falls, North Carolina. His father, Isaac Crouch, was a Baptist minister and a Civil War veteran. The family moved north and settled in Dover, Delaware, where the young Crouch came into contact with immigrant groups and radical politics during the post–World War One red scare. At first he was wary of radicalism, especially after anarchists allegedly began sending bombs to the homes of political leaders, including U.S. Attorney General Mitchell Palmer. But raids and deportations quickly followed, and Crouch developed sympathy with the argument that violence might be needed to counter the state's power. This argument, he later wrote, moved him toward the "Communist point of view."[57]

After the Crouch family moved back to North Carolina, eighteen-year-old Paul took a job at a textile mill in Winston-Salem. Like the other millworkers, he endured long hours and low wages, but he enjoyed the camaraderie and unsuccessfully tried to organize a union. After leaving the mill, he worked for a time as a journalist, then joined the army and was shipped to Hawaii. Here, Crouch became acquainted with other soldiers who were interested in radicalism, and they formed a "loose association of army radicals" who met to discuss politics. His views led to his expulsion from the army; and in 1924, at age twenty-one, he joined the Communist Party. Crouch worked as an organizer for the party for the next seventeen years, traveling throughout the United States and into the Soviet Union. He trained other party members to "infiltrate the military," organize strikes, and participate in union activism, and he wrote "countless screeds against American capitalism." He met Poyntz during this time, and he later described her as one of his and his wife Sylvia's best friends. Crouch and Poyntz worked together on party projects , most notably during the Gastonia textile strike in 1928.[58]

Paul and Sylvia (who was also a party member) wanted to settle down and earn an income outside of the party, but in 1942 the CPUSA ordered them to move to Los Angeles. Crouch refused and was expelled from the party. He later claimed that he had already been frustrated by its constant policy shifts and its obeisance to the USSR rather than to the American working class. It was dominated, he said, by people who had "no regard whatever for the American people," and it did not respect the basic "laws of human decency." Crouch feared that if Stalinism took over, the world would return to "slavery, tyranny, and unbridled despotism."[59]

According to Taylor, Crouch may have been frustrated by the party's line in 1942, but his real shift to anti-communism came later. After he was expelled, he stayed quiet for five years. Then, motivated by "financial incentives, the desire for fame, vengeance, fear," and a "true change of heart," he decided to become an informant. His reasoning was similar to that of other ex-communist witnesses, whose motivations for talking varied from fear to opportunism. Certainly, in his case, finances were an important trigger: Crouch had lost his job at Pan Am and needed to support his family. But he also saw this as an opportunity to "avenge personal slights" and to "save the nation" from a group that he now believed presented a true threat. Essentially, writes Taylor, Crouch "end[ed] up simply exchanging one ideology for another."[60]

On May 11, 1949, Hoke Welch, the editor of the *Miami Daily News*, testified before an executive session of HUAC, during which time he entered an affidavit from Crouch into evidence. Two days earlier, his newspaper had published the first in a series of articles by Crouch that leveled sensational accusations against the CPUSA, including its culpability in Poyntz's murder. Crouch himself had testified before HUAC a week before his articles appeared. The information he shared galvanized both the national press and law enforcement. One HUAC official described it as a "break bigger than the Whittaker Chambers and Liz Bentley cases combined." It is not clear why the same had not happened when Gitlow's book was published in 1948.[61]

In the affidavit that Welch shared with HUAC, Crouch called "Julia" (his name for Poyntz) not just a party co-worker but "one of my closest personal friends in the movement." The friendship among Crouch, Poyntz, and Sylvia had blossomed while all three were in Gastonia for the strike. Crouch claimed that even by 1929 Poyntz was expressing "bitter disappointment" in the CPUSA's leadership and the "dictatorship which . . . controlled the party." So ten years after these intimate conversations, he was not surprised to learn (he said) that she was going to break with the party. In other words, his affidavit asked HUAC to believe that Poyntz had spent a decade simultaneously behaving like a devoted communist—even agreeing to move into the underground—while also remaining disillusioned with the party.[62]

When Poyntz went missing in 1937, Crouch was serving as a district organizer in North Carolina. Despite the close friendship he alleged, the two had not seen each other for several years. He knew that she was doing "special work," party code for members "who had become GPU agents." He read about her disappearance in the newspaper; and when he attended the next party conference in New York in 1938, he made inquiries. His questions about her were met with "silence, frowns, and polite intimations to 'mind my own business.'" Some people told him that Poyntz was a traitor. In his affidavit, he recalled that a man named Epstein, the editor of *Freiheit,* was one of the attendees who evaded his questions. If his timeline is accurate, this is a very surprising claim about Schachno Epstein. Crouch was in New York sometime after Poyntz's disappearance was first publicized in December 1937. By January 1938, Tresca was loudly accusing Epstein of being involved in her murder and having left the United States in August 1937 using a false passport. After A. A. Rubens was arrested in Moscow in December 1937 and his passport ring was exposed, the FBI made alleged attempts to find Epstein and speak to him about the false passport. Yet Crouch places him in New York City in 1938, conspicuously visible among his communist colleagues.

Memory is always unreliable, but many of the ex-communist witnesses did like to claim a place for themselves in the midst of the most sensational happenings in the party.[63]

Crouch came to believe that Poyntz had been murdered because she knew too much and wanted to break with the party. In 1948, six years after he was expelled from the CPUSA, he spoke with the former communist Herbert Zam and the former socialist Paul Krebs at the home of Milton Zitensky. Zitensky's wife was also a former communist, and during this get-together the group pieced together what they believed had happened to Poyntz. They speculated that Epstein had lured her from her boardinghouse aided by a woman named Martha Stone. She was then shot by the "notorious GPU agent" George Mink. The group did not agree on where Mink had disposed of her body. Some thought that she was buried in or near Yonkers, outside of New York City, while others believed her body had been thrown into Manhattan's East River.[64]

This version of the story closely resembled Tresca's, though the addition of Martha Stone was new. She was the wife of Phil Frankfeld, CPUSA's district organizer in Maryland. As Crouch learned from others at the meeting, she had once worked for the GPU and had reportedly been involved in Trotsky's assassination in Mexico. She may have been the same woman whom Budenz called "Miss Y" in his book, where he said he had introduced her to certain GPU agents. In his book he claimed he did not want to name her because he had made a "religious pledge not to injure innocent people." One wonders how someone involved in an assassination could be "innocent." Moreover, Budenz named hundreds of so-called secret communists to the FBI, so his "religious pledge" is questionable. In any case, he allegedly gave her name to the New York district attorney's office. Mink's name, however, often came up in accounts of Poyntz's disappearance, though not always in the same role. In this version, he was the trigger man. Crouch claimed he had known Mink and believed he was of "extremely low personal character." According to the affidavit, Mink had threatened to "get rid of" CPUSA people who did not like him, and he had once served a prison sentence in Denmark for rape.[65]

On May 10, 1949, a day before Hoke's testimony, Crouch had aired these accusations in an article in the *Miami Daily News.* Mincing no words, he began, "Juliet Stuart Poyntz was murdered by a Russian secret police agent and her body was thrown into East River in New York City." Unlike his affidavit, the article displayed no doubts about where her body had been dumped. This, he noted, was what happened to communists such as "Julia" and himself, who broke with the party and chose to expose it. Her murder, he wrote, was why he did not take exposing it lightly. He reiterated for readers that Poyntz was one of his "best friends in the Party" and from a "well known Virginia family." Not knowing where his "best friend" was actually from was Crouch's first big mistake, and it would not be his last. He said that she had confided to him that she wanted the American party to be independent from the Soviets and that she had effected her break with the party before her disappearance. He declared that Poyntz, a devoted underground agent, was nonetheless frustrated by "Moscow domination" and was prepared to expose it.[66]

The inconsistencies in Crouch's testimonies and articles would later become notorious, but already he was revealing them. In his affidavit, he had claimed that his conversations with Poyntz about party leadership had taken place in Gastonia in 1928 and 1929. The May 10 article left his readers with the impression that he and Poyntz had spoken together right before her disappearance, which was not what his affidavit indicated. Did Crouch know or not know what had happened to her? Both Budenz and Gitlow had already told the story of her disappearance, and both of their accounts parroted Tresca's initial claims, which had been circulating for eleven years. The only major difference between Crouch's story and theirs was that he had inserted himself into it as Poyntz's intimate friend and confidant. But was Poyntz really such a careless spy? If breaking with the party was a capital crime, why was she so flagrantly talking about it?[67]

In his May 10 article, Crouch claimed that he had made a "long and intensive investigation" of her disappearance. A "high-ranking" party official, someone he said he had later heard might have been involved in her murder, had told him that she was a "traitor," giving Crouch the impression that he should leave the story alone. He did not name Mink in the article but referred to the man who took the "actual shot" as a "notorious GPU agent." Three days later, in a May 13 article, he did reveal the murderer's name, opening the piece with the sensational news that "George Mink, an American citizen in the pay of the Russian secret police, fired the shot which killed Julia Stuart Poyntz in 1937." This, he wrote, was an "irrefutable fact."[68]

The information in the May 13 article repeated Crouch's affidavit almost verbatim. This time, however, he was clearer about when Poyntz had told him about her disillusionment with the party: in 1928 and 1929, years before she entered the underground and then disappeared. Readers unfamiliar with the case probably never noticed the strange inconsistencies in both his and Gitlow's timelines. In the article, Crouch said that Epstein and "a woman" were responsible for luring Poyntz from her boardinghouse, while Mink committed the actual murder. However, he confusingly claimed that Poyntz's body was buried near Yonkers but later dug up and thrown into the East River. He did not name Stone but did note that the woman who had lured Poyntz from her room had taken part in Trotsky's assassination. He described Mink as a "drunkard" who was "dissolute in his personal life" and had boasted to Crouch that he could get rid of people who did not like him.[69]

To lend credence to Crouch's accusations, the *Miami Daily News* ran a May 16 article in which the "former red spy queen" Elizabeth Bentley confirmed his story. Describing Poyntz as a "socialite," Bentley claimed that three people in the underground had told her that Poyntz was "six feet under." Bentley said that she had seen Poyntz with a "dark-complexioned man" before her disappearance, and she thought that man was Mink. This story, which was different from the account that Bentley shared later in *Out of Bondage* (1951), was "remarkably similar" to Crouch's. She told the paper she was interested because Poyntz had been the first person to try to recruit her into the underground.[70]

Taylor notes a particularly large discrepancy in Crouch's tale: his claim that communist leaders had refused to tell him what had happened to Poyntz while he was still in the party but did tell him the truth after he was out. Why would any party leader have shared such information with an ex-member? But such inconsistencies did not seem to bother HUAC and other committee officials who cited Crouch's testimony in the years that followed. The press also took his credibility for granted, and suddenly people everywhere were paying attention to Poyntz's long-closed case.[71]

Law enforcement officials began sending tips to the FBI about unidentified dead women who had appeared about the time that Poyntz had gone missing. A "badly decomposed" body found in Long Island Sound in August 1937 was exhumed from her pauper's grave to see if it could be Poyntz. When it had first been discovered, police thought she might have been Alice McDonnell Parsons, a socialite who had gone missing. But the body was not hers, and no trace of Parsons was ever found. Now, prompted by Crouch's disclosures, a police captain from New London, Connecticut, reopened the investigation and ordered the exhumation. When found, the body was five foot, two inches tall, four inches shorter than Poyntz had been, but investigators thought that maybe the two months it had spent in the sound had made it shrink. They pinned their hopes on dental records, which showed that both Poyntz and the body had silver fillings, but it was not identified as hers.[72]

Congress took notice of Crouch's accusations and recalled him to testify before HUAC, and the Senate Judiciary Committee announced plans to subpoena him. Nonetheless, despite the fervor Crouch created, nothing definitive came out of the investigations into Poyntz's disappearance. Notably, his articles had not focused on why so little notice had been taken of her disappearance in 1937, why federal agencies at that time had had little interest in a missing communist who was allegedly working for the Soviet underground.[73] Even in this new Cold War climate, not everyone saw such claims as credible. The FBI kept copies of Crouch's *Miami Daily News* articles in its Poyntz file but had doubts about his testimony. An internal memo described the articles as "highly colored" and "written for public consumption." It noted that their information "appear[ed] to be fabricated," basing that suspicion on an early interview with Crouch, when he told the agent he had no information about Poyntz's disappearance. The bureau took issue with several of his articles, given that he had shared none of that material with them when given the chance. Agents did not feel it was worth their time to interview him again.[74]

Crouch spent the next few years working as a professional informant. He was "renowned" for his services and made a good living from anticommunism. In 1951, he reported earning $4,840 as an informant; in 1953, he brought in $8,000. In 1954, he collected $9,675 from the Justice Department alone. He lived rent-free in an apartment in Hawaii owned by the "Chinese National Archbishop," and both he and his wife gave speeches and wrote articles for money. Yet even by the early 1950s, doubts about Crouch's testimony were emerging in the mainstream press.[75] Like other ex-communist witnesses, he often spoke in generic terms about the CPUSA's Soviet-related activities and loyalties. Rather than testifying about an individual's participation in the party, he implicated many people by association. Reporters and defense attorneys noted the inconsistencies that resulted from such universalizing, sometimes within the same hearing. For instance, in 1954, Crouch testified that a man named David Davis was a communist. Davis's attorney reached out to other defense attorneys who had defended individuals against Crouch's accusations. The attorney learned that, in 1949, during testimony against the Australian labor leader Harry Bridges, Crouch had declared on the stand that he had no information about Davis. When confronted, Crouch could not offer an answer. Though diehard anti-communists continued to support him, the press began to question his reliability, and U.S. Attorney General Herbert Brownell decided to "investigate the entire informer system."[76]

Things got worse for Crouch as his informant income began to wane. He attempted to publish a manuscript about his revelations, but publishers told him that the market for ex-communist witness accounts had dried up. In the manuscript, he mentioned Poyntz, but only briefly. He discussed his "research" about her disappearance, which amounted to trading stories with other former communists. His conclusions were exactly what he and others had been saying since 1937. He did claim that Poyntz had intended to leak information to a newspaper reporter, but he did not say how he knew this.[77] Meanwhile, William Thompkins, the head of the Justice Department's Internal Security Division, told Brownell that he should no longer use Crouch as a witness. Then, in 1955, Harvey Matusow, another ex-communist turned informer, published *False Witness,* which revealed that he had perjured himself on the witness stand, often with the encouragement of Senator Joseph McCarthy. Matusow accused his friends Crouch and Bentley of lying on the stand as well. The mainstream media uncovered falsified and exaggerated testimony, and "The Crouch Appendix," a document listing the contradictions and inconsistences in his testimony, started circulating. Crouch began an eager campaign to defend himself, but his health was rapidly declining. On November 18, 1955, he died from lung cancer. His death, largely unnoticed in the press, was a relief to the FBI, which would no longer have to deal with his persistent requests for help in clearing his name.[78]

Crouch had spent seventeen years in the Communist Party, and there was likely some element of truth in his testimony and in the claims of other ex-communists. But his desperate need to earn an income required new information, and that is what concerned Herbert Packer in *Ex-Communist Witnesses.* What was true, what was exaggeration, and what was an outright lie? Did the witnesses themselves even know the difference? These one-time communists planted terror in the hearts of the American public, a conviction that communism would undermine everything they held dear. Stories about Poyntz's mysterious disappearance stoked that fear. Chambers, Crouch, Budenz, and Bentley were all accused of lying, but their testimony was nonetheless influential. Packer concluded that the witnesses he examined in his book all presented "detailed assertions" that were "difficult, if not impossible," to verify with evidence. But it was clear that they and the many other ex-communists who became informants were passionate about their beliefs. They had forsaken "one set of absolutes for another." Each was seeking "self-vindication," and anyone who challenged their stories was clearly "against them." This black-and-white thinking was exploited by congressional and judicial "interrogators" for their own "immediate political purposes."[79] Packer, himself an anti-communist, questioned the ability of Congress and the media to uncover the truth amid the hysteria. The only solution was to create "objective" public agencies to gather information and test it without "gaining present political advantage."[80]

The need to continually offer up new information to sustain a career in anti-communism became a particular problem for Elizabeth Bentley. Like Crouch, she often exaggerated and fabricated her information to remain relevant. But she faced other barriers in her attempt to remain a viable professional witness. As Packer noted, she was one of the most influential anti-communist witnesses during the Cold War, but she was also one of the most notorious. In her struggle against gender conventions, which male anti-communists did not face, she found a new use for Poyntz—not as a sympathetic victim, but as depraved and dangerous.

CHAPTER SEVEN

THE LADY SPY

In the late spring of 1936, Elizabeth Bentley was at home entertaining friends when she answered a knock at her door. She opened it and found that the newcomers were Juliet Stuart Poyntz (whom she knew as Juliet Glazer) and a woman named Pauline Rogers. Poyntz insisted on speaking with Bentley, so she escorted the pair away from her guests and into her bedroom. After closing the door, she turned to look at Poyntz, whose face was "distorted with hate and rage." Poyntz was angry that Bentley and a colleague had called her a counterrevolutionary, an insult with deadly consequences in the Communist Party, and "launched into a vituperative diatribe" that left Bentley stunned. Poyntz accused Bentley herself of being a "Trotskyite" and a counterrevolutionary. Staring at her with "concentrated fury," she threatened that if Bentley ever meddled in her affairs again she would see to it that Bentley was "taken care of" and "put six feet under." The episode left Bentley "weak and shaking" but not exactly afraid because she did not know then that Poyntz was a Soviet agent.[1] It was the last time she ever saw Poyntz alive.

This incident is described in Bentley's 1951 book *Out of Bondage*. Like much of the rest of her book, its accuracy is questionable. Bentley's version of Poyntz was radically different from the naïf described by male anti-Stalinists and anti-communists. Their construction of her as a victim erased all blame from her for being a communist and painted the Soviet Union as the unquestioned culprit in her disappearance. Chambers, Budenz, Crouch, and Gitlow had all used this "innocent woman" narrative to dramatize the communist threat. For them, Poyntz embodied a fear that had become central in American anti-communism: that women were more vulnerable than men to communist propaganda, that American masculinity had to step up to preserve patriarchal institutions against communist infiltration, and that communism sought to undermine traditional gender order and had to be defeated.

Bentley, however, was wrestling with different gender expectations, and she had to convince the American public of her own virtue and her good intentions. For male anti-communists, merely defecting from the party was enough to earn public forgiveness for spying; for Bentley, the situation was more complicated because she had not followed the proper gendered script expected of women in Cold War America. She was unmarried, sexually promiscuous, and a hard drinker, traits that were tolerated and sometimes admired in men but not in women. The press almost never mentioned a male anti-communist's personal appearance, but they saw Bentley's as a disappointment. She was bookish and homely, not sultry and seductive. In other words, she was trapped: she neither looked the part of a female spy nor acted the part of a middle-class white housewife. With no other choice, she had to create a new image for herself.

Bentley wanted to forge a career in anti-communism. So in recounting her life in the party and later in the underground, she used Poyntz as a foil to her own self-constructed image as a naïve, well-behaved, reformed, Christian woman. This was not easy. While male anti-communists managed to carve lucrative careers from public testimony, books, and public appearances, Bentley faced intense scrutiny, and every personal fault became fodder for critics and the press, even after her death. So while trying to capitalize on her past in the Soviet underground, she put enormous energy into controlling her public image. She did this by deploying existing gendered constructs to her advantage, using Poyntz to represent the Soviet machinery and describing herself as its victim.[2]

Female Spies

In 1945, Bentley, who was at that time still working in the Soviet underground, contacted the FBI because she was afraid the Soviets were suspicious of her loyalties. At the bureau's behest, she remained in the underground for another two years as an FBI informant. She left the underground in 1947 when she was subpoenaed to appear before a federal grand jury. In 1948, she made her public debut as a witness for HUAC. According to the historian Veronica Wilson, it was at this point that the Truman administration began to see her as a "genuine threat." She was, after all, accusing its officials of passing information to the Soviets. The media pounced on Bentley, accusing her of "mud-slinging" and "slander" and employing "reductive, sexist diatribe[s]" when discussing her. Newspaper articles filled an inordinate amount of space with descriptions of her physical appearance, characterizing her as a "pathetic Rebel Girl" and deriding her "scraggly hair."[3]

Popular culture tended to depict female spies as alluring and sexy, but the reality was often very different. Bentley's biographer, Kathryn Olmsted, believes that her representation in the media set the standard for how other female spies of the era—among them Priscilla Hiss, Ethel Rosenberg, and Judith Coplan—were publicly depicted. According to Olmsted, few media accounts focused on their actual work as spies; rather, they painted the women in gendered terms as "shrewish wives, neurotic old maids, and voluptuous young vixens." Olmsted argues that this obsession with looks tells us very little about how these women operated in the Soviet underground, it does reveal a great deal about gender expectations at midcentury.[4]

Images from pulp fiction and films were largely responsible for the stereotypes that journalists employed when writing about female spies. In such tellings, these women were portrayed as hypersexual sirens who used their bodies to lure unsuspecting men. According to Olmsted, the femme fatale trope was "especially prevalent" after World War II, given the anxiety that was arising around the changing relations between men and women. The stereotype fit into anti-communist warnings about gender upheaval and exacerbated "oversimplified" reactions to the Communist Party's stance on gender equality. Women communists were seen as hostile, "cold, ruthless and above all humorless." The political scientist Herbert Krugman notes that the media often depicted female communists as talentless "haters," and much anti-communist propaganda described married communist women as "dominant" over their husbands and children.[5]

Such preoccupations led to overgeneralizations about women whose behavior failed to meet traditional expectations, and it also meant that the media and politicians took women's information and experiences less seriously. This gender trap was what compelled Bentley to write *Out of Bondage.* In the book, she became an innocent who had been lured into the Soviet underground by manipulative agents such as Poyntz, whom she described as a communist succubus. Her motivation for using Poyntz was clear: she had to defend herself from extreme public criticism, so she appropriated the sexist standards being used against her and applied them to Poyntz. Both the man-eating femme fatale stereotype and the humorless communist trope appeared in Bentley's descriptions of her interactions with Poyntz, who was not around to challenge them. In her desperate attempt to capitalize on anti-communism, Bentley did not describe the real Poyntz for her readers. Instead, she described herself.[6]

Elizabeth Bentley and Communism

Elizabeth Bentley was born on January 1, 1908, in New Milford, Connecticut, the only child of Charles Bentley, a dry-goods merchant, and May Charlotte Turrill, a teacher. As a young woman, she won a scholarship to Vassar College. Though she was a mediocre student there, she did discover an interest in politics. She briefly joined the League for Industrial Democracy, a socialist student organization, and later claimed to have been influenced by faculty member Hallie Flanagan, an "influential leftist." After graduating with degrees in English, Italian, and French, Bentley taught for two years at Foxcroft Preparatory and Finishing School for Girls in Middleburg, Virginia. She left Foxcroft to pursue a graduate degree at Columbia University and in 1933 won a "prestigious" scholarship to the University of Florence in Italy. By this point both of her parents had died, and Bentley, already an alcoholic, had begun to display her drunkenness in public. She engaged in frequent affairs with married and single men, had gained a reputation for borrowing (but not repaying) money from friends, and was rumored to have had more than one illegal abortion.[7]

While studying in Italy, Bentley became enamored of Mussolini and was so involved with a fascist student organization that she began to neglect her studies. During this period, she began an affair with her academic advisor, Mario Casella, whose assistant wrote most of her master's thesis. Casella turned Bentley against fascism, but she was still unable to focus on her studies. After nearly being expelled from the university for failing a class, she sank into depression and tried to kill herself. Now a "confirmed alcoholic," she returned to New York in 1934 with a plagiarized thesis and few job prospects.[8]

Unable to find work, Bentley took a typing class at Columbia. There she met a woman named Lee Fuhr, a communist involved with the American League against War and Fascism (ALWF), an organization with a strong communist presence. With Fuhr's encouragement, Bentley became involved in the ALWF and in 1935 decided to join the party. Her time spent in fascist Italy and her Italian language skills were useful to the communists and attracted the interest of Poyntz, who was then locating and recruiting Columbia students who had connections in Europe. At this time Poyntz attempted, without success, to recruit Bentley into the underground.[9]

In 1938, Bentley was introduced to Jacob Raisin, better known as Jacob Golos, who became both her handler and her lover. Golos was a devoted communist and a high-level CPUSA official. He was tasked with ensuring that the American cadre followed the Stalinist line, and he passed information from informants to Soviet intelligence. Though Golos had a wife and child in Moscow, her affair with him was Bentley's longest and most important relationship. For five years, she aided him in his work. She served as a mail drop for agents, and Golos also trained her to get documents from "high placed agents" and "debrief and control" them. When his health began to deteriorate, she began to take over the management of his spy ring in Washington, D.C.[10]

Golos died in 1943, and Bentley blamed his death on the pressure he had endured from the Soviets, who were eager for inside information from American military intelligence. She now took complete charge of his spy ring, but her alcoholism and loneliness increased. She took to hitting on women and complained to her Soviet handlers about her lack of a "male companion." Unlike other agents, she was not an "ideologue." She paid little attention to CPUSA politics, and her commitment to the Soviet Union and to communism had been tied to Golos and the other people she knew in the party. Moreover, by 1945, she feared that the FBI was monitoring her activities. At the same time the Soviets were suggesting that she move to Moscow, and she knew that recall orders meant death. So in August, Bentley approached agents at the bureau office in New Haven, Connecticut, and began her career as an anti-communist informant. The FBI kept her working as an insider until 1948, when she publicly accused communists of spying, thus officially ending her connection with the Soviets.[11]

As soon as Bentley became a public defector and delivered her opening testimony to a grand jury, she set to work at controlling her media image. Her first move was to contact Nelson Frank and Frederick Woltman, two ex-communists who now worked for the anti-communist *New York World-Telegram,* which often tried to find links between communists and the Democratic Party. Bentley shared her story with the reporters, but they had to hold off on publishing it until July 1948, when the grand jury decided to make indictments. Frank and his editorial assistant, Norton Mockridge, then ran a series of articles constructing a narrative about Bentley that she would never live up to.[12]

The first article, headlined "Red Ring Bared by Blond Queen," created a version of Bentley known as the "red spy queen." She was described (without an accompanying photo) as a "svelte and striking blonde," a "New England born" all-American girl, and a "graduate of an outstanding woman's college," whose life had veered in the wrong direction when she became a communist. The "beautiful blonde" turned to the FBI for help because of her "squeamishness" and "growing feeling of revulsion" about betraying the country of her birth.[13] Though Frank had met Bentley and knew that the articles had misrepresented her, subsequent articles continued to describe her as "good looking." Because he could not yet reveal her name, he often referred to her simply as "the blonde."[14]

There was no material evidence to prove Bentley's allegations about the Communist party, but the articles in the *New York World-Telegram* seemed to give them credence. They also made her seem more sympathetic. In one article, Frank and Mockridge wrote that she, like other women, had been tricked and manipulated into becoming a spy. Bentley told the reporters that the CPUSA would gradually involve its members in spying by asking them to perform simple tasks. This, she said, was how she had become trapped, by not "fully realiz[ing]" she had been drawn in until it was too late. She noted that at first she had been happy to do the work because of her "hatred of fascism," thus playing on American anxieties about Hitler.[15] In these accounts, Bentley was cleverly deflecting the blame for her years of work in the underground onto others whom she claimed had manipulated her. Yet in the end it was not her involvement in spying that caused her public undoing; it was her flaunting of gendered expectations. When Bentley finally decided to "drop her mask," journalists and the public were sorely disappointed by her appearance and her unconventional life. Despite her attempts to change their focus, both remained a preoccupation in the press.[16]

Time's 1948 exposé on Bentley began with its disappointment in her appearance. She was not a "Mata Hari" who had "vampired" information out of men. Neither was she "blond, beautiful," or "glamorous." In reality, she was "plump" and had a "sharp nose and receding chin." She was, in short, "not so exciting," as she had been described or imagined in other articles. The leftwing *New Leader* felt compelled to describe Bentley as "not so young."[17] Some newspapers depicted her as a "sex-starved, man-eating temptress" or as a "sexually repressed, man-hating spinster." As Wilson writes, even in death Bentley could not escape scrutiny. Her 1963 *New York Times* obituary described her as a "plump, brown-haired, rather dowdy woman."[18] Had Poyntz gone missing in the postwar years, she, too, might have faced this unforgiving press and public.

It could not have been easy for Bentley to see her appearance become a media focus. Though she continued to try to manipulate "her image and story to her own advantage," she was repeatedly described as physically unattractive, dismissed as a "professional informer," and labeled as a "betrayer of [both] liberalism" and communism. She was criticized for remaining unmarried and for her "loose" sexuality. She was painted as an unreliable, unsavory woman who "should not be taken seriously." Though much of what Bentley revealed was not a lie, her appearance and behaviors so preoccupied politicians and the media that the information she shared was not taken seriously. Male ex-communist witnesses did not receive this kind of dismissive treatment. They, too, did not fit popular culture images of male spies, but their looks were never the point.[19]

In her testimony, Bentley named about eighty alleged spies. J. Edgar Hoover knew that her information was correct, and the information she shared "effectively shut down Soviet Espionage in North America." But as the *New Leader* reported in 1948, a lack of "incontrovertible" material proof partly explained why there were so many public questions about Bentley's accusations. In addition, it was much easier to discount her because she had stepped outside the era's accepted roles for women.[20]

Unlike former male spies, who were celebrated for their ideological reversals, Bentley found that her work in the Soviet underground had seriously tainted her image. Liberal and leftwing critics often accused her of being part of a "conservative conspiracy" to "undermine" the Truman presidency and attack the New Deal.[21] Being a woman Cold Warrior was a handicap, and Bentley's hand was forced. In Poyntz, she discovered the perfect foil in her attempt to remake herself as a woman who had been led astray but was desperate to get back onto the right path.

Out of Bondage

Bentley's book *Out of Bondage* did not mention her many affairs, her drinking problem, or her falsified master's degree but began with a description of her return to New York from Italy and her introduction to American communism. Bentley described meeting Fuhr and her enticement into the party via the ALWF, which offered shelter to the unmarried, orphaned young woman. She was enthusiastic about the CPUSA's anti-fascist popular front program and the party's new identity as the leader of a "coalition of progressive forces to beat back the tide of war and fascism." She claimed that she had been "taken in by this clever propaganda."[22]

In 1935, Bentley landed a permanent job at the Home Relief Bureau, a government welfare agency. Here, she was approached by a co-worker and communist named Pauline Rogers, who asked her to consider focusing more of her energies on Italian anti-fascism. Rogers, in turn, introduced her to Poyntz, known to Bentley by her married name, Juliet Glazer.[23] In a 1945 FBI deposition, Bentley recalled that Rogers had suggested that her time spent in fascist Italy and her knowledge of Italian could be valuable in anti-fascist circles. Poyntz then asked Bentley to help her do "research work" on Italian fascism and to assist in translation because Poyntz did not know Italian. According to Bentley, she later learned that Poyntz had approached others at Columbia "along the same lines." Though she was not quite sure what Poyntz wanted from her, she told the FBI that it was her "opinion" that she was recruiting for "underground work in Italy."[24]

The pair's first meeting was in Poyntz's room; a "gentleman" was also there, but Bentley did not indicate if she was introduced to him. The meeting was short; and after a brief conversation with Poyntz, Bentley left. She said that she saw Poyntz and the unnamed gentleman again at dinner, but her deposition to the FBI did not mention the purpose of the dinner or any conversation during it. Bentley saw Poyntz again twice but did not indicate to the FBI that she ever again had any significant contact with her or with the gentleman. In 1937, she learned that Poyntz had disappeared, with some "indication that she had been kidnapped by NKVD agents." She read a newspaper story alleging that Schachno Epstein, a "prominent European," had been involved and that Poyntz had never been heard from since.[25]

By this time Bentley was involved with Golos, who encouraged her to cut off contacts with fellow communists and focus on her work as an informant in the Italian propaganda organization. Bentley told the FBI that she had mentioned Poyntz during her first meeting with Golos, and he responded by claiming that she was a "German Agent" and had been "liquidated." "In his circles," he said, when someone went missing, people noted "that so and so" was "playing pinochle." Bentley mentioned the disappearance to Louis Sass, the head of the Harlem Section of the CPUSA, who also called Poyntz a German spy.[26]

On the whole, Bentley's 1945 deposition did not concentrate much attention on Poyntz. While she claimed to have learned about the alleged murder just as she was entering the underground, that news did not appear to concern her much or affect her actions. Nor did Poyntz merit any detailed description, though the FBI agent did make a note of the deposition in Poyntz's FBI file. This lack of detail stands in stark contrast to the narrative that Bentley constructed in her 1951 memoir *Out of Bondage,* in which Poyntz evolved from a side note to a sexually corrupted, aggressive, terrifying communist agent.

The text of the book first appeared in serial form in *McCall's,* a popular women's magazine. According to Olmsted, Bentley portrayed herself in these excerpts as a "sort of Communist June Cleaver," playing down her "spinsterhood" by portraying her long-term relationship with Golos as a marriage. She tried to depict herself as a "conventional housewife" who "meekly obeyed her 'husband.'" She claimed they regretted never having had children together and thus settling into a proper family life. She made no mention of her many sexual liaisons, instead describing herself as a "defender of traditional sexual morality." As her biographers have demonstrated, Bentley was no dupe, no matter how she appeared in the media. She was the primary author of her own story, and her memoir proved that she was "shrewd enough" to write and rewrite her narrative as she saw fit.[27]

Bentley, however, was not solely responsible for *Out of Bondage*'s writing. Her first draft was allegedly rewritten by the poet John Gilland Brunini, a prominent Catholic anti-communist and the jury foreman during the William Remington hearings. (Bentley had accused him of spying.) At this time Bentley was desperate for income as she was unable to hold down steady employment while in service to the federal government. According to her, Brunini suggested writing the book. Certainly, she had been floating the idea of a memoir for years, but the FBI had made it clear they did not want her to publish a tell-all. Though Brunini denied writing the finished manuscript, evidence suggests that he at least did a very heavy revision. Olmsted documents a letter Bentley wrote to Brunini describing her frustration about his slow progress. The biographer also believes that Thomas Sloane, the editor at Devin-Adair Publishing Company, played a large role in sculpting the manuscript. The two helped to write a memoir "aimed at female readers," constructing a melodramatic narrative in which Bentley appeared to be a victim of the communist apparatus, not what she actually was: one of its functionaries.[28]

In the book, Bentley claimed that Pauline Rogers warned her not to speak about Poyntz with others because she was in "direct contact" with underground anti-fascists in Italy, and talk could make her and them vulnerable. This information contradicts what Bentley told the FBI, when she said she did not know anything about Poyntz's work. In the book version, Rogers introduced Bentley to Poyntz at tea and then quickly excused herself, leaving the others alone together. Bentley's unflattering description of Poyntz is reminiscent of the media's characterization of Bentley herself: a "rather heavy-set woman" with a shapeless "brown hat" and "non-descript brown tweed coat," "straggly brown hair," and a "rather plain face." When Poyntz tried to ease the awkwardness created by Rogers's quick departure, Bentley did note that she had "beautiful brown eyes."[29] She also described Poyntz somewhat sympathetically as a "widow" with "cultured" speech, which she incorrectly labeled as a New England accent. While there is no question that Poyntz's looks did not match the prevailing stereotype of female spies, many who knew her claimed that the force of her personality often overpowered any awareness of her physical appearance. Bentley, however, had been publicly humiliated on that point many times over. Now she turned the tables and did the same to Poyntz.[30]

Poyntz's appearance may have been unremarkable, but the book made it clear that her behavior as a Soviet spy was not. In the pair's next few meetings, Bentley recalled far more interaction than she had mentioned to the FBI in 1945. During one session, for instance, Poyntz offered her a highball, mocking her as a "Puritan" when she refused a second drink. Bentley, the notorious alcoholic, primly explained that she "just didn't like alcohol." During the meeting, Poyntz went on to describe underground work in Europe, saying that women agents had to perform "unpleasant tasks," which included "drinking and sleeping with many men." Thus, in the space of a page, Poyntz morphed from a plain, bookish woman to a sexually promiscuous, hard-drinking female spy.[31]

Bentley's feigned disgust is amusing. She claimed that she had never seen herself as a "prude," but she was "nauseated" by Poyntz's "choice of subjects" and her "obvious relish" in describing them. She said that the "ugly details" seemed straight out of a "lurid book," and Poyntz took "morbid delight" in describing them as Bentley tried desperately to move away from the subject. Laughing, Poyntz called her a "hothouse flower," counseling her that if she wanted to work in the underground, she would have to accept them as part of her work. As Olmsted notes, the book is filled with such "improbable moments." Though Bentley described herself as an "innocent schoolgirl" "appalled" by the communists' "flouting of traditional sexual mores," she was well acquainted with hard drinking and sexual promiscuity.[32]

Throughout the book, Bentley returned to the theme of sexual prudishness, setting herself up as a defender of "traditional sexual morality." She was particularly blunt about this in her narrative about an underground agent named Mary Price, who was beginning to find the work "dehumanizing and isolating." Bentley agreed; she wrote that people in the underground were not "living like human beings," so she tried to help Price return to open party work. Golos, however, told her that the Soviets had another task in mind for Price. Because she was "attractive and single" as well as "intelligent and a trusted worker" they wanted to set her up in an apartment with nice clothes and prostitute her to men who might be "useful to the cause."[33]

The story of Mary Price appeared in several forms over the course of Bentley's life. A 1944 Soviet telegram confirms that she really did try to get Price out of the underground, but the Soviets suspected this was because she "did not like Mary." Price herself claimed that Bentley wanted her out because Price had "rejected her homosexual advances." In the version of the story that appears in Bentley's 1945 FBI deposition, Price saved herself. In the 1951 book version, Golos was appalled that the Soviets expected him to set up Price as a prostitute. Bentley wrote that they accused him of being a "sentimentalist" while she "struggle[ed] with a wave of disgust." In another improbable scene, Bentley noted she had no idea the party "used women" as prostitutes, though Poyntz had already told her that in an earlier section of the book. In other words, Golos and Bentley, an unmarried couple, were presented as defenders of American morality, particularly women's sexual purity, against their corrupt Soviet handlers. Golos made Bentley promise not to let the Soviets get Price into their clutches, and he swore to "fight this thing to the end." Bentley wrote that she was so shaken by the episode that she lay awake remembering what Poyntz had told her: that communism could cost a woman not just her soul but her body as well.[34] These contradictions in the text and Bentley's feigned disgust at so-called immoral behavior cast doubt on both her memory of the incidents and her reliability as a witness.

Throughout the book, Bentley continued to describe Poyntz in the most unlikable of terms. Poyntz, she wrote, was a stern disciplinarian and a bully, who mocked Bentley and told her that she needed to exhibit "sterner stuff" if she wanted to be a "good revolutionary." According to the book, even before their early interactions, Bentley was trying to avoid Poyntz, but she could not locate Rogers to convey the message. So she decided to meet with Poyntz again; and if she did not have any actual anti-fascist work for Bentley to do, she would walk away.[35]

Bentley repeatedly emphasized her doubts about working with Poyntz. During one interaction, she wondered if Poyntz was crazy or drunk. So if Poyntz had turned her away from any interest in underground work, why did she become involved anyway? One answer is that Bentley and possibly her male ghostwriters were creating a narrative in which she served as a pawn in other people's games. Meek and easily manipulated, this version of Bentley had little control over her own actions. Without a male figure to keep her in line, she made dangerous decisions without understanding their consequences. It was the ultimate deferential female role. This was certainly intentional and perhaps written by her male ghostwriters.[36]

In his interview with Herbert Solow, Poyntz's recruit Mark Graubard mentioned a Soviet general known to him as "Phillips." This figure appeared in Bentley's book as "Mr. Smith." Bentley met Smith at Poyntz's apartment, where he offered to take the women out to dinner. Bentley described it as one of the most "unpleasant evenings" she ever had. Smith was "amorous," moving close to her on the couch at the apartment and ogling her at dinner while Poyntz sat by looking amused. After Smith left, Poyntz told Bentley that Smith wanted to give her a better-paying job so that she could help in the underground.[37] Among other communists, Phillips/Smith had a reputation for sexually assaulting women, so this scenario may well have been true. If so, it implicates Poyntz in his behavior. Yet she was an activist with a long history as a women's rights advocate. Graubard found it unlikely that she would have approved of such behavior; and when he confronted Phillips about it, the general dismissed Poyntz as his lackey. So Phillips might have behaved like a predator toward Bentley, but there is doubt as to whether he would have done so in front of Poyntz.[38]

Disgusted by Smith's behavior, Bentley refused the job offer, claiming that her position at the Home Relief Bureau would soon put her on the civil service rolls with job security and a pay raise. Poyntz was immediately alarmed; she warned Bentley not to go on the rolls because that action would require fingerprinting. Bentley's supposed response revealed a naïveté that one would not expect from a grown woman. Bentley, who knew Poyntz worked in the underground, became confused as to why Poyntz would object to her being fingerprinted. While she decided that Poyntz was not insane, she was scared by her "ugly talk" of the underground and Poyntz's claim that Bentley "didn't behave the way a Communist should." She instantly tried to break with Poyntz, but the recruiter continued to hound her, even showing up unannounced at her apartment a month later. At this meeting Bentley told Poyntz she had already been fingerprinted. Poyntz called her a "fool" and left.[39]

In her book, Bentley wrote that she now decided to go to Columbia to pursue a graduate degree in sociology. This led to her reassignment to the university's CPUSA unit. One day, while she was with her friend Lee Fuhr and two other communist women, she spotted Poyntz having lunch with a party member named Land. Fuhr was surprised to see Land and Poyntz together and told Bentley that Poyntz was "no good." According to Fuhr, Poyntz had tried to lure her into the underground, offering to fund her education in nursing so that Fuhr could become useful to the communist movement. Fuhr declined the offer, claiming that she had an "uncanny feeling" that she should not accept it. With some hesitation, she told Bentley that Poyntz had been too eager. As a nurse, Fuhr was familiar with the "queer quirks" of people. She believed that Poyntz was a "homo," and she "didn't want to be mixed up in anything like that."[40]

By accusing Poyntz of being a homosexual, Bentley was invoking another specter for Cold War audiences: sexual perversion. For her contemporary readers, normative sexuality was strictly heterosexual; anything else was a threat to the American social and political order. As the historian Jane Sherron DeHart writes, "strict boundaries" had to be erected to prevent "gender revolution, illicit sexuality, especially homosexuality, and . . . race-mixing." Anti-communist ideologues warned that homosexuality was a disease that would "weaken the nation from within." They labeled homosexuals as deviants and thus easy targets for the Soviets, who could recruit them by threatening to reveal their sexuality. As a result of such arguments, the State Department and other government agencies purged homosexuals from their staffs.[41]

The historian K. A. Cuordileone argues that the Cold War was permeated with a "dualistic imagery" that portrayed anti-communism as "masculine toughness" and anything else as soft and feminine. This "heightened concern" with masculinity further fueled anti-homosexuality. In contrast to female spies, who were stereotyped as hypersexual and deviant, the quintessential anti-communist private investigator showed "contempt for things effete," such as "intellectuals, professionals, homosexuals, and the 'pansy' bureaucracy" that tied law-and-order's hands. "Fears of sexual disorder" were powerful because they could be easily personalized. Amid the social changes taking place among women and minorities and the increasing visibility of homosexuals, a conservative emphasis on nuclear family and a renewed celebration of "American manhood" appeared ever more urgent.[42]

Bentley did not simply allege that Poyntz was homosexual; she also accused her of being an adulterer. In the book, she tells the tale of Meg Hinkley, who was outside the restaurant with Fuhr and Bentley. According to Bentley, Land had introduced Meg and her husband Bill to Poyntz shortly after they had joined the CPUSA. Poyntz wanted their help in some "project she was engaged in," but they were disturbed when she began making passes at Bill. Meg became distraught when she saw Poyntz with Land. The group of women decided that there was something wrong with Poyntz and that they should investigate to see if she might be a counterrevolutionary sent into party ranks to "corrupt the comrades." But the investigation came to nothing, and Poyntz "disappeared" from the Columbia campus.[43]

Bentley may have been recounting a real incident, but it reads as gaslighting. She painted Poyntz as not only bisexual but also as a woman who was willing to have an affair with a comrade's husband—a level of sexual deviance that surely no good American could forgive. More importantly, by describing Poyntz as deviant she linked Soviet communism to deviance. At the same time, she set herself up as a contrasting paradigm of sexual and moral virtue, though she had lived with a married man for years and had been accused of coming on to other women. Bentley had decided that Poyntz would take the fall. Who was left to challenge her?

According to the book, Bentley had no more contact with Poyntz until they ran into each other on a trolley car in the spring of 1936. Bentley, now committed to investigating Poyntz as a counterrevolutionary, set up a tea date with her. She then told Louis Sass about her suspicions. After asking the local leadership, he, too, came to believe that Poyntz was a counterrevolutionary and said that no one at the district center had ever heard of her. This is hard to believe, given that she had been a visible party leader for years. Sass instructed Bentley to bring along a young party member named Comrade C to confront Poyntz. When Comrade C accused Poyntz of being a counterrevolutionary, her face went "chalk white," and she had a look of "naked terror" in her eyes. There seemed to be a man in the apartment's back room, which made Bentley more nervous. When Poyntz turned angrily toward Bentley, Comrade C pushed her out of the apartment, and the two dramatically fled to find a telephone and inform Sass of what had happened.[44]

Days later Poyntz appeared at Bentley's door with Pauline Rogers and launched into a "vituperative diatribe," accusing Bentley of being a counterrevolutionary and a "Trotskyite." Bentley was shaken. The visitors at her house described her as "white as a ghost" and "trembling" so much she could not even light her own cigarette. Bentley never saw her again.[45]

Poyntz was Bentley's first, but not last, contact with the Soviet underground. Others confirmed for her that Poyntz had worked for the OGPU and had recruited young "innocents" for underground tasks. She learned from a Soviet agent that Poyntz was now herself "six feet under," where she had once threatened to put Bentley. And when Bentley began to consider her own defection from the underground, she remembered what had happened to dissenters such as Poyntz.[46]

The sales of *Out of Bondage* were "disappointing." Writing for the *New York Times*, John Oakes described the book as "surprisingly dull," offering little information about what exactly she had passed on to the Soviets while working in the underground. He described the writing as not "particularly interesting, exciting, or convincing," though Bentley did at times describe things in "theatrical terms." He had expected more from a "spy thriller" but instead found a narrative similar to those of other former communists.[47] Joseph Alsop opened his review in *Commonweal* by saying that it was difficult to decide whether the text was "tragic, or . . . ludicrous, or . . . terrifying, or . . . . pathetic." To him, the book had a "smell of phoniness," making it difficult to take seriously, yet he acknowledged that it was a "symptom of our times." Bentley, in his view, was an "obviously" unstable person who had joined the party out of "loneliness and frustration." He questioned her depiction of her disillusionment, refusing to believe that a woman who had been a CPUSA member for ten years and had worked in its underground could remain so naïve about the party and its links to Moscow.[48] Adopting much of the language then used to describe her, he took issue with the book's "girly" tone and the way in which its most important information (what her Washington contacts had given her to pass on to Moscow) was stated in "femininely vague" terms. Alsop remained unconvinced that a "professional spy" had not known or cared about what she was handing over to the Soviets. He rejected the sentimental tropes of innocence in which she cloaked herself. Nonetheless, he did believe the general outline of the story and offered some sympathy for what Bentley had endured. It was her alleged victimhood and naïveté he could not savor.[49]

The CPUSA press derided Bentley, describing her as part of a professional anti-communist apparatus tasked with undermining the party and its goals of gender, race, and class equality. Party spokespeople claimed that her "elastic memory" often shocked even "conservative" Americans, and they savored news stories that exposed her falsehoods. Articles alleged that she, Chambers, Budenz, and others belonged to an anti-communist informer racket and reviled them as stoolpigeons for the FBI. They noted that the jury foreman in the Remington trial had helped to write her memoir and suggested that her publisher was a "smut house." The party released a satirical book announcement for *Out of Bondage* in which a "federal district attorney" would provide illustrations, a judge would compose its accompanying screenplay, and federal court judges would own its television serialization rights. Party leadership saw Bentley as an "unstable" element in the anti-communist machinery.[50]

Despite Bentley's best efforts, attacks on her appearance and her lifestyle continued. In his 1952 study of HUAC, the law professor and political scientist Robert Carr demonstrated how difficult it was to move beyond midcentury constructions of femininity. According to Wilson, he reduced Bentley to the level of a "frumpish" and "romantically insecure spinster."[51] In the book, he pasted her with the label of "ex-spy queen," following the lead of the *New York World-Telegram*. In Carr's view, Bentley had first stepped out of her womanly role in the 1930s, when she tried to "lead the life of an intellectual." Instead, she became "a sadly confused idealist . . . used by persons shrewder and cleverer than herself." While Carr saw her as Chambers's "feminine counterpart" and acknowledged that their testimony was "not dissimilar," he described her narrative as filled with "confusion and naivete," a contrast to Chambers's "assurance and sophistication." Yet Carr also noted that the committee had privileged Chambers's testimony over Bentley's and that some of the people she had named went uninvestigated.[52]

Commentators continued to focus on Bentley's unmarried status and her affairs with married men. For instance, according to Wilson, the historian John Patrick Diggins (in *The Proud Decades: American in War and Peace, 1941–1960)* regurgitated old and "unsubstantiated rumors" about her motivations for joining the Communist Party and the underground, which he called an attempt to find "male companionship." Thus, once Golos (one of her few long-term relationships) died, he found it natural for her to switch her loyalties to the FBI. Yet such representations were not solely constructed by others; Wilson argues that some were the result of Bentley's own machinations. Starting with her testimony, she worked to represent herself as a naïve victim. She allowed the committee members to make assumptions about "her passivity and irrationality" and "reinforced . . . sexist and simplistic assumptions." She continued to do so in her memoir, purposely choosing terms that would resonate with a Cold War reading audience.[53]

Aware that sexual purity and teetotaling were not enough to solidify her obeisance to gendered expectations, Bentley eventually claimed that a "religious experience" had motivated her to approach the FBI. In 1948, encouraged by Budenz, she converted to Catholicism. Yet she was influenced more by the hope of creating ties with the "anti-communist lobby" than by "ideology," and she found it difficult to forge a career in Catholic anti-communism. After her conversion, she used her connections with religious leaders to land a teaching job at Mundelein College, a Catholic institution for women in Chicago. But she did not last long in the job: she was fired for living with a man and for "loose morals," which Olmsted suspects also referred to her alcoholism. Because she could not hold down a regular job and her book sales were not strong, Bentley repeatedly asked the FBI to help her with money. But her personal struggles were making her a liability: she was ignoring subpoenas to testify, and the FBI was forced to negotiate to get her cooperation. As her life continued its downward spiral, she became less manageable and more demanding. In 1955, when Harvey Matusow admitted to lying on the stand about his communist past, he also accused Bentley of lying. That same year, the IRS confiscated her bank accounts because she had failed to pay taxes on her book royalties. In 1963, after years of struggling to stay afloat, she died of abdominal cancer at the age of fifty-five.[54]

Bentley's life was characterized by turbulence, depression, and alcoholism. While her legacy is connected to her personal struggles, gender assumptions continue to influence her place in recorded history. She herself may not have recognized that she was deeply embedded within a gendered system that had set her up to fail, but it is clear she could never have been as successful as her male peers were. Her story as well as the narrative she crafted about Poyntz are a reminder that women often devote themselves to the very expectations that confine and limit them.

CONCLUSION

What did happen to Juliet Stuart Poyntz? Was she kidnapped in Central Park, taken to some remote location, and murdered? Was she spirited to the Soviet Union, held in a gulag, and eventually executed? Did the Nazis kill her? Did George Mink lure her to the Soviet Union? Did Schachno Epstein do the deed? Did her handler Lena tell the Soviets that Poyntz was a threat? Was she interrogated or summarily killed? Did she suffer? Was she aware of the danger she was in? Or did she assume another name, go into hiding, and live to an advanced age unmolested? Was her end not so remarkable at all?

We will probably never be able to answer these questions or prove anything with actual evidence. But in Cold War America, what really happened to Poyntz quickly became less important than the *meaning* of what had happened to her. When Carlo Tresca accused the CPUSA of killing his friend on Soviet orders, he laid the foundation for a narrative that lasted well into the Cold War years and even into the present. Thanks to his dogged efforts to get Poyntz's name before the American public and her case into the hands of law enforcement, he made her a lasting influence on conservatives and former Marxists and linked his own fate to hers forever. Long after her disappearance and his own murder, Poyntz would be invoked regularly as proof that a communist evil was lurking to undermine American institutions.

In 1951, the British Trotskyite Hugo Dewar published *Assassins at Large*, a study of Soviet assassinations. Dewar had been a life-long socialist but became a committed anti-Stalinist after he was expelled from the British Communist Party in 1931. He devoted an entire chapter of his book to Poyntz's disappearance. Titled "The Lady Vanishes," it revealed nothing new, but Dewar quoted Tresca at length as well as Budenz and Gitlow. His account was modeled closely on Tresca's, linking Poyntz's disappearance to the Robinson-Rubens case and suggesting that Tresca's assassination might have been retribution for his accusations against the party. In the chapter, Dewar cited several Soviet defectors who claimed that the foreign parties under the Comintern were subservient to Moscow, thus suggesting that the CPUSA was implicated in her disappearance. His account is a verbatim version of the story that Tresca and Solow were circulating in the prewar years and that Budenz and Gitlow repeated without reservation. During the Cold War years, everyone took it for granted that Poyntz had been murdered by the Soviets.[1]

In 1953, Grace Lumpkin, a former communist fellow traveler and the wife of Mike Intrator (the man who appeared on Solow's doorstep with Whittaker Chambers in 1938), testified before the U.S. Senate's Permanent Subcommittee on Investigations, telling its members that for a time she had been under "Communist Discipline" and was therefore guilty of the party's crimes. She believed that being even "remotely connected with the party" meant that you "g[a]ve your inner consent to murder." Leaving the party did not cleanse a person of the "underlying corruptions" that had occurred in the subconscious. Although Lumpkin did not tell the subcommittee what murder she was guilty of, she did tell the *Chicago Daily Tribune* that she had been referring to Poyntz's. It is interesting to note that she did not tell the committee because that could have made her liable to perjury, but airing her suspicions to the press carried no risk. Lumpkin was not confessing to pulling the trigger—if indeed there had been a trigger. Instead, she was claiming that all communists were guilty by association, an assumption that lawmakers commonly made about rank-and-file communists throughout the Cold War.[2]

In 1955, the conservative journalist Ralph de Toledano fictionalized Poyntz's murder in his anti-communist novel *Day of Reckoning,* which focused on Tresca's assassination and attempts to find the killer. In the novel, Poyntz's murder is taken for granted and is the precipitating event for Tresca's. De Toledano accused communists of both murders and claimed that the women's rights and civil rights movements were fronts for communism, a popular prejudice among Americans, but also a dangerous one, given that FBI Director J. Edgar Hoover was expending a great deal of energy on trying to make the same link.[3]

Day of Reckoning had a lukewarm reception and seems to have been largely ignored, though de Toledano (incorrectly) blamed the unpopularity of anti-communism as a reason for poor sales. In the *New York Times,* the anti-communist Granville Hicks wrote a short, lackluster review, offering no analysis of the text other than noting that it contained events "reminiscent" of Tresca's murder and Poyntz's disappearance. Despite these "historical parallels," he concluded, the book belonged in the category of "manufactured melodrama." George Sokolsky, de Toledano's friend and a committed conservative journalist, tried to make a case for the book in his nationally syndicated column. The value of *Day of Reckoning*, he argued, was that it told the reader how these things were done. He tried to sell the novel as a piece of history, one that confirmed anti-communist claims that communism was violent.[4]

In an undated document, Joseph Freeman, a communist intellectual and a former editor of the *New Masses,* wrote about a run-in he had had with Tresca over the Poyntz case. At the time of her disappearance, Freeman was an active, well-connected member of the CPUSA. In his recollections, he noted that he had also been a long-time friend of Schachno Epstein, whom he had known since he "was a boy." He met Poyntz through Epstein and once went on an outing to New Jersey with the two of them, along with a third person, unnamed, who was carrying a gun. When asked why, the unnamed man showed it to Freeman, telling him it was a fake to scare people off. During the next few months, Epstein visited Freeman frequently to check on "whether he [had] got on to something," and Freeman was suspicious of his friend's actions. Soon thereafter, Poyntz disappeared and Epstein's visits ended.[5]

Freeman believed that Fiorello La Guardia, the former mayor of New York City, had asked Tresca to investigate what had happened to Poyntz. Tresca apparently felt that Freeman might have been an "innocent" accomplice or at least knew something about her disappearance, so he visited him regularly. Trying to get Freeman to spill, Tresca "begged, talked and threatened," but Freeman apparently knew nothing, although he accepted Tresca's allegations that Epstein must have been involved in Poyntz's murder. On Tresca's last visit, he asked Freeman to walk with him to Bryant Park. In the park, Freeman noticed that Tresca had arranged for two men to listen in on their conversation and take notes. Angered, he left. For a time, Tresca continued to make threatening telephone calls, and Freeman continued to claim he knew nothing. It is remarkable, however, that he accepted Tresca's accusations against his childhood friend.[6]

In 1983, David Lesser, a former communist who was obsessed with the Soviet secret police presence in the United States, penned a sensational account of Poyntz's murder. In an unpublished manuscript titled "The Extenders: A True Memoir of the Actual State of Things," he claimed to be the last person to see Poyntz alive. According to him, on an unusually warm day in January 1938, a full seven months after she had gone missing and a month after newspapers reported her disappearance, Lesser saw a woman walking on a pier along the Hudson River. She was accompanied by Professor Rauch, a teacher at New York University and a well-known communist. Lesser described her as several inches taller than Rauch, simply and "conservatively dressed," and smoking. She apparently smiled at Lesser as they walked past.[7]

Lesser had been reading Tresca's and Solow's articles, and it occurred to him that the woman with Rauch might have been Poyntz. He went to the Rand School's library and looked through old copies of the *Socialist Call* in search of pictures, which confirmed for him that Poyntz was the woman he had seen on the pier. (Apparently he was not concerned that the pictures were more than twenty-five-years old and the incident took place months after Poyntz went missing.) Fearing for his own safety, Lesser told no one. In his manuscript, he claimed that his silence triggered a nervous breakdown.[8]

Former Soviet agents also fueled the Poyntz mystery with difficult-to-prove claims. Walter Krivitsky, the Soviet secret police operative for whom Poyntz had worked as a recruiter, defected to the United States in 1937 and was found dead in 1941 from an assumed suicide that anti-communists alleged was actually a political hit. Before his death he claimed that Poyntz had been General Viovt Putna's lover and that she had been killed soon after he was liquidated in the USSR. Chambers, too, had mentioned Putna, linking him to the Poyntz and Robinson-Rubens cases. But Krivitsky also admitted that he had no evidence of the connection and said he was just repeating a rumor he had heard in the underground.[9]

Alexander Vassiliev, a former KGB agent, teamed up with the historians Harvey Klehr and John Earl Haynes on two books about the operations of the Soviet underground in the United States. While doing research in the KGB archives, he found some interesting information. When Elizabeth Bentley defected to the FBI, Moscow Center (a euphemism for KGB headquarters) ran a check on Poyntz's history. These documents alleged that in October 1934 she was recruited by the Intelligence Directorate

Red Army (GRU) in Moscow, and in November she returned to the United States to begin her work in the underground. She traveled again to Moscow in November 1936 and remained there until February 1937, when she returned to the United States. Tresca believed that she was interrogating show trial witnesses with Mink during this time. Presumably at some point between February and June 1937, when she was last seen, Poyntz met with a GRU representative. The documents declared that the "circumstances of her disappearance" were not known to Moscow Center. Klehr, Haynes, and Vassiliev believe that this statement "strengthens" suspicions that the GRU had her killed because the documents purposely distanced the Soviets from knowledge of her whereabouts.[10]

Poyntz's disappearance has intrigued journalists as well. In 1967, marking the thirtieth anniversary of the mystery, Richard Sterling published an article in the *New York Independent* about the case, along with a reprint of Poyntz's passport picture (which today widely circulates on the Internet) and an image of her 1934 face-off with Mayor La Guardia. Sterling noted other unusual events linked to Poyntz and her family, mentioning a missing file at the Masonic home where her father died and a 1937 fire at her sister's home that destroyed most of the family's personal effects, including pictures of Poyntz. In fact, however, the Masonic home still possesses a file on J. J. Points, which includes his cause of death, thus raising suspicions about Sterling's research. The journalist did reflect on Poyntz's place in "American memory," noting that her name still came up occasionally in the press but that the Communist Party had been successful in "erasing all trace of her and her past." Now, he lamented, Poyntz only lived on in the writings of the "past and the memories" of those who had known her.[11]

Sterling was not wrong. Well into the 1970s Poyntz's name regularly came up whenever anti-communists wanted to highlight the bad behavior of communists. In an article about keeping American intelligence agencies up to date on Soviet weapons technology, the journalist Gerald Raftery listed the KGB murders that had occurred on U.S. soil, including Poyntz's and Krivitsky's. The anti-feminist conservative Phyllis Schlafly invoked Poyntz's murder in an article about the 1976 assassination of General Joaquin Zenteno Anaya in Paris. Anaya had been in charge of the Bolivian army in Santa Cruz, where Che Guevara was captured and killed. Schlafly believed that Anaya's killing was proof that an international communist assassination squad was still in operation, and she cited Poyntz's disappearance and Krivitsky's alleged murder as evidence that such squads had been operating for a long time. She concluded by warning readers that communists made murder "highly profitable," using it to intimidate their opponents and secure their goal of worldwide conquest.[12]

In 1988, Dorothy Gallagher had published a book about Tresca and noted his obsession with the Poyntz case. Two years later, she used Poyntz's FBI file as the basis for her essay "Disappeared." Gallagher's piece focused on the strange narrative of Mary Delmar/Lena/Tina and also briefly considered Tresca's accusations against the Communist Party. While the essay did not reveal any new information, it did share the Poyntz mystery with a new audience. Nearly two decades later, in June 2017, the *Liberty Conservative,* an online journal, published Ron Capshaw's short synopsis of the case, which also served as an attack on so-called Stalin apologists in academia. The article revealed the enduring appeal of anti-communist hysteria among American conservatives, with Capshaw insisting, without evidence, that we "know the culprits." He did recognize what many had forgotten in the eighty years since Poyntz's disappearance: that her case had far-reaching consequences.[13]

By 2018, at a time of weakened American leadership, the Russian secret service appeared to be at it again: killing its former agents abroad with no fear of consequences. In March, the former spy Sergei Skripal and his daughter were poisoned in England with a Russian nerve agent. (They both survived.) Then in April, Poyntz's name returned to the public eye when Masha Gessen, writing for the *New Yorker,* likened the Skripals' attempted assassinations to Stalin's Great Terror. Gessen evoked Trotsky's assassination in Mexico, which took place at a time when the Soviets often "killed suspected traitors"—for instance, the American communist Juliet Stuart Poyntz.[14] Such accounts assume that Poyntz's disappearance was, without doubt, murder at the hands of the Soviet secret police. Even historians have accepted this version of events.[15]

As a foundational narrative, Poyntz's story proved to Cold War anti-communists that communism was against democracy. With that assumption, they did not require actual evidence in order to indict the Soviets and, by extension, American communists. In addition, her story highlighted midcentury American anxiety about changing gender roles. If containing communism was an imperative, containing women in heterosexual familial institutions was a way to do so. That is why linking demands for social change to communism weakened the left, including the women's and civil rights movements. Yet fears around Poyntz's disappearance also demonstrated that members of the American left were as quick as the right to link communists to assumed crimes. Anti-Stalinists such as Tresca were central to the creation and reification of Cold War anti-communism, and at the heart of this imagining was Juliet Stuart Poyntz: not the woman, the communist, or the devoted social justice activist, but the victim—the terrified, defenseless, middle-aged "girl." Amid their hatred of and anxiety about Stalin, anti-Stalinist leftists turned their backs on anti-racism, anti-sexism, and worker's rights, thus empowering the anti-communist right and the forces that were working to undermine civil rights.

When Poyntz walked out of her boardinghouse into that June night, she walked into one of the most enduring stories in anti-communist history. Her disappearance inspired a generation of American Marxists to move to the political right, with lasting consequences for the American left. The story of her alleged murder frightened Americans in the Soviet underground, and many who defected to become mouthpieces for a conservative anti-communism that continues to this day. Even as Poyntz the real woman has been forgotten and her friends and defenders have passed away, her name remains a powerful symbol. This makes it all the more important to give her the last word. As she reminded her union readers in 1918, though "tongues may be silenced," the "desire for a better world can never be crushed."[16]

NOTES

Introduction

1. "Plan Business Women's Clubhouse with 800 Rooms to Cost $2,500,000," *New York Times*, June 18, 1922; "Reception to Open Women's Clubhouse," *New York Times*, April 7, 1929; Elias Lieberman, "The Mysterious Disappearance of Juliet or a Lady Communist Vanishes (A True Story)," 2–3, Elias Lieberman Manuscript Collection, Kheel Center, Cornell University (hereafter cited as Lieberman Collection).
2. Federal Bureau of Investigation, memo, NY 100–59538, Sam Tanenhaus Papers, box 53, folder 1, Hoover Institution Archives, Stanford University (hereafter cited as Tanenhaus Papers).
3. Lieberman, "The Mysterious Disappearance of Juliet," 2–3; Federal Bureau of Investigation, "What Was the Fate of Red Julia Poyntz," February 8, 1962, Tanenhaus Papers, box 53, folder 1.
4. Andrew Meier, *The Lost Spy: An American in Stalin's Secret Service* (New York: Norton, 2008), 45.
5. Ellen Schrecker, *Many Are the Crimes: McCarthyism in America* (New York: Little, Brown, 1998); Landon Storrs, *The Second Red Scare and the Undoing of the New Deal Left* (Princeton, NJ: Princeton University Press, 2015); Michael Kimmage, *The Conservative Turn: Lionel Trilling, Whittaker Chambers, and the Lessons of Anti-Communism* (Cambridge, MA: Harvard University Press, 2009); Kirsten Marie Delegard, *Battling Miss Bolsheviki: The Origins of Female Conservatism in the United States* (Philadelphia: University of Pennsylvania Press, 2012); Kim E. Nielsen, *Un-American Womanhood: Antiradicalism, Antifeminism and the First Red Scare* (Athens: Ohio University Press, 2001).
6. Judy Kutulas, *The Long War: The Intellectual People's Front and Anti-Stalinism, 1930–1940* (Durham, NC: Duke University Press, 1995), 2–3, 14–17, 106–10, 112.
7. Schrecker, *Many Are the Crimes,* 112–41; Alan Wald, "Herbert Solow: Portrait of a New York Intellectual," *Prospects* 3 (October 1978): 421.
8. John Earl Haynes and Harvey Klehr, *Early Cold War Spies: The Espionage Trials That Shaped American Politics* (Cambridge: Cambridge University Press, 2006), 1, 6–10.
9. Ibid., 6–10.
10. Schrecker, *Many Are the Crimes,* 137.
11. Nick Fischer, *Spider Web: The Birth of American Anticommunism* (Urbana: University of Illinois Press, 2016); Delegard, *Battling Miss Bolsheviki,* 8.
12. Delegard, *Battling Miss Bolsheviki,* 8–9, 20; Storrs, *The Second Red Scare,* 12.
13. Delegard, *Battling Miss Bolsheviki,* 21, 28; Fischer, *Spider Web,* 7; Nielsen, *Un-American Womanhood,* 30.
14. Delegard, *Battling Miss Bolsheviki,* 22.

15. Storrs, *The Second Red Scare,* 12.
16. Nielsen, *Un-American Womanhood,* 10.
17. Kimmage, *The Conservative Turn,* 2–5.
18. Kathryn Olmsted, "Blond Queens, Red Spiders, and Neurotic Old Maids: Gender and Espionage in the Early Cold War," *Intelligence and National Security* 19, no. 1 (2004): 79.
19. Elaine Tyler May, *Homeward Bound: American Families in the Cold War* (New York: Basic Books, 2008); Robbie Lieberman, "The Long Black and Red Scare: Anti-Communism and the African American Freedom Struggle," in *Little Red Scares: Anti-Communism and Political Repression in the United States, 1921–1946,* ed. Robert Justin Goldstein (New York: Taylor and Francis, 2019), 266–67.

Chapter One: The Family

1. Douglas County Health Department, birth register, vol. 1, October 12, 1885–June 25, 1887, Omaha Public Library Archives, Omaha, NE (hereafter OPLA); Elias Lieberman, "The Mysterious Disappearance of Juliet or a Lady Communist Vanishes (A True Story)," 9, Lieberman Collection.
2. John Points, private, Boswell's Kentucky militia, volunteers, reference card, 1812, in index to "Compiled Service Records of Volunteer Soldiers Who Served during the War of 1812," RG 94, ser. M602, National Archives and Records Administration, Washington, DC (hereafter NARA).
3. John Points, private, Huston's battalion, mounted volunteers, enlistment card, 1794, in index to "Compiled Service Records of Volunteer Soldiers Who Served from 1784–1811," RG 84, Records of the Adjutant General's Office, 1962–84, ser. M905, NARA; John Points, Brookside, Indiana, April 15, 1823, U.S. General Land Office Records, 1796–1907, U.S. Bureau of Land Management, Eastern States, Springfield, VA.
4. Obituary of Thomas R. Points, *Westmoreland Recorder,* March 26, 1896.
5. "Index to Marriage Record," Delaware County, IN, 1827–1942.
6. "Biographical Sketch of Reverend T. R. Points," *Westmoreland Recorder,* January 3, 1907.
7. James Madison, *Hoosiers: A New History of Indiana* (Indianapolis: Indiana University Press, 2014), 72–73; "Biographical Sketch of Reverend T. R. Points," 3.
8. G. W. Kemper, ed., *A Twentieth-Century History of Delaware Country, Indiana* (Chicago: Lewis, 1908), 114.
9. John Points, land deeded to Thomas Points, June 2, 1841, Delaware County, Indiana, Delaware County Historical Society, Muncie, IN.
10. "Biographical Sketch of Reverend T. R. Points," 3.
11. James McPherson, *Battle Cry of Freedom: The Civil War Era* (Oxford: Oxford University Press, 1988), 145; "Biographical Sketch of Reverend T. R. Points," 3.
12. McPherson, *Cry of Freedom,* 152–53.
13. U.S. Bureau of the Census, population statistics, San Diego, California, 1920, in *Fourteenth Census of the United States,* NARA; "Biographical Sketch of Rev. T. R. Points," 3. The house was allegedly haunted by a man who had fired bricks during its

construction. He was murdered after a fight in a bar. The home is still remembered as haunted.

14. "Biographical Sketch of Rev. T. R. Points," 3.
15. Obituary of Thomas R. Points, 3.
16. "Mrs. Thomas Points Dead," *Westmoreland Register,* June 21, 1906.
17. "Kansas State Agricultural College" (Worcester, MA: American Antiquarian Society, 1865), 11; Kansas Office of the Census, agricultural statistics for Pottawatomie, 1860, Kansas State Historical Society Archives, Topeka.
18. "Kansas State Agricultural College" (Worcester, MA: American Antiquarian Society, 1877), 39; *Handbook of the Kansas State Agricultural College* (Worcester, MA: American Antiquarian Society, 1874), 1874; "Kansas State Agricultural College," *Walnut Valley Times,* August 4, 1871; "General News," *Hutchinson News,* March 12, 1910, 11.
19. "General News," 11; Kansas State Agricultural College, Alice Stewart's records, Hale Library Archive, Morse Department of Special Collections, Manhattan, KS.
20. W. David Baird and Danny Goble, *The Story of Oklahoma* (Norman: University of Oklahoma Press, 2007), 158.
21. Ibid., 158.
22. Marriage announcement for Charles Stewart and Juliette Slate, *Hartford Daily Courant,* November 1849; Marlynn Ann Fleck-O'Keefe, *Fort Towson Indian Territory: A Link to the West* (Towson, OK: Lakeside, 2001), 91–92.
23. Baird and Goble, *The Story of Oklahoma,* 158. Family lore holds that Charles and Juliette had five children; reportedly, two were twins, and both died as infants. Alice may have been named after one of her older dead siblings, but there is no evidence to support this story.
24. Ibid., 158; U.S. Bureau of the Census, population statistics, Hartford, Connecticut, 1860, in *Eighth Census of the United States,* NARA.
25. U.S. Bureau of the Census, population statistics, Riley, Kansas, 1870, in *Ninth Census of the United States,* NARA.
26. Lawrence H. Larsen and Barbara J. Cottrell, *The Gate City: A History of Omaha* (Lincoln: University of Nebraska Press, 1997), 5.
27. Omaha City Schools, "Annual Report of the Board of Education" (Omaha, NE: Herald), iv–v; *Omaha City Directory* [for 1874–75] (Omaha, NE: Wolfe, 1874), 195; *Centennial Brown's Directory of Omaha, Nebraska* (Omaha, NE: Brown, 1876), 233; *Wolfe's Omaha City Directory* [for 1878–79, 1879–80, 1880–81, 1881–82,1883–84] (Omaha, NE: Herald, 1878–1884), 236, 274, 278, 311, 304.
28. "Legislators," *Evening World Herald,* November 5, 1892; Omaha City Schools, "Eleventh Annual Report of the Board of Education of the City of Omaha" (Omaha, NE, 1884), 8–9.
29. Omaha City Schools, "Eleventh Annual Report, " 8–9.
30. "Index to Marriages in Douglas County, 1856–March 1905," book 10, 108, Archives of the Historical Society of Douglas County, Omaha, NE; Nebraska Office of the Census, population of Omaha, 1885, RG M352, NARA.

31. Omaha City Schools, "Annual Report of the Board of Education, 1886" (Omaha, NE: Rees, 1886), 9–12; Omaha School Board, "Annual Report of the Board of Education, Year Ending August 1, 1885" (Omaha, NE: Rees, 1886), vii–8.
32. Omaha City Schools, "Annual Report of the Board of Education, 1889" (Omaha, NE: Gibson, Miller, and Richardson, 1889), 1. The Points family home on South Twenty-Eighth Street no longer exists. By the 1930s, the neighborhood was in decline and, in the 1950s, parts were targeted for demolition to make way for a road that would eventually become Interstate 480. Thanks to vociferous opposition, half of the homes on the street were saved, but the highway lies where the Points home once stood. See Janet R. Daly-Bednarek, *The Changing Image of the City: Planning for Downtown Omaha, 1945–1973* (Lincoln: University of Nebraska Press, 1992), 152–54.
33. Douglas County Health Department, death register, vol. 2, July 3, 1887–November 29, 1887, OPLA; obituary of John Points, *Omaha Daily World*, August 29, 1887.
34. Douglas County Health Department, birth register, vol. 2, July 1, 1881–December 29, 1892, OPLA; Douglas County Health Department, death register, vol. 2, February 7, 1893–May 22, 1893, OPLA; Louis Baumann, "Prospect Hill Cemetery Burial Records from Earliest Known to December 31, 1975" (Omaha, NE: Greater Omaha Genealogical Society, 1977), record 5717. John and Charles were buried in unmarked graves in the Masonic Relief Section of Forest Lawn Memorial Park in Omaha.
35. Douglas County Health Department, birth register, vol. 2, July 1, 1881–December 29, 1892, OPLA.
36. "Douglas Democrats," *Omaha Daily World*, May 1, 1888.
37. Richard White, *It's Your Misfortune and None of My Own: A New History of the American West* (Norman: University of Oklahoma Press, 1991), 371–74.
38. "People's Independent," *Sunday World-Herald*, October 3, 1897.
39. Omaha City Schools, "Omaha Public Schools' Annual Reports, 1892" (Omaha, NE: Megeath, 1892), 5; Omaha City Schools, "Omaha Public Schools' Annual Reports, 1893" (Omaha, NE: Festner, 1893), 134; Omaha City Schools, "Omaha Public Schools' Annual Reports, 1894" (Omaha, NE: Klopp and Bartlett, 1895), 108; Omaha City Schools, "Omaha Public Schools' Annual Reports, 1895" (Omaha, NE: American Publishing Company, 1895), 139; *Omaha City Directory* [for 1896] (Omaha: NE: Omaha Printing Company, 1896), 427.
40. "Populist Delegates," *Omaha World-Herald*, September 21, 1900; "Douglas County Populists Offer State Platform Names Delegates and Requests Them to Push Resolutions," *Omaha World-Herald*, June 1, 1902; "Hitchcock Indorsed by Populist Convention Congressional Nominee of the Democrats Unanimously Nominated by Douglas County," *Omaha World-Herald*, October 9, 1904; "Official Canvas of the Vote of Douglas County," *Omaha World-Herald*, November 19, 1904.
41. *Omaha Directory Company's Omaha City Directory* [for 19014–15] (Omaha, NE: Omaha Directory Company, 722, 698; "Single Taxers Had No Fear of Hoodoo '23,"

Omaha World-Tribune, September 3, 1912; "Male Suffragists Form Organization," *Omaha World-Herald,* January 15, 1914.

42. "Kansas Deaths and Burials, 1885–1930," http://ancestry.com. It's not clear if the available death certificate for A. Stewart refers to Alice's brother, though the birth information matches.
43. U.S. Bureau of the Census, mortality statistics for Arkansas, 1880, *Tenth Census of the United States,* NARA; U.S. Bureau of the Census, population statistics for Township 6, Choctaw Nation, Indian Territory, 1900, *Twelfth Census of the United States,* NARA.
44. U.S. Bureau of the Census, population statistics for Hampden, MA, 1900, *Twelfth Census of the United States,* NARA.
45. "Woman Reds Are Accused of Slaying Had Been a J. C. Girl," *Jersey City Journal,* May 18, 1949; "School No. 9," *Jersey City Journal,* May 2, 1898.
46. "Society Notes," *Jersey City Journal,* March 30, 1903; "High School Class of 1903 Gives Dance," *Jersey City Journal,* February 14, 1903; "Society Notes," *Jersey City Journal,* April 7, 1903.
47. "Miss J. S. Points a Barnard Officer," *Jersey City Journal,* May 31, 1901.
48. Marian Churchill White, *A History of Barnard College* (New York: Columbia University Press, 1954), 15, 34; "1907 Elections," *Barnard Bulletin,* November 9, 1903; "Scenery Committee," *Barnard Bulletin,* November 2, 1903; "1907 Elections," *Barnard Bulletin,* April 11, 1904.
49. Mary E. Stoval, "The *Chicago Defender* in the Progressive Era," *Illinois Historical Journal,* 83, no. 3 (1990): 159.
50. "College Settlement Associations," *Barnard Bulletin,* December 8, 1906, 1.
51. "Silver Bay Conference," *Barnard Bulletin,* October 6, 1906.
52. Juliet Stewart Poyntz, valedictory speech, box 1, folder 1, Undergraduate Association Collection, Barnard College Archives and Special Collections, New York (hereafter cited as BCA).

Chapter Two: The Communist

1. "1907 Personals," *Barnard Bulletin,* October 2, 1907; Juliet Stuart Poyntz, alumna update, Alumnae Biographical Files Collection, box 1, folder 1, BCA; James S. Pula, "American Immigration Policy and the Dillingham Commission," *Polish American Studies* 37, no. 1 (1980): 7–8; Katherine Benton Cohen, *Inventing the Immigration Problem: The Dillingham Commission and Its legacy* (Cambridge, MA: Harvard University Press, 2018), 138–39, 163–66.
2. Poyntz, alumna update.
3. Ethel Pupper Howes, "College Equal Suffrage League Described by an Authority," *Columbia Daily Spectator,* November 1, 1915; Juliet Stuart Poyntz, "Resolution Submitted by Comrade Poyntz on Statement Made at CEC Meeting," May 12, 1925, 2,

Jay Lovestone Papers, box 204, folder 8, Hoover Institution Archives, Stanford University, Stanford, CA (hereafter cited as Lovestone Papers).

4. "Form League for Suffrage," *Post Standard* (Syracuse, NY), February 8, 1910.
5. "Prominent Speakers Who Will Be at Big Suffrage Convention," *Oakland Tribune,* March 9, 1910, "President Taft Hissed by Woman Suffragists," clipping from unidentified newspaper, April 15, 1910, Ann Lewis Women's Suffrage Collection, https://lewissuffragecollection.omeka.net; "Women Apologize to President Taft," *Ogden Daily Standard,* April 16, 1910.
6. Juliet Stuart Poyntz, "Suffragism and Feminism at Barnard," *Barnard Bear* 9, no. 7 (1914): 3–4.
7. Ibid., 4.
8. Juliet Stuart Poyntz, "Conditions among the Immigrants of Milwaukee, Wisconsin," master's thesis, Columbia University, 1, 4–5, Columbia University Archives, New York (hereafter cited as CUA).
9. Ibid,. 20–31, 32–50.
10. Ibid., 50–51.
11. "The Club Woman," *Sunday State Journal,* March 20, 1910; Elias Lieberman, "The Mysterious Disappearance of Juliet or a Lady Communist Vanishes (A True Story)," 2, Lieberman Papers; Juliet Stuart Poyntz, alumna card and appointment card, CUA.
12. "The Club Woman"; Poyntz, alumna update; "Society Notes," *Jersey City Journal,* June 28, 1911.
13. Poyntz, alumna update; Arthur Irwin, "Woman Red Leader Vanishes Here," *New York World Telegram,* December 17, 1937.
14. Arnold B. Van Bergen, "Juliet Stuart Poyntz," n.d., 1, Federal Bureau of Investigation Files, Washington, DC (hereafter cited as FBI Files); William B. Welte, Jr., "Juliet Stuart Poyntz," n.d., box 5, folder 1, 3, Tanenhaus Papers; Lieberman, "The Mysterious Disappearance," 10; marriage certificate of Frederick Franz Ludwig Glaser and Juliet Stuart Poyntz, 1913, New York City Municipal Archives, Department of Records and Information Services; Werner Abelshauser, Wolfgang von Hippel, Jeffrey Allan Johnson, and Raymond Stokes, *Germany Industry and Global Enterprise: BASF, the History of a Company* (Cambridge: Cambridge University Press, 2009), 215.
15. Nancy Cott, *Public Vows: A History of Marriage and the Nation* (Cambridge, MA: Harvard University Press, 2000), 143; Nancy Cott, "Marriage and Women's Citizenship in the United States, 1830–1934," *American Historical Review* 103, no. 5 (1998): 1470.
16. Lieberman, "The Mysterious Disappearance," 10–11, 26; Irwin, "Woman Red Leader Vanishes Here"; naturalization certificate for Juliet Stuert [sic] Glaser, *New York, New York County, Supreme Court Naturalization Petition Index, vol. 628, 1907–1924,* 198, http://ancestry.com.
17. Van Bergen, "Juliet Stuart Poyntz," 1.
18. Lieberman, "The Mysterious Disappearance," 26–27; John A. Salmond, *Gastonia, 1929: The Story of the Loray Mill Strike* (Chapel Hill: University of North Carolina Press, 2009), 82.

19. John L. Recchiuti, "The Rand School of Social Science during the Progressive Era: Will to Power of a Stratum of the Intellectual Class," *Journal of the History of the Behavioral Sciences* 31 (April 1995): 149, 152; "New Instructors," *Barnard Bulletin,* October 9, 1912; "Alumnae Notes," *Barnard Bulletin,* April 8, 1914; "Socialist-Feminist Scandal," *Barnard Bulletin,* October 11, 1915; Recchiuti, "The Rand School," 153, 155.
20. J. Dennis Chasse, "The American Association for Labor Legislation and the Institutionalist Tradition in National Health Insurance," *Journal of Economic Issues* 28, no. 4 (1994): 1065; "Question Twice Discussed," *Boston Globe,* February 2, 1915.
21. Lieberman, "The Mysterious Disappearance," 12–13; John Thomas Maguire, "Maintaining the Vitality of a Social Movement: Social Justice Feminism, and the Bryn Mawr Summer School for Women Workers, 1921–1924," *Pennsylvania History* 76, no. 4 (2009): 401.
22. Lieberman, "The Mysterious Disappearance," 14; "Report of the Ladies' Waist and Dressmakers' Union," box 1, folder 34, 12, International Ladies Garment Workers Union Manuscript Collection, Kheel Center, Cornell University, Ithaca, New York; Maguire, "Maintaining the Vitality of a Social Movement," 401, "Lone Woman in Strike Conference Urged Walkout," *Fort Wayne Daily News,* October 9, 1916; Susan Stone Wong, "From Soul to Strawberries: The International Ladies Garment Workers Union and Worker's Education, 1914–1950," in Joyce L. Kornbluh and Mary Frederickson, eds., *Sisterhood and Solidarity: Worker's Education for Women, 1914–1984* (Philadelphia: Temple University Press, 1984), 39.
23. "Lone Woman in Strike Conference"; Wong, "From Soul to Strawberries," 39–40.
24. Juliet Stuart Poyntz, "The Unity Movement—The Soul of a Union," in Kornbluh and Frederickson, *Sisterhood and Solidarity,* 59–60; Lieberman, "The Mysterious Disappearance," 14.
25. Wong, "From Soul to Strawberries," 44–45; Poyntz, "The Unity Movement," 58–59.
26. Poyntz, "The Unity Movement," 59–60.
27. Ibid., 59; Wong, "From Soul to Strawberries," 45–46.
28. Wong, "From Soul to Strawberries"; Juliet Stuart Poyntz, "The Feminist Revolution," *Message,* October 11, 1918.
29. Juliet Stuart Poyntz, "Why Should Women Vote?," *Message,* November 2, 1917.
30. Ibid.
31. Juliet Stuart Poyntz, "Victory?," *Message,* November 16, 1917; "Our Suffrage Jubilee," *Message,* November 16, 1917.
32. Carlo Tresca, "Where Is Juliet Stuart Poyntz?," *Modern Monthly* 10 (March 1938): 17; Tony Michels, *Jewish Radicals: A Documentary Reader* (New York: New York University Press, 2012), 256–57; Elias Lieberman, "Bon Voyage! My Dear Friend Epstein," *Message,* June 8, 1917; "The Operators', Tuckers', and Pressers' Branches Express Their Gratitude to Comrade S. Epstein," *Message,* June 22, 1917.
33. Juliet Stuart Poyntz, "Goodbye to *The Message,*" *Message,* January 3, 1919.
34. Wong, "From Soul to Strawberries," 40; Poyntz, "Goodbye to *The Message*"; Lieberman, "The Mysterious Disappearance," 19.

35. Lieberman, "The Mysterious Disappearance," 19–20; Harvey Klehr and John Earl Haynes, *Storming Heaven Itself: The American Communist Movement* (New York: Twayne, 1992), 15.
36. Klehr and Haynes, *Storming Heaven Itself,* 14–15.
37. Juliet Stuart Poyntz, "Industrial Peace and War," *Nation* 108, no. 2798 (1919): 246.
38. Juliet Stuart Poyntz, "The World and the Practical Man," *Nation* 113, no. 2928 (1921): 164.
39. Klehr and Haynes, *Storming Heaven Itself,* 19–23.
40. Lieberman, "The Mysterious Disappearance," 22–23; Klehr and Haynes, *Storming Heaven Itself,* 35.
41. Lieberman, "The Mysterious Disappearance," 24–25; Klehr and Haynes, *Storming Heaven Itself,* 35–37.
42. Marriage record of Eulalie Points and Raymond McClelland, 1911, http://ancestry.com; "Society Notes," *Jersey City Journal,* May 16, 1911.
43. Richard Sterling, "Juliet Stuart Poyntz: Red NKVD Agent from Omaha, Nebraska," *New York Independent,* August 21, 1967; "Missing Red Leader Sought," *Mansfield News Journal,* October 2, 1939.
44. Klehr and Haynes, *Storming Heaven Itself,* 40–41.
45. Ibid., 41; Robert Service, *A History of Twentieth-Century Russia* (Cambridge, MA: Harvard University Press, 2003): 154–55.
46. Service, *A History of Twentieth-Century Russia,* 106–107.
47. Lieberman, "The Mysterious Disappearance," 28; Klehr and Haynes, *Storming Heaven Itself,* 40–41.
48. Workers' Party of America (WPA), "Statement Regarding Comrade Juliet Stuart Poyntz," May 26, 1925, box 137, folder 2, 1, Herbert Romerstein Papers, Hoover Institution Archives, Stanford University, Stanford, CA (hereafter cited as Romerstein Papers. The statement is also archived with the Comintern Papers, FOND 515, DELO 366, 84.
49. Wong, "From Soul to Strawberries," 40; WPA, "Statement Regarding Comrade Juliet Stuart Poyntz," 2.
50. Poyntz, "Resolution Submitted by Comrade Poyntz," 1–3.
51. Benjamin Gitlow, *I Confess: The Truth about American Communism* (New York: Dutton, 1940), 249.
52. Juliet Stuart Poyntz, "Speech by Comrade Poyntz at CEC Meeting," May 13, 1925, box 204, folder 8, 1, Lovestone Papers.
53. Ibid., 2–3.
54. Gitlow, *I Confess,* 249.
55. "Poyntz Sheds Further Light on the History and Continuation of the Foster-Lore Alliance," n.d., box 204, folder 8, Lovestone Papers; Gitlow, *I Confess,* 252–53; "Poyntz Appointed to Women's Department and Poyntz's Appointment as Delegate to the Sixth World Congress," n.d., box 137, folder 2, Romerstein Papers; "Smaller Parties Present Platforms," *Barnard Bulletin,* October 30, 1925; "Candidates Nominated by the Workers' Party," *Syracuse Herald,* October 31, 1928.

56. "Minor Parties Hold Joint Meeting," *Barnard Bulletin,* November 6, 1928.
57. Service, *A History of Twentieth-Century Russia,* 162, 176.
58. Klehr and Haynes, *Storming Heaven Itself,* 41, 46, 65.
59. Ibid.; "Labor Officials Come to Defense," *Altoona Mirror,* June 10, 1929; Margaret Larkin, "Tragedy in North Carolina," *North American Review* 228, no. 6 (1929): 686.
60. Klehr and Haynes, *Storming Heaven Itself,* 41, 65; "Labor Officials Come to Defense"; Larkin, "Tragedy in North Carolina," 689.
61. Klehr and Haynes, *Storming Heaven Itself,* 41, 65; "Labor Officials Come to Defense"; Larkin, "Tragedy in North Carolina," 689.
62. "Labor Officials Come to Defense"; "Plans to Defend Strikers Held for Killing Aderholt," *Thomasville Times Enterprise,* June 10, 1929; "Textile Strikers to Defense Suspects," *Decatur Daily News,* June 10, 1929; Bill Dunne, "Gastonia," *New Masses* (July 1929): 4–5.
63. Salmond, *Gastonia,* 84.
64. Ibid., 84, 87, 93.
65. Special agent in charge (SAC), New York office of the Federal Bureau of Investigation, memo to J. Edgar Hoover, June 16 1949, box 53, folder 1, Tanenhaus Papers.
66. Walter M. Trumbull, "In the Gastonia Strike Area," *Labor Defender* (August 1929): 161.
67. "The Gastonia Striker's Case," *Harvard Law Review* 44 (May 1931): 1120–23; Salmond, *Gastonia, 1929,* 167–72.
68. "The Gastonia Strikers' Case," 1120–23; Salmond, *Gastonia,* 167–72.
69. Canadian police, "Memo: Relating to Robinsons/Rubens," October 19, 1938, Robinson and Rubens File, National Archives of the United Kingdom, Kew, England; J. Edgar Hoover, memo to E. J. Brennan, September 21, 1922, box 53, folder 1, Tanenhaus Papers; Greek legation, memo to Henry Stimson, December 29, 1930, RG 59, entry 205C, NARA; "15,000 at Union Square," *New York Times,* August 10, 1927; SAC, New York, memo to Hoover, June 16, 1949.
70. "Women Reds Here in Soviet Holiday," *New York Times,* March 5, 1928; Minor Parties Hold Joint Meeting," *Barnard Bulletin,* November 6, 1928; "Conference on Labor Problems," *Barnard Bulletin,* April 12, 1929.
71. "Woman Workers Form Federation," *New York Times,* May 20, 1928.
72. Lieberman, "The Mysterious Disappearance," 32.
73. "LaGuardia Asks Albany to Give Him Full Power over the City's Finances," *New York Times,* January 3, 1934; "LaGuardia Spurns Jobless Delegations' Demands for Relief," *Daily Worker,* January 3, 1934.
74. "LaGuardia Asks Albany."

Chapter Three: The Anarchist

1. Arthur Irwin, "Woman Red Leader Vanishes Here: Had Lived in Fear Since Losing Sway in Party Councils," *New York World-Telegram,* December 17, 1937.
2. "Think Robinsons Quit Communists: U.S. Follows Theory They Joined Trotsky," *New York World-Telegram,* December 17, 1937.

3. Nunzio Pernicone, *Carlo Tresca: Portrait of a Rebel* (New York: Palgrave Macmillan, 2005), 7–9, 11, 14–15.
4. Ibid., 18–19.
5. Ibid., 28–29.
6. Ibid., 124, 135; Nunzio Pernicone, ed., *The Autobiography of Carlo Tresca* (New York: City University of New York Press, 2003), xvii.
7. Pernicone, *Carlo Tresca,* 164; Carlo Tresca, "The Gentleman of the Federal Grand Jury," 1938, Herbert Solow Papers, box 10, folder 8, Hoover Institution Archives, Stanford University, Stanford, CA (hereafter cited as Solow Papers).
8. Pernicone, *Carlo Tresca,* 198.
9. Donald Rayfield, *Stalin and His Hangmen: The Tyrant and Those Who Killed for Him* (New York: Random House, 2004), 248.
10. Ibid., 277.
11. Vadim Rogovin, *1937: Stalin's Year of Terror* (Oak Park, MI: Mehring, 1998), 164.
12. Rayfield, *Stalin and His Hangmen,* 293.
13. Terry A. Cooney, *The Rise of the New York Intellectuals: "Partisan Review" and Its Circle, 1934–1945* (Madison: University of Wisconsin Press, 1986), 104, 126; Pernicone, *The Autobiography of Carlo Tresca,* xvii; Commission of Inquiry into the Charges Made against Leon Trotsky in the Moscow Trials, *Not Guilty* (New York: Ishi, 2008), 308.
14. John Patrick Diggins, *Mussolini and Fascism: The View from America* (Princeton, NJ: Princeton University Press, 1975), 411.
15. Herbert Solow, "One Year of the Poyntz Mystery," 1938, box 10, "Juliet Stuart Poyntz" folder, 6, Solow Papers.
16. Andrew Meier, *The Lost Spy: An American in Stalin's Secret Service* (New York: Norton, 2008), 228; Esther Iverem, "Alexander J. Barmine Dies; Early High-Level Soviet Defector," *New York Times,* December 28, 1987.
17. John Earl Haynes and Harvey Klehr, *Venona: Decoding Soviet Espionage in America* (New Haven, CT: Yale University Press, 1999), 50.
18. Meier, *The Lost Spy,* 226–27, 28.ß
19. Rogovin, *1937,* 360.
20. Pernicone, *Carlo Tresca,* 229–30.
21. Pernicone, *The Autobiography of Carlo Tresca,* xvii.
22. "Soviet Is Pressed to Find Robinsons," *New York Times,* December 11, 1937.
23. Irwin, "Woman Red Leader Vanishes Here"; "Think Robinsons Quit Communists."
24. Elias Lieberman, "The Mysterious Disappearance of Juliet or a Lady Communist Vanishes (A True Story)," 2. Lieberman Papers; Irwin, "Woman Red Leader Vanishes Here"; "Police Tracing Julia S. Poyntz," *New York Sun,* January 12, 1938; Carlo Tresca, "The Communazi Lady Vanishes," box 10, "Juliet Stuart Poyntz" folder, 3, Solow Papers.
25. Lieberman, "The Mysterious Disappearance," 4–5; Marie B. MacDonald, letter to Carlo Tresca, July 25, 1940, box 10, "Juliet Stuart Poyntz" folder, Solow Papers.

26. Federal Bureau of Investigation (FBI), memo, New York 100–59538, box 53, folder 1, Tanenhaus Papers.
27. "Police Department Description Card for Juliet Stuart Glaser—née Julia Poyntz," c. 1938, in *Guide to Carlo Tresca,* box 2, folder 43, Tamiment Library Archives, New York University, New York (hereafter TLA); Lieberman, "The Mysterious Disappearance," 44.
28. "Police Department Description Card"; Lieberman, "The Mysterious Disappearance," 44; Russell L. Cecil, ed., *A Textbook of Medicine* (Philadelphia: Saunders, 1941), 523–528. According to the police card, Poyntz also had false teeth, brown eyes and hair, and a sallow complexion; Tresca, "The Communazi Lady Vanishes," 3.
29. Tresca, "The Communazi Lady Vanishes," 3.
30. Ibid.
31. Lieberman, "The Mysterious Disappearance," 44; Tresca, "The Communazi Lady Vanishes," 3; "Police Tracing Julia S. Poyntz," *New York Sun,* January 22, 1938.
32. Irwin, "Woman Red Leader Vanishes Here"; "Woman Communist Missing 7 Months," *New York Times,* December 18, 1937.
33. Carlo Tresca," Where Is Juliet Stuart Poyntz?," *Modern Monthly* 10, no. 11 (1938): 12.
34. "CP denies any knowledge of Juliet Poyntz," *Daily Worker,* December 18, 1937.
35. "X," letter to J. Edgar Hoover, December 24, 1937, enclosed in J. Edgar Hoover, letter to Cordell Hull, December 29, 1937, RG 59, entry 205C, NARA; "2 Passport Sets Believed Used by 'Robinsons,'" *New York World-Telegram* December 28, 1937.
36. "U.S. Jury Will Sift Poyntz Mystery," *New York Times,* February 8, 1938; "TMC/The Militant—Robinson-Rubens/Poyntz," n.d., *Guide to Carlo Tresca,* box 2, folder 43, TLA; Pernicone, *Carlo Tresca,* 233.
37. "'Mrs. Robinson' Identified as Missing Mrs. Rubens," *New York World-Telegram,* December 29, 1937.
38. "2 Passport Sets Believed Used by 'Robinsons'"; "Identities of 'Robinsons,' 'Rubens' and 'Robbins' Tangled in Mystery That Leads to Moscow," *New York World-Telegram,* December 31, 1937; "'Key Man' Bared in Case of 'Robinsons,'" *New York World-Telegram,* January 6, 1938; "Asks U.S. to Prod Soviet on Answer," *New York World-Telegram,* January 11, 1938; "Spy Tale Unfolds in Jury Trial," *New York Times,* April 13, 1939.
39. "U.S. Can't See Wife of Rubens," *Sunday Mirror,* January 23, 1938; "Report Mrs. Rubens Slain, Husband, 'A Spy,' Escaped," *Daily Mirror,* February 2, 1938; Hugo George Robol, "Rubenses Will Confess or Else," *Daily Mirror,* February 8 ,1938; "Mrs. Rubens Tells Envoy She Doesn't Want Help," *Daily Mirror,* February 11, 1938.
40. "Poyntz, FBI Memo," n.d., *Guide to Carlo Tresca,* box 2, folder 43, TLA.
41. Tresca, "The Gentleman of the Federal Grand Jury."
42. Ibid.
43. "The Sun Finds a Trotzkyite Expert," *Daily Worker,* February 10, 1938; Tresca," Where Is Juliet Stuart Poyntz?," 17.

44. "Italian Anti-Fascists Lash Tresca's USSR 'Plot' Tales," *Daily Worker,* February 14, 1938.; Judy Kutulas, *The Long War: The Intellectual People's Front and Anti-Stalinism, 1930–1940* (Durham: Duke University Press, 1995).
45. "Trotzkyite Tries to Shunt U.S. Inquiry from 'Robinson' Trail," *Daily Worker,* February 18, 1937; "Soviet Press Points to Trotzkyite Link in Case of 'Robinson' Pair," *Daily Worker,* February 18, 1937.
46. "Spy Tales Unfold in Passport Trials," *New York Times,* April 13, 1939; "Rubens Case Led to Trial of 3 Here," *New York Times,* June 10, 1939.
47. "Soviet Is Pressed to Find Robinsons"; "'Mrs. Robinson' Identified as Missing Mrs. Rubens."
48. Kathryn Olmstead, "Blond Queens, Red Spiders, and Neurotic Old Maids: Gender and Espionage in the Early Cold War," *Intelligence and National Security,* 19, no. 1 (2004): 79.
49. "'Mrs. Robinson' Identified as Missing Mrs. Rubens."
50. Arthur Irwin, "Nazi Angle Rises in Poyntz Disappearance," *New York World-Telegram,* December 18, 1937.
51. Tresca, "The Communazi Lady Vanishes," 4.
52. Ibid., 5.
53. Tresca, "Where Is Juliet Stuart Poyntz?," 17.
54. Ibid.
55. Tresca, "The Communazi Lady Vanishes," 11; Tresca," Where Is Juliet Stuart Poyntz?," 18.
56. Tresca, "The Communazi Lady Vanishes," 11–12.
57. Ibid., 12–13.
58. Tresca," Where Is Juliet Stuart Poyntz?," 18.
59. Carlo Tresca, letter to Vito Marcantonio, December 15, 1938, and Vito Marcantonio, letter to Carlo Tresca, January 7, 1939, box 10, "Juliet Stuart Poyntz" folder, Solow Papers.
60. Robert H. Thayer, letter to Carlo Tresca, January 11, 1939, box 10, "Juliet Stuart Poyntz" folder, Solow Papers.
61. Tresca, "The Communazi Lady Vanishes," 1.
62. Ibid., 2–7; Herbert Solow, "Memo," December 1939, box 10, "Juliet Stuart Poyntz" folder, Solow Papers.
63. Lieberman, "The Mysterious Disappearance," 4–5.
64. Ibid., 39–41.
65. Tresca, "The Communazi Lady Vanishes," 3.
66. Ibid., 13.
67. Tresca Memorial Committee, "Who Killed Carlo Tresca?," October 1945, 1, Carlo Tresca Papers, New York Public Library, New York; "Three Theories on the Tresca Assassination," *PM,* January 13, 1943.
68. Pernicone, *Carlo Tresca,* 285.
69. Carlo Tresca Memorial Committee, "Who Killed Carlo Tresca?," 10–11.

70. Ibid., 10–14.
71. Ibid., 12–14; Pernicone, *Carlo Tresca,* 269–73, 293.
72. Tresca, "The Gentleman of the Federal Grand Jury."

Chapter Four: The Intellectual and the Feds

1. Alan Wald, *The New York Intellectuals: The Rise and Decline of the Anti-Stalinist Left from the 1930s to the 1980s* (Chapel Hill: University of North Carolina Press, 1987), 37–38; U.S. Bureau of the Census, population statistics, Manhattan, NY, 1920, in *Fourteenth Census of the United States,* NARA; Alan Wald, "Herbert Solow: Portrait of a New York Intellectual," *Prospects* 3 (October 1978): 421.
2. Wald, *The New York Intellectuals,* 50–54; Wald, "Herbert Solow," 52, 421.
3. Wald, *The New York Intellectuals,* 39, 41–42.
4. Ibid., 50–54; Wald, "Herbert Solow," 52, 421.
5. Wald, *The New York Intellectuals,* 37–43.
6. Wald, "Herbert Solow," 421; Herbert Solow, untitled manuscript, n.d. box 1, folder 6, Solow Papers.
7. Wald, *The New York Intellectuals,* 50–54; Wald, "Herbert Solow," 421;.
8. Terry Cooney, *The Rise of the New York Intellectuals: Partisan Review and Its Circles, 1934–1945* (Madison: University of Wisconsin Press, 1986), 109.
9. Neil Jumonville, *The New York Intellectuals Reader* (New York: Routledge, 2007), 5; Cooney, *The Rise of the New York Intellectuals,* 113.
10. Wald, *The New York Intellectuals,* 128–33, 139.
11. Harvey Teres, *Renewing the Left: Politics, Imagination, and the New York Intellectuals* (Oxford: Oxford University Press, 1996), 65; Cooney, *The Rise of the New York Intellectuals,* 102.
12. Wald, *The New York Intellectuals,* 150.
13. Herbert Solow, "New Evidence Reveals Rubens-Soviet Tie Up," *New Leader,* February 19, 1938.
14. Herbert Solow, "Rubens Drama Craftily Staged," *New York Sun,* February 9, 1938.
15. Herbert Solow, "Mrs. Rubens Seen Resisting," *New York Sun,* February 10, 1938.
16. Solow, "Mrs. Rubens Seen Resisting."
17. Herbert Solow, "Fate of Mrs. Rubens Pondered," *New York Sun,* February 11, 1938.
18. Herbert Solow, "Memo of Interview with Melach Epstein," 1938, box 10, folder 8, Solow Papers.
19. Solow, "Fate of Mrs. Rubens Pondered."
20. J. Edgar Hoover, letters to Herbert Solow, May 5, 1938, November 2, 1938, November 22, 1939, and July 29, 1938, box 10, folder 8, Solow Papers.
21. E. A. Tecu, letter to J. Edgar Hoover, March 7, 1938, box 53, folder 1, Tanenhaus Papers. I have twice requested Poyntz's FBI file through the Freedom of Information Act. The first time, the FBI returned a short fourteen-page file that included a writing sample from Poyntz and a verification that it was her writing. The second time, I received the exact same materials. However, while doing research in the

Tanenhaus Papers at the Hoover Institution in the summer of 2016, I found an FBI file on Poyntz containing more than two hundred pages, which according to its label had once been archived with the Harvey Klehr Papers at Emory University. The FBI is not the only agency that is being secretive. I have made three separate requests for the New York State missing persons file on Poyntz and have received three rejections.

22. Tecu, letter to Hoover, March 7, 1938.
23. Herbert Solow, notes, 1938, box 10, folder 8, Solow Papers.
24. Herbert Barnes, letter to J. Edgar Hoover, May 17, 1949, box 53, folder 1, Tanenhaus Papers.
25. Special agent in charge (SAC) , New York office of the Federal Bureau of Investigation (FBI), letter to J. Edgar Hoover, June 2, 1949, and SAC, Boston office of the FBI, letter to J. Edgar Hoover, July 15, 1949, box 53, folder 1, Tanenhaus Papers.
26. Marie B. MacDonald, letter to Herbert Solow, 1938, box 10, folder 8, Solow Papers; Solow, notes.
27. Solow, notes, 1938.
28. Richard M. Fried, "Springtime for Stalin: Mosinee's 'Day under Communism' as Cold War Pageantry," *Wisconsin Magazine of History* 77, no. 2 (1993–94): 87.
29. Joseph Zack, letter to Herbert Solow, February 13, 1938, box 10, folder 8, Solow Papers; Federal Bureau of Investigation (FBI), document NY100–59538, box 53, folder 1, 3, Tanenhaus Papers.
30. Mark Graubard, letter to Herbert Solow, November 1, 1939, and Herbert Solow, "Personal Memo—Graubard Interview," 1938, box 10, folder 8, Solow Papers.
31. Herbert Solow, letter to Mark Graubard, November 2, 1939, box 10, folder 8, Solow Papers.
32. Solow, "Personal Memo—Graubard Interview"; Herbert Solow, letter to Mark Graubard, November 10, 1939, box 10, folder 8, Solow Papers.
33. Solow, "Personal Memo—Graubard Interview"; Herbert Solow, "Memo—Worcester," 1938, box 10, folder 8, Solow Papers.
34. Solow, "Personal Memo—Graubard Interview"; Mark Graubard, letter to Herbert Solow, November 8, 1939, box 10, folder 8, Solow Papers.
35. Solow, "Personal Memo—Graubard Interview."
36. Ibid.; Solow, letter to Graubard, November 10, 1939; Elizabeth Bentley, *Out of Bondage: KGB Target: Washington, D.C.* (New York: Ivy Books, 1988), 32–36.
37. Solow, "Personal Memo—Graubard Interview"; Solow, "Memo—Worcester"; Herbert Solow "Memo—Interview with Lore," December 26, 1939, box 10, folder 8, Solow Papers; Mark Graubard, letter to Herbert Solow, November 15, 1939, box 10, folder 8, Solow Papers.
38. Solow, "Personal Memo—Graubard Interview"; Solow, "Memo—Worcester"; Solow, letter to Graubard, November 10, 1939; Graubard, letter to Solow, November 15, 1939.

39. Herbert Solow, letter to William Harlan Hale, box 10, folder 8, Solow Papers.
40. FBI, document NY100–59538, 1.
41. SAC, memo, WFO (BSM) Airtel Urgent NY (100–59538), November 5, 1953, box 53, folder 1, Tanenhaus Papers; FBI, document NY100–59538.
42. Ibid.; A. H. Bujmont [sic], letter to W. A. Branigan, November 5, 1953, box 53, folder 1, Tanenhaus Papers; Federal Bureau of Investigation (FBI), "Juliet Stuart Poyntz File," December 7, 1953, box 53, folder 1, 8, Tanenhaus Papers; Federal Bureau of Investigation (FBI), Washington, D.C., field office, to J. Edgar Hoover and New York field office, November 6, 1953, box 53, folder 1, Tanenhaus Papers; Federal Bureau of Investigation (FBI), Washington, D.C., field office, "Juliet Stuart Poyntz" [memo], December 7, 1953, box 53, folder 1, 1–4, Tanenhaus Papers.
43. FBI, Washington, D.C., field office, "Juliet Stuart Poyntz," December 7, 1953, 1–8.
44. Ibid.
45. Ibid.; Solow, "Personal Memo—Graubard Interview"; Solow, "Memo—Worcester."
46. Hebert Solow, "Statement," n.d., box 10, folder 8, Solow Papers; Solow, "Memo—Worcester"; Herbert Solow, "Interview—Hennessey," December 2, 1939, box 10, folder 8, Solow Papers.
47. Solow, "Memo—Interview with Lore"; A. J. Nicholas, letter to Herbert Solow, May 1, 1940, box 10, folder 8, Solow Papers; Herbert Solow, "Memo—Lunch with Hale," November 10, 1939, box 10, folder 8, Solow Papers; Arthur Irwin, "Woman Red Leader Vanishes Here: Had Lived in Fear Since Losing Sway in Party Councils," *New York World-Telegram,* December 17, 1937.
48. Arnold B. Van Bergen, "Juliet Stuart Poyntz," September 1944, box 534, folder 1, 1, Tanenhaus Papers.
49. Herbert Solow, memo, n.d., box 10, folder 8, Solow Papers.; Rhodri Jeffreys-Jones, *The FBI: A History* (New Haven: Yale University Press, 2007), 101–2.
50. Solow, "Memo of Interview with Melach Epstein"; Herbert Solow, "Memo—Shub," 1938, and "Memo of Talk with Karl," 1938, box 10, folder 8, Solow Papers.
51. Herbert Solow, "Stalin's Spy Scare—American Edition," n.d., box 10, folder 8, 1–3, Solow Papers.
52. Herbert Solow, "Missing a Year! Where Is Julia Poyntz?," *New Leader,* June 20, 1938; Herbert Solow, "One Year of the Poyntz Mystery," 1938, box 10, folder 8, 4, Solow Papers.
53. Solow, "Missing a Year!," 7–10; Solow, "Memo of Interview with Melach Epstein."
54. FBI, document NY100–59538, 13–15.; Elias Lieberman, "The Mysterious Disappearance of Juliet, or a Lady Communist Vanishes (A True Story)," 49, Lieberman Papers.
55. Wald, "Herbert Solow," 445; Herbert Solow, "Communist Hostilities," n.d., box 10, folder 8, Solow Papers.
56. Herbert Solow, letter to Eleazar Lipsky, February 28, 1945, box 11, folder 4, Solow Papers; Ray Doyle and Adrian Spies, "Mystery Woman Ruled Dead; Lost Since Break with Reds," *New York Daily Mirror,* November 13, 1944.

57. Herbert Solow, letter to Joseph M. Proskauer, January 15, 1953, box 11, folder 4, Solow Papers; Jay Maeder, "Joseph Scottoriggio Rain on the Grave," *New York Daily News,* April 28, 1999.

Chapter Five: The Witness

1. Herbert Solow, untitled manuscript, 1952, box 5, folder "Whittaker Chambers," 1, 4–5, Solow Papers.
2. Alan Wald, "Herbert Solow: Portrait of a New York Intellectual," *Prospects* 3 (October 1978): 422.
3. Ellen Schrecker, *Many Are the Crimes: McCarthyism in America* (Princeton, NJ: Princeton University Press, 1998), 120–21; Nick Fischer, *Spider Web: The Birth of American Anticommunism* (Urbana: University of Illinois Press, 2016).
4. Whittaker Chambers, *Witness* (Washington, DC: Regnery,1952), 194; Whittaker Chambers, "The Faking of Americans," 28, box 5, folder "Whittaker Chambers," Solow Papers.
5. Sam Tanenhaus, *Whittaker Chambers: A Biography* (New York: Random House, 1997), 31, 43, 45; Chambers, *Witness,* 194.
6. Tanenhaus, *Whittaker Chambers,* 31, 43, 45; Chambers, *Witness,* 194–95.
7. Chambers, *Witness,* 204.
8. Herbert Solow, "Affidavit on Whittaker Chambers," November 12, 1938, 1–3, box 5, folder "Whittaker Chambers," Solow Papers; Maurice Isserman, *Which Side Are You On? The American Communist Party during the Second World War* (Urbana: University of Illinois Press, 1993), 6–7.
9. Solow, "Affidavit on Whittaker Chambers," 5.
10. Ibid., 6; Solow, untitled manuscript, 1952, 5.
11. Solow, "Affidavit on Whittaker Chambers," 6–7 ; Solow, untitled manuscript, 1952, 1–5.
12. Solow, untitled manuscript, 1952, 6–7.
13. Solow, "Affidavit on Whittaker Chambers," 8–9. It is not clear if Tresca knew Chambers in February 1938. But after Chambers left the underground, Solow recalled at least one occasion when he and Chambers attended a party with Tresca, so they certainly knew each other afterward.
14. Ibid., 6–7.
15. Ibid., 10–11.
16. Ibid., 3–5; Herbert Solow, letter to Del, September 19 [no year], box 5, folder "Whittaker Chambers," Solow Papers.
17. Solow, "Affidavit on Whittaker Chambers," 13–15; Herbert Solow, "Supplement 1 to Chambers Story," November 3, 1938, 1–2, box 5, folder "Whittaker Chambers," Solow Papers.
18. Solow, "Affidavit on Whittaker Chambers," 13–15; Solow, "Supplement 1 to Chambers Story," 3; Chambers, "The Faking of Americans," 3; Whittaker Chambers, "Background to Unpublished MS 1938 on Soviet Espionage by Karl [Whittaker Chambers]," box 5, folder "Whittaker Chambers," Solow Papers.

19. Chambers, "The Faking of Americans," 3, 22.
20. Ibid., 25; Herbert Solow, "Memo in RE Rudewitz-Rubens-Braun," box 11, Folder "Spies-General," Solow Papers; Chambers, "The Faking of Americans," 27
21. Chambers, "The Faking of Americans," 27; Roman Brackman, *The Secret File of Joseph Stalin: A Hidden Life* (London: Routledge, 2001), 188; Schrecker, *Many Are the Crimes,* 137.
22. "2 Passport Sets Believed Used by 'Robinsons,'" *New York World-Telegram,* December 31, 1937; "Identities of 'Robinsons,' 'Rubens,' and 'Robbins' Tangled in Mystery That Leads to Moscow," *New York World-Telegram,* December 31, 1937; "'Key Man' Bared in Case of 'Robinsons,'" *New York World-Telegram,* January 6, 1938; Schrecker, *Many Are the Crimes,* 137.
23. Chambers, "The Faking of Americans," 7; "'Mrs. Robinson' Identified as Missing Mrs. Rubens," *New York World-Telegram,* December 29, 1937; marriage certificate of Adolph A. Rubens and Ruth B. Braman, May 18, 1935, New York City Marriage Index, 1866–1937, New York City Department of Records, Municipal Archives; birth certificate of Ruth Boerger, May 27, 1908, Commonwealth of Pennsylvania, Bureau of Vital Statistics, New Castle.
24. Chambers, "The Faking of Americans," 3–4.
25. Ibid., 29, 35.
26. Robert W. Thurston, *Life and Terror in Stalin's Russia, 1937–1941* (New Haven, CT: Yale University Press, 1996), 35, 50, 52, 57.
27. Chambers, "The Faking of Americans," 35; Herbert Solow, letter to Herbert L. Packer, July 11, 1962, box 5, folder "Whittaker Chambers," Solow Papers; Rhodri Jeffreys-Jones, *The FBI: A History* (New Haven: Yale University Press, 2007), 101–2.
28. Chambers, "The Faking of Americans," 31.
29. "Long Term Foreseen for Rubens by Wife," *New York Times,* July 1, 1939; "Mrs. Rubens Takes Soviet Citizenship," *New York Times,* November 17, 1939; "Mrs. Ruth Rubens Gives Up Hope for her Seized Mate," *Cumberland Evening Times,* June 30, 1939; "Mrs. Ruth Rubens Will be Freed by Soviet Officials," *Independent Record,* June 10, 1939; illegible writer, letter to Herbert Solow, February 11, 1938, box 11, folder "Spies-General," Solow Papers.
30. Solow, untitled manuscript, 1952, 1; John Earl Haynes, Harvey Klehr, and Alexander Vassiliev, *Spies: The Rise and Fall of the KGB in America* (New Haven, CT: Yale University Press, 2009), 17.
31. John Earl Haynes and Harvey Klehr, *Venona: Decoding Soviet Espionage in America* (New Haven, CT: Yale University Press, 1999), 66–67.
32. Chambers, *Witness,* 463–69; Haynes and Klehr, *Venona,* 89–90.
33. Haynes and Klehr, *Venona,* 90–92.
34. John Earl Haynes and Harvey Klehr, *Early Cold War Spies: The Espionage Trials That Shaped American Politics* (Cambridge: Cambridge University Press, 2006), 92, 132; Jonathan P. Herzog, *The Spiritual-Industrial Complex: America's Religious Battle against Communism in the Early Cold War* (New York: Oxford University Press, 2011), 40.

35. Chambers, *Witness,* 248–49.
36. Matthew Dunne, *A Cold War State of Mind: Brainwashing and Postwar American Society* (Amherst: University of Massachusetts Press, 2013), 211.
37. Chambers, *Witness,* 35–36.
38. Ibid., 43, 47.
39. Ibid., 36.
40. Ibid.
41. Ibid.
42. Ibid.
43. Ibid.
44. Ibid., 439.
45. Marie Delegard, *Battling Miss Bolsheviki: The Origins of Female Conservatism in the United States* (Philadelphia: University of Pennsylvania Press, 2012); Kim E. Nielsen, *Un-American Womanhood: Antiradicalism, Antifeminism, and the First Red Scare* (Athens: Ohio University Press, 2001); Elaine Tyler May, *Homeward Bound: American Families in the Cold War* (New York: Basic Books, 2008). Nielsen, in particular, argues that anti-communist women constructed ideas of "natural" roles for women that eschewed radical politics and embraced conservative gender roles.
46. Herzog, *The Spiritual-Industrial Complex,* 40–41.
47. Sidney Hook, "The Faiths of Whittaker Chambers," *New York Times*, May 25, 1952.
48. Schrecker, *Many Are the Crimes*, 120.
49. Robert Friedman, "Whittaker Chambers—'Witness' for War and Fascism," *Daily Worker,* May 25, 1952.
50. Julia Allen, *Passionate Commitments: The Lives of Anna Rochester and Grace Hutchins* (Albany: State University of New York Press, 2013); Grace Hutchins, letter to Random House, printed in *Daily Worker*, July 27, 1952.
51. Wald, "Herbert Solow," 446–49.
52. "Chambers Is Dead; Hiss Case Witness," *New York Times,* July 12, 1961; "Herbert Solow Dies; Former Fortune Editor," *Hartford Courant,* November 28, 1964; Haynes and Klehr, *Early Cold War Spies,* 132–35.
53. Wald, "Herbert Solow," 452.

Chapter Six: The Informers

1. Herbert L. Packer, *Ex-Communist Witnesses: Four Studies in Fact Finding* (Stanford, CA: Stanford University Press, 1962), 3–4.
2. Ibid., 4-6.
3. Ibid.
4. Ibid., 6.
5. Ibid., 121–22; Louis Budenz, *This Is My Story* (New York: McGraw-Hill, 1947), 7–8.
6. Packer, *Ex-Communist Witnesses,* 121–22; Budenz, *This Is My Story,* 10, 18; Jonathan P. Herzog, *The Spiritual-Industrial Complex: America's Religious Battle against Communism in the Early Cold War* (New York: Oxford University Press, 2011).

7. Packer, *Ex-Communist Witnesses,* 121–22; Budenz, *This Is My Story*, 20.
8. Packer, *Ex-Communist Witnesses,* 122–23; Budenz, *This Is My Story*, 123–24.
9. Packer, *Ex-Communist Witnesses,* 123.
10. Ibid., 122–23; Herzog, *The Spiritual-Industrial Complex*, 42–43.
11. Robert Lichtman, "Louis Budenz, the FBI, and the 'List of 400 Concealed Communists': An Extended Tale of McCarthy Era Informing," *American Communist History* 3, no. 1 (2004): 25, 29; Packer, *Ex-Communist Witnesses,* 124.
12. Louis Budenz, testimony, Executive Session, House Committee on Un-American Activities, April 3, 1946, RG 233, box 1, NARA (hereafter cited as HUAC).
13. Ibid.
14. Ibid. The transcriptions are littered with misspellings, especially of names. He may have been talking about General Nikolai Yezhov, who was executed in 1940.
15. "Calls Communists Here Soviet Spies," *New York Times,* April 4, 1946.
16. Budenz, *This Is My Story,* 133, 234–35.
17. Ibid., 234, 238.
18. Ibid., 244, 259, 263–64.
19. Ibid., 263–64.
20. Ibid., 263.
21. "Budenz Outlines Trotsky Murder," *New York Times,* March 14, 1947; Herbert Solow, "Kremlin Cloak-and-Dagger: What John Chamberlain Missed about the House on 13th Street," *New Leader* (1947).
22. Herbert Solow, "Statement," March 17, 1947, box 10, folder 8, Solow Papers.
23. "Communist Inquiry Is Demanded Here," *New York Times,* March 18, 1947; "Charge Soviet Secret Police Aided Slayers," *New York Times,* March 18, 1947; Solow, "Statement."
24. "Budenz Gives Jury Communism Data," *New York Times,* June 6, 1947.
25. Samuel Sillen, "Hypocrite's Progress: The Story of Budenz," *Worker,* March 23, 1947.
26. James S. Allen, "A Puny Soul Seeks Salvation in Fascism," *Sunday Worker*, May 4, 1947.
27. Andrew Meier, *The Lost Spy: An American in Stalin's Secret Service* (New York: Norton, 2008); Lichtman, "Louis Budenz," 53.
28. Lichtman, "Louis Budenz," 51; Robert D. McFadden, "Editor of Daily Worker," *New York Times*, April 28, 1972; "Budenz Sees Church as Able Foe of Reds," *New York Times,* April 27, 1947.
29. Benjamin Gitlow, *I Confess: The Truth about American Communism* (New York: Dutton, 1940), 4–6, 12–13.
30. Ibid., 25; Harvey Klehr and John Earl Haynes, *Storming Heaven Itself: The American Communist Movement* (New York: Twayne, 1992), 43; Marc Lendler, "The Time to Kill a Snake: *Gitlow v. New York* and the Bad-Tendency Doctrine," *Journal of Supreme Court History* 36 (March 2011): 11–12.
31. Lendler, "The Time to Kill a Snake," 15.
32. Ibid., 11, 23–24.
33. Ibid., 23–25.

34. Ibid.; Granville Hicks, "Communism, American Model," *New York Times Book Review,* October 17, 1948.
35. Gitlow, *I Confess,* 84, 249; Dorothy Parnell, "How to Avoid Falling into Communist Trap," n.d., Benjamin Gitlow Papers, box 5, Hoover Institution Archives, Stanford University, Stanford, CA (hereafter cited as Gitlow Papers).
36. Gitlow, *I Confess,* 249.
37. Ibid., 253; Harvey Klehr, John Earl Haynes, and Fridrikh Igorevich Firsov, *The Secret World of American Communism* (New Haven, CT: Yale University Press, 1995), 43.
38. Hicks, "Communism, American Model."
39. Ibid.; Benjamin Gitlow, *The Whole of Their Lives* (Boston: Western Islands Press, 1948), 338.
40. Gitlow, *The Whole of Their Lives,* 338–39.
41. Ibid.
42. Ibid., 340.
43. Ibid.
44. Ibid.
45. Ibid., 340–41.
46. Ibid., 341.
47. Ibid.
48. Ibid.
49. Ibid., 342–44.
50. Ibid., 347–48.
51. Norman Thomas, letter to J. Edgar Hoover, November 15, 1948, box 53, folder 1, Tanenhaus Papers; "Jury Hears Gitlow: Former Communist Leader Talks Tresca Slaying," *New York Times,* February 9, 1949.
52. Benjamin Gitlow, "The Poyntz Mystery," n.d., box 5, Gitlow Papers.
53. Ibid.
54. Hicks, "Communism, American Model"; Raymond Rosenthal, "The Iron Tradition," *Commentary,* January 1, 1948.
55. "Benjamin Gitlow Is Dead at 73; Leader in U.S. Communist Party," *New York Times,* July 20, 1965.
56. Gregory S. Taylor, *The Life and Lies of Paul Crouch: Communist, Opportunist, Cold War Snitch* (Gainesville: University Press of Florida, 2014), 1–7.
57. Ibid., 14–15.
58. Ibid., 7, 24.
59. Ibid., 7, 109–10.
60. Ibid., 7, 114.
61. "Paul Crouch Exposes Red Intrigue Here," *Miami Daily News,* May 7, 1949; Hoke Welch, testimony, May 11, 1949, RG233, box 9, "Hoke Welch" folder, HUAC.
62. Paul Crouch, affidavit, May 11, 1949, RG233, box 9, "Hoke Welch" folder, 1, HUAC.
63. Ibid., 2.
64. Ibid., 3.

65. Ibid., 3–4; Budenz, *This Is My Story,* 262; Lichtman, "Louis Budenz," 51.
66. Paul Crouch, "Red Agent Slew U.S. Woman, Crouch Says," *Miami Daily News,* May 10, 1949.
67. Ibid.
68. Ibid.; Paul Crouch, "GPU Agent Mink Called Poyntz Killer," *Miami Daily News,* May 13, 1949.
69. Crouch, "GPU Agent Mink Called Poyntz Killer."
70. "Ex-Spy Queen Confirms Crouch Story on Slaying," *Miami Daily News,* May 16, 1949.
71. Taylor, *The Life and Lies of Paul Crouch,* 135.
72. James Carter, "Seek Poyntz Clue in Pauper Grave," 1947, Federal Bureau of Investigation (FBI) Files, box 53, folder 1, Tanenhaus Papers.
73. Edward K. Nellor, "Hill to Probe Crouch Story of Red Slaying," 1947, FBI Files, box 53, folder 1, Tanenhaus Papers.
74. H. B. Fletcher, memo to D. M. Land, May 26, 1949, FBI Files, box 53, folder 1, Tanenhaus Papers.
75. Taylor, *The Life and Lies of Paul Crouch,* 155, 243, 245.
76. Ibid., 235–37, 245.
77. Paul Crouch, "Stalin Upsets the Apple Cart," n.d., 2–3, and "Shadow of Murder; Eisler Jumps Bail," n.d., 1, 1A, 2, Paul Crouch Papers, box 1, Hoover Institution Archives, Stanford University, Stanford, CA.
78. Taylor, *The Life and Lies of Paul Crouch,* 265–67.
79. Packer, *Ex-Communist Witnesses,* 225–26.
80. Ibid., 226–27.

Chapter Seven: The Lady Spy

1. Elizabeth Bentley, *Out of Bondage: KGB Target, Washington, D.C.* (New York: Ivy Books, 1988), 51.
2. Veronica Wilson, "Elizabeth Bentley and Cold War Representation: Some Masks Not Dropped," *Intelligence and National Security* 14, no. 2 (1999): 49.
3. Ibid., 53, 56–57.
4. Kathryn Olmsted, "Blond Queens, Red Spiders, and Neurotic Old Maids: Gender and Espionage in the Early Cold War," *Intelligence and National Security* 19, no.1 (2004): 79.
5. Ibid., 80–81, 89.
6. Ibid.
7. Kathryn Olmsted, *Red Spy Queen: A Biography of Elizabeth Bentley* (Chapel Hill: University of North Carolina Press, 2002), 1–6.
8. Ibid., 6–8.
9. Ibid., 8–15.
10. Ibid., 18–20, 25–27, 36, 43.
11. Ibid., 65–68, 55, 89.

12. Ibid., 123–24.
13. Nelson Frank and Norton Mockridge, "Red Ring Bared by Blond Queen," *New York World-Telegram,* July 21, 1948.
14. Nelson Frank and Norton Mockridge, "Super-Secrecy Veiled Russia's Spy Cells Here," *New York World-Telegram,* July 22, 1948.
15. Olmsted, *Red Spy Queen,* 123–24; Nelson Frank and Norton Mockridge, "Citizens Tricked into Spy Ring by U.S. Reds," *New York World-Telegram,* July 23, 1948.
16. Olmsted, "Blond Queens, Red Spiders, and Neurotic Old Maids," 78–79.
17. "The Network," *Time* 52, no. 6 (1948): 16; Ralph de Toledano, "The Bentley-Chambers Story," *New Leader,* August 14, 1948.
18. Olmsted, "Blond Queens, Red Spiders, and Neurotic Old Maids," 82; Wilson, "Elizabeth Bentley and Cold War Representation," 49; "Elizabeth Bentley Is Dead at 55; Soviet Spy Later Aided U.S.," *New York Times,* December 4, 1963.
19. Wilson, "Elizabeth Bentley and Cold War Representation," 50.
20. Toledano, "The Bentley-Chambers Story," 1; John Earl Haynes and Harvey Klehr, *Early Cold War Spies: The Espionage Trials That Shaped American Politics* (New York: Cambridge University Press, 2006), 87–88.
21. Olmsted, "Blond Queens, Red Spiders, and Neurotic Old Maids," 82; Wilson, "Elizabeth Bentley and Cold War Representation," 50–51.
22. Bentley, *Out of Bondage,* 3–5.
23. Ibid.; Olmsted, *Red Spy Queen,* 8–9, 13.
24. Bentley, *Out of Bondage,* 30; Elizabeth Bentley, deposition to the Federal Bureau of Investigation (FBI), November 30, 1945, FBI file 65–56402, serial 220, NARA.
25. Bentley, deposition, 3.
26. Olmsted, *Red Spy Queen,* 20–26; Wilson, "Elizabeth Bentley and Cold War Representation," 51; Bentley, deposition, 4.
27. Wilson, "Elizabeth Bentley and Cold War Representation," 59–60; Olmsted, *Red Spy Queen,* 166–67.
28. Olmsted, *Red Spy Queen,* 158–61, 168–69; Kalman Seigel, "Foreman of Remington Grand Jury Helped on Book, Bentley Says," *New York Times,* January 11, 1951.
29. Bentley, *Out of Bondage,* 30.
30. Ibid., 30–31.
31. Ibid., 31.
32. Olmsted, *Red Spy Queen,* 16; Bentley, *Out of Bondage,* 31–32.
33. Olmsted, *Red Spy Queen,* 167; Bentley, *Out of Bondage,* 137.
34. Olmsted, *Red Spy Queen,* 167–68; Bentley, *Out of Bondage,* 137–38
35. Bentley, *Out of Bondage,* 32.
36. Ibid., 32–33.
37. Ibid., 35–36.
38. Olmsted, *Red Spy Queen,* 17; Mark Graubard, letter to Herbert Solow, November 8, 1939, box 10, "Poyntz" file, Solow Papers.

39. Bentley, *Out of Bondage,* 36–37.
40. Ibid., 42.
41. Jane Sherron DeHart, "Containment at Home: Gender, Sexuality, and National Identity in Cold War America," in *Rethinking Cold War Culture,* ed. Peter J. Kuznick and James Gilbert (Washington, DC: Smithsonian Institute Press, 2001), 124–26.
42. K. A. Cuordileone, *Manhood and American Political Culture in the Cold War* (New York: Routledge, 2005), xix, xxi–xxiii.
43. Bentley, *Out of Bondage,* 3.
44. Ibid., 49–50.
45. Ibid., 51–52.
46. Ibid., 61, 176–77.
47. Olmsted, *Red Spy Queen,* 173; John Oakes, "Elizabeth Bentley's Own Story," *New York Times,* September 23, 1951.
48. Joseph Alsop, "Miss Bentley's Bondage," *Commonweal* (November 1951): 120.
49. Ibid., 120–21.
50. "Moron Sorbell," *Sunday Worker,* July 19, 1953; "Where Red Spy Queen Tripped Up," *Sunday Worker,* May 8, 1955; Alan Max, "Smut House Announces," *Daily Worker,* January 12, 1951.
51. Wilson, "Elizabeth Bentley and Cold War Representation," 53, 56–57.
52. Robert Carr, *The House Committee on Un-American Activities, 1945–1950* (Ithaca: Cornell University Press, 1952), 88, 90, 94–95.
53. Wilson, "Elizabeth Bentley and Cold War Representation," 57, 59.
54. "Miss Bentley Cites College Atheism," *New York Times,* February 19, 1949; Bentley, *Out of Bondage,* 154, 170–90; Olmsted, *Red Spy Queen,* 146–55, 194–202.

Conclusion

1. Hugo Dewar, *Assassins at Large* (Whitefish, MT: Literary Licensing, 2013). "The Lady Vanishes" is available at https://www.marxists.org.
2. Grace Lumpkin, testimony, April 2, 1953, U.S. State Department Information Program, NARA; William Moore, "Forced by Reds to O.K. Killing, Author Says," *Chicago Daily Tribune,* April 3, 1953,.
3. Ralph de Toledano, *Day of Reckoning* (New York: Holt, 1955), 22–24.
4. "Book Bias Is Charged," *New York Times,* April 12, 1955; Granville Hicks, "The Hunter Hunted," *New York Times,* April 3, 1955; George Sokolsky, "*Day of Reckoning* Praised; Ignored by Book Reviewers," *Syracuse Post Standard,* April 3, 1955; James M. Gillis, "Why I Like Sokolsky," 1–3, and "Debate: Is Communism a Menace?," George Sokolsky Manuscript Collection, boxes 1 and 87, Hoover Institution Archives, Stanford University, Stanford, CA.
5. Joseph Freeman, untitled manuscript, Joseph Freeman Manuscript Collection, box 179, folder 6, Hoover Institution Archives, Stanford University, Stanford, CA.
6. Ibid.

7. David Lesser, "The Extenders: A True Memoir of the Actual State of Things," 1983, 133–35, David Lesser Papers, Tamiment Library, New York University.
8. Ibid.
9. Gary Kern and Walter Krivitsky, eds., *MI5 Debriefing and Other Documents on Soviet Intelligence* (Las Cruces, NM: Xenos, 2004), 97.
10. John Earl Haynes, Harvey Klehr, and Alexander Vassiliev, *Spies: The Rise and Fall of the KGB in America* (New Haven, CT: Yale University Press, 2009), 534–35.
11. Richard Sterling, "Juliet Stuart Poyntz, Red NKVD Agent from Omaha, Nebraska," *New York Independent,* August 21, 1967.
12. Gerald Raftery, "Always a Few Bad Apples," *Bennington Banner,* October 6, 1975; Phyllis Schlafly, "Ambassador Killed: International Communists Still Have Assassination Squads," *[Prescott, Arizona] Daily Courier,* June 5, 1976.
13. Dorothy Gallagher, "Disappeared," *Grand Street,* 9, no. 2 (1990): 142–54; Ron Capshaw, "On Our Soil: The Liquidation of Juliet Poyntz," July 3, 1937, https://libertyconservative.com.
14. Masha Gessen, "Under Russian Terror, All Exiles Are Fearful and All Deaths are Suspicious," *New Yorker,* April 13, 2018.
15. Rosalyn Baxandall, "The Question Seldom Asked: Women and the CPUSA," in *New Studies in the Politics and Culture of United States Communism*, ed. Michael E. Brown, Randy Martin, Frank Rosengarten, and George Snedenker (New York: Monthly Review Press, 1993), 145.
16. Juliet Stuart Poyntz, "Reflections on May Day," *Message,* April 26, 1918.

INDEX

Page references in *italics* refer to figures.

Index

Index